JESUS AND PAUL RECONNECTED

JESUS AND PAUL RECONNECTED

Fresh Pathways into an Old Debate

Edited by

Todd D. Still

William B. Eerdmans Publishing Company
Grand Rapids, Michigan / Cambridge, U.K.

Published 2007 by
Wm. B. Eerdmans Publishing Co.
2140 Oak Industrial Drive N.E., Grand Rapids, Michigan 49505 /
P.O. Box 163, Cambridge CB3 9PU U.K.

Printed in the United States of America

12 11 10 09 08 07   7 6 5 4 3 2 1

Library of Congress Cataloging-in-Publication Data

Jesus and Paul reconnected: fresh pathways into an old debate / edited by Todd D. Still.
        p.   cm.
    Includes bibliographical references and index.
    ISBN 978-0-8028-3149-1 (pbk.: alk. paper)
    1. Christianity — Origin.   2. Jesus Christ.   3. Paul, the Apostle, Saint.
    I. Still, Todd D.

    BR129.J47   2007
    225.6 — dc22

                                                    2007028193

www.eerdmans.com

Contents

Contributors

John M. G. Barclay   Lightfoot Professor of Divinity, Department of Theology and Religion, University of Durham, Durham, England, UK

Markus Bockmuehl   Fellow of Keble College and Professor of Biblical and Early Christian Studies, Oxford University, Oxford, England, UK

Beverly Roberts Gaventa   Helen H. P. Manson Professor of New Testament Literature and Exegesis, Princeton Theological Seminary, Princeton, New Jersey, USA

Bruce W. Longenecker   Senior Lecturer, School of Divinity, St. Mary's College, University of St. Andrews, St. Andrews, Scotland, UK

Francis Watson   Professor of New Testament Exegesis and Kirby Lang Chair in New Testament, Department of Divinity and Religious Studies, University of Aberdeen, Aberdeen, Scotland, UK

Stephen Westerholm   Professor of New Testament, Department of Religious Studies, McMaster University, Hamilton, Ontario, Canada

Preface

The essays that comprise this volume had their origin as plenary addresses given at the George W. Truett Theological Seminary of Baylor University in November 2004 under the auspices of the Minette and Huber Lelland Drumwright, Jr., Endowed Colloquium in New Testament Studies. This prefatory note affords the opportunity to express appreciation to a number of persons who made that occasion and this collection possible.

Pride of place must be given to the contributors themselves. But for their willingness to offer their papers, this book would not have come to be. I am deeply indebted to each of them for their exemplary work, warm collegiality, and enthusiastic support of this project.

I would also like to extend my sincere gratitude to Mrs. Minette Drumwright Pratt, to Mr. Bill Pratt, and to their family and friends whose fiscal generosity to honor the memory of the late New Testament scholar Huber Lelland Drumwright, Jr., enabled the Colloquium to occur, and by way of extension, this book to come to fruition.

The administration of Baylor University and Truett Seminary also merit mention here. Both Dr. Robert B. Sloan, Jr., and Dr. David Lyle Jeffrey, who at the time of the Colloquium served the University as President and Provost respectively, extended encouragement and earmarked monies for the event. In fact, Dr. Sloan, himself a New Testament scholar, and Mrs. Sue Sloan graciously invited conference participants into the presidential home for a delightful dinner and lively "table talk." Then Dean Paul W. Powell and Associate Dean David E. Garland (who now serve Truett Seminary as Special Assistant to the Dean and as Dean, respectively), the latter of whom is also an accomplished New Testament scholar and a generous mentor, also enabled the Colloquium by providing monetary and other less tangible, though no less important, forms of support.

The Baylor University Press and its Director, Dr. Carey C. Newman, who, too, is a recognized New Testament scholar, treated Colloquium contributors to an excellent meal at a wonderful restaurant, for which I remain grateful. It is the spirit of collaboration and hospitality exemplified by Carey and others at the Press that makes Baylor such an enjoyable place to work.

Additionally, I would like to say thank you to seminary and university colleagues and students, too numerous to mention here by name, for their assistance and attendance during the Colloquium. Among many others, I would be remiss if I failed to single out Ms. Margaret "Meg" Ramey, who skillfully and cheerfully served as my graduate assistant from the fall of 2003 through the summer of 2005. She was tremendously helpful and extremely competent both during the Colloquium and in the preparation of this volume for publication. It is also appropriate to express thanks to my current graduate assistant, Mr. Bradley Arnold, who compiled the indices for this volume in the summer of 2007.

Lastly, a word of appreciation is in order for Dr. Allen C. Myers, Senior Editor at Eerdmans. When I approached Allen about the possibility of Eerdmans publishing this volume, I was met with courtesy and professionalism. His interest in and support of this project aided my work as the editor of these excellent essays. I trust those who read these pieces will profit as much as I have in editing them.

Abbreviations

AB	Anchor Bible
BETL	Bibliotheca ephemeridum theologicarum lovaniensium
Bib	*Biblica*
BibInt	*Biblical Interpretation*
BJRL	*Bulletin of the John Rylands University Library of Manchester*
BNTC	Black's New Testament Commentaries
BTZ	*Berliner Theologische Zeitschrift*
BZNW	Beihefte zur Zeitschrift für die neutestamentliche Wissenschaft
CBQ	*Catholic Biblical Quarterly*
EKKNT	Evangelisch-katholischer Kommentar zum Neuen Testament
ETS	Erfurter theologische Studien
HNTC	Harper's New Testament Commentaries
HR	*History of Religions*
HTKNT	Herders theologischer Kommentar zum Neuen Testament
HTR	*Harvard Theological Review*
HUT	Hermeneutische Untersuchungen zur Theologie
IBS	*Irish Biblical Studies*
ICC	International Critical Commentary
Int	*Interpretation*
JBL	*Journal of Biblical Literature*
JSNT	*Journal for the Study of the New Testament*

JSNTSup	Journal for the Study of the New Testament: Supplement Series
JTS	*Journal of Theological Studies*
KEKNT	Kritisch-exegetischer Kommentar über das Neue Testament
NCB	New Century Bible
Neot	*Neotestamentica*
NICNT	New International Commentary on the New Testament
NIV	New International Version
NovT	*Novum Testamentum*
NovTSup	Novum Testamentum Supplements
NRSV	New Revised Standard Version
NTL	New Testament Library
NTTS	New Testament Tools and Studies
NTS	*New Testament Studies*
OBT	Overtures to Biblical Theology
RSV	Revised Standard Version
SANT	Studien zum Alten und Neuen Testaments
SNTSMS	Society for New Testament Studies Monograph Series
SNTW	Studies of the New Testament World
SP	Sacra pagina
THKNT	Theologischer Handkommentar zum Neuen Testament
TNTC	Tyndale New Testament Commetaries
TSAJ	Texte und Studien zum antiken Judentum
TynBul	*Tyndale Bulletin*
WBC	Word Biblical Commentary
WUNT	Wissenschaftliche Untersuchungen zum Neuen Testament
ZNT	*Zeitschrift für Neues Testament*

Introduction

If some scholars regard inquiry into the relationship between Paul and Jesus as part and parcel of the task that is New Testament studies, others are far more wary. While the latter may well regard such a scholarly enterprise desirable, they may well wonder, especially if they are inclined to see a historical and/or theological chasm between the two, if such a comparison will prove profitable or if such a project is even possible. Be that as it may, though such comparative analysis long lay dormant, perhaps due in no small part to the shadow cast upon such work by late nineteenth- and early twentieth-century (German) NT scholarship,[1] it presently appears that "Scholarly interest in tracing lines of historical continuity and discontinuity between Jesus and Paul is on the rise."[2] Hopefully this volume, which is comprised of six essays written by established Jesus and Paul scholars, who not only explore historical congruity between this illustrious pairing but also examine potential connections in their thought, relationships, and practices, will ride this detected tide while illustrating intriguing and stimulating ways to compare this incomparable pair.

The initial essay, written by John M. G. Barclay, considers the radical grace of God as declared by both Jesus and Paul. After setting the stage for his study, and in effect, the five that follow, Professor Barclay examines ap-

1. Cf. James D. G. Dunn, "Introduction," in *The Cambridge Companion to St. Paul,* ed. James D. G. Dunn (Cambridge: Cambridge University Press, 2003), 1-15 (on 8).

2. So Bruce N. Fisk, "Paul: Life and Letters," in *The Face of New Testament Studies: A Survey of Recent Research,* ed. Scot McKnight and Grant R. Osborne (Grand Rapids: Baker Academic, 2004), 283-325 (on 312). See also n. 113 on 312-13.

plicable portions of the Parable of the Prodigal Son (Luke 15:11-32), Galatians 1, and Romans 9–11 in turn. Although Dr. Barclay detects "no direct lines of continuity in tradition from Jesus and Paul" in the texts he treats, he maintains that "one cannot help being struck by the *congruity* between Jesus and Paul" on the topic of divine grace. Both Jesus and Paul, Barclay concludes, announced simultaneously, if paradoxically, divine judgment and mercy. In so doing, they welcomed "sinful" outsiders and unsettled "comfortable" insiders. The caustic grace that Jesus and Paul espoused and enacted pushed back theological frontiers even as this message called into question traditional expectations and customs. Far more than contending for "covenantal nomism," Jesus and Paul, this article argues, confronted their audiences with a God of kindness and severity (Rom. 11:22), whose mercy is both "offensive and uncanny."

Stephen Westerholm is the author of this book's second essay. In his paper Professor Westerholm considers the complex, and at times confounding, relationship between law and gospel in Jesus and Paul. To do so with respect to Jesus' ministry, Westerholm turns to the Gospel of Matthew. There he gives special attention to the account of the "rich young ruler." To treat the notoriously knotty pairing of law and gospel in Paul, Dr. Westerholm examines pertinent passages in Galatians. For all of the differences between the Matthean Jesus and the Paul of Galatians on these intimately related topics — differences that our author neither denies nor ignores — there are, according to Westerholm, striking theological similarities. Among the most striking is the devaluing of the so-called "ritual" or "ceremonial" aspects of the law and the underscoring of the law's moral demands. Furthermore, this article, not unlike the one before it, notes that Jesus as well as Paul proclaimed a gospel which embraced and redressed sinful people in their respective plights. The good news announced by and about Jesus, though not *wholly* divorced from or antithetical to the law, clearly de-emphasized the law, if not in intent (Paul in Galatians), at least in effect (Jesus in Matthew). All the while, the gospel message they declared centered upon the transformative and enduring grace of God revealed in the person and through the mission of Jesus the Christ.

Whereas the first two essays address the message of Jesus and Paul to those who found themselves spiritually disenfranchised, Bruce W. Longenecker's study seeks to establish the centrality of the materially destitute in the ministries of Jesus and Paul respectively. To do so, Dr. Longenecker concurs with and expands upon the view held by not a few Jesus specialists, namely, that the economically needy, downtrodden, and vulnerable "were of special significance and concern to Jesus." This is demonstrated through Longenecker's treatment of programmatic passages in Matthew and particularly in Luke, where special attention is given to Jesus' Nazareth sermon. Textual lines are also drawn between the Matthean and Lukan texts under consideration and Isaiah 61. Turning to Paul, the paper considers in some detail various Pauline passages that bear upon the topic to hand. Surprisingly, Longenecker notes, the abiding concern for the poor shown by Paul and his communities has typically escaped the notice of scholars. Be that as it may, textual evidence from the Pauline letter corpus and Acts indicates that the apostle was in both theory and practice eager to remember the poor. Longenecker then proceeds to show that what was true of Jesus and Paul was also true of the earliest believers in Jerusalem and of James, their leader. By way of conclusion, the results of the study are reiterated and a challenge for contemporary Christians to care for the poor and oppressed in their midst is issued.

The fourth essay in this collection is by Markus Bockmuehl. That we may by way of introduction dispense entirely with a survey of the state of the scholarly discussion regarding Jesus and Paul is due in no small part to Professor Bockmuehl's contribution. In his densely documented paper regarding the role that the Apostle Peter occupies in the published work of E. P. Sanders, John Dominic Crossan, N. T. Wright, and James D. G. Dunn on Jesus and Paul, Bockmuehl offers an overview and critique of the aforementioned scholars' treatment (or lack thereof) of Simon Peter. In doing so, he simultaneously provides an entrée into and appraisal of both the "Third Quest" for the Historical Jesus and the "New Perspective" on Paul. In addition to the thousands of pages of scholarly work synthesized and analyzed in his essay, with care and verve Dr. Bockmuehl raises afresh the question whether and in what ways Peter may serve as a "bridge figure" between Jesus and Paul as well as a catalyst for much needed and long overdue conversation between "Third Questers" and "New Perspective Paulinists."

If Professor Bockmuehl's paper considers the prospects of Peter as something of a mediating figure between Jesus and Paul (and those who study them), Francis Watson's essay proposes that Paul was the recipient of unmediated instruction from the risen Jesus regarding the Last Supper. In his tightly argued, provocative essay, Dr. Watson maintains, in contradistinction to NT scholarship, that the instruction Paul reiterates to the Corinthians concerning the Lord's Supper in 1 Cor. 11:23-25 came to the apostle via divine revelation, not Christian tradition. To support this original thesis Dr. Watson not only maintains that what Paul says, and fails to say, in 11:23a must be taken with utmost seriousness, but he also seeks to demonstrate that: 1 Cor. 11:23 and 1 Cor. 15:3 are not incompatible; Paul's statements regarding revelatory encounters elsewhere in his letters make it conceivable that the apostle could be referring to a similar experience in 11:23, especially in light of his claim at the outset of the verse ("I received from the Lord . . ."); and the Markan eucharistic narratives are dependent upon Paul, a position made all the more plausible in light of Luke's prioritization of Paul in his redaction of Mark. By way of conclusion Professor Watson draws out the implications of his work for Pauline Christology, namely, that the heavenly Lord from whom Paul received a revelation regarding the Last Supper and who Christian believers continue to experience in the Eucharist is none other than the earthly Jesus who was "crucified in weakness, but lives by the power of God" (2 Cor. 13:4).

While Dr. Watson's paper considers the origin of Paul's instruction to the Corinthians regarding the institution of the Lord's Supper, which, according to Paul, functions as a proclamation of the Lord's death until he comes (1 Cor. 11:26), in the final essay of this volume Beverly Roberts Gaventa raises and responds to the question "Who was responsible for Jesus' death?" Using Mel Gibson's hugely popular and controversial film *The Passion of the Christ* as the point of entry into her treatment of this query, Professor Gaventa proceeds to devote the lion's share of her essay to a close reading of Rom. 8:32. In treating this pivotal text, Gaventa enters into dialogue with other Pauline scholars and marshals an impressive array of parallels both within and without Romans and the Pauline corpus. Despite the misgivings of some contemporary Christians, Gaventa contends that Paul, at least in Rom. 8:32, views God as the one responsible for delivering his Son over to death. A brief foray into Luke's Gospel, coupled with Col. 2:14-15 and various remarks made by Irenaeus in his *Against Heresies,* strongly suggests that this "apocalyptic" interpretation of Jesus' crucifixion was not unique to Paul. Furthermore, by way of conclusion, Dr. Gaventa maintains that an apocalyptic understanding of Jesus' death, that is, a view that regards God as orchestrating his Son's deliverance to and subsequent triumph over anti-god powers, coheres with the human plight and holds forth the prospect of liberating modern persons from captivity to narcissism and despair.

A bibliography of works cited as well as an index of authors and subjects and an index of Scriptures and other ancient literature concludes this book. It is hoped, however, that the important observations made in this volume will foster further conversation and will result in additional contributions to a long-neglected but now growing area of New Testament research.

TODD D. STILL

Chapter 1

"Offensive and Uncanny": Jesus and Paul on the Caustic Grace of God

John M. G. Barclay

One hundred years ago, the theme of our conference — Jesus and Paul — was one of the central and most hotly debated issues in NT scholarship. At stake was the theological coherence of Christianity, as well as the status of Paul, the wellspring of (at least) the Protestant tradition. Was the theology of Paul in tune with the simple message of Jesus, despite the obvious differences in vocabulary? Or did Paul's complex, and perhaps "Hellenistic," concepts of salvation make him, in effect, the "second founder" of Christianity, the one who, in Wrede's opinion, "exercised beyond all doubt the stronger — not the better — influence"?[1] It is a curious but notable fact that this debate, despite its potential historical and theological significance, has fallen almost entirely silent in contemporary academic circles, to the extent that Todd Still's proposal of our topic made many of us stop and think about questions on which we have barely reflected for years. One could point to many explanations for this shift in scholarly interests. Perhaps we have become narrowly focused in sub-specialisms and have grown suspicious of the attempt to construct grand syntheses about early Christian theology. Perhaps we now have so many different Jesuses in contemporary scholarship, along-

---

1. William Wrede, *Paul* (London: P. Green, 1907), 180. For an overview of the history of debate, see my "Jesus and Paul," in *Dictionary of Paul and His Letters*, ed. Gerald F. Hawthorne, Ralph P. Martin, and Daniel G. Reid (Downers Grove: InterVarsity, 1993), 492-503; cf. Victor Paul Furnish, "The Jesus-Paul Debate: From Baur to Bultmann," in *Paul and Jesus: Collected Essays*, ed. A. J. M. Wedderburn, JSNTSup 37 (Sheffield: Sheffield Academic Press, 1989), 17-50.

side several different Pauls, to the extent that we are simply too uncertain, or too much in disagreement, about both sides of the comparison to be able to engage in meaningful dialogue on this matter. Perhaps the theological motor of this debate has simply run out of fuel: even where contemporary theology retains an interest in the historical Jesus, this may be couched in terms which accommodate various reconstructions of that Jesus and which allow for considerable diversity in earliest Christianity, even between Jesus and Paul. And if Paul is the object of theological and ideological attack, as he continues to be, there are far easier ways to undermine his authority than the claim that he corrupted or misconstrued the message of Jesus.[2]

The waning of interest in our topic is ironic in at least one respect. Contemporary scholarship, for all its diversity, is practically unanimous in affirming that, for both Jesus and Paul, a focal point of attention was the status and condition of Israel in the purposes of God. If the "third quest" of the historical Jesus has achieved anything, it has enabled re-engagement with the reality of "Jesus the Jew," even if the reconstruction of his aims, concerns, and self-understanding remains a matter of controversy between Sanders, Vermes, Crossan, Wright, Allison, and others.[3] At least we cannot imagine now describing Jesus' message in the old abstract categories of "the Fatherhood of God" and "the infinite value of the human soul"! Similarly, the postwar shift in Pauline studies, promoted by Stendahl and Sanders, has reconceived Paul as a Jew wrestling with thoroughly Jewish questions, and even those who take Paul to be heavily influenced by late Hellenistic rhetoric and philosophy support the broad consensus that the Letter to the Romans is *primarily* about God, Jews, and Gentiles, not ab-

---

2. For a defense of Paul as vitally connected to the teaching of Jesus see David Wenham, *Paul: Follower of Jesus or Founder of Christianity?* (Grand Rapids: Eerdmans, 1995). The heftiest attacks on Paul today concern his relationship to power: see, e.g., Elizabeth A. Castelli, *Imitating Paul: A Discourse of Power* (Louisville: Westminster/John Knox, 1991); Stephen D. Moore, *God's Beauty Parlor: And Other Queer Spaces in and around the Bible* (Stanford: Stanford University Press, 2001), 133-72.

3. E. P. Sanders, *Jesus and Judaism* (London: SCM, 1985); Geza Vermes, *Jesus the Jew* (London: SCM, 1973); Vermes, *The Religion of Jesus the Jew* (London: SCM, 1993); J. D. Crossan, *The Historical Jesus* (Edinburgh: T&T Clark, 1991); N. T. Wright, *Jesus and the Victory of God* (London: SPCK, 1996); Dale C. Allison, *Jesus of Nazareth: Millenarian Prophet* (Minneapolis: Fortress, 1998). Cf. John P. Meier, *A Marginal Jew*, 3 vols. (New York: Doubleday, 1991, 1994, 2001); James D. G. Dunn, *Jesus Remembered* (Grand Rapids: Eerdmans, 2003).

stract *loci* of systematic theology.[4] The scholarly terrain is thus well-suited to the attempt to compare Jesus and Paul in their understanding of Israel, her history, present standing, and current challenge in the sight of God. Of course, there is a large difference in Paul's construal of these questions, given his calling to be an apostle to the Gentiles and his experience of the Gentile mission. But I shall argue here that, despite this obvious difference in setting and focus, and whatever may or may not connect Paul to Jesus in the transmission of early Christian tradition, a fundamental similarity can be seen in their understanding of the challenge of divine grace to Israel's own traditions and boundaries.

We may begin to circle in on our topic by a brief consideration of two of the giants of twentieth-century scholarship. Contrary to popular opinion, Rudolf Bultmann was extremely interested in the message of Jesus and, at least in his earlier work, gave sustained attention to its force and impact on Jesus' contemporaries. Strongly influenced by the discovery of the apocalyptic Jesus by Weiss and Schweitzer, Bultmann insisted that Jesus was both radical and offensive to his contemporaries (*not* the liberal preacher of sweet generalities).[5] Unfortunately, the terms in which he understood this offense to function are set off against a caricature of "late Judaism." Against the Jewish contentment with single acts of law-observance and outward obedience, argues Bultmann, Jesus enunciated the total demand of God, a radical obedience which claims the whole self. Against Jewish self-satisfaction, expressed in boasts in one's own righteousness and the attempt to make oneself secure, Jesus insisted that we become aware of our nothingness before God, his apocalyptic message being a mythological expression of the encounter with God which shatters our sense of ourselves and our futures. Thus, says Bultmann,

> When Jesus juxtaposes the repentant publican to the self-satisfied Pharisee, or the "prodigal" son to the correct elder son, he makes clear

4. Krister Stendahl, *Paul among Jews and Gentiles* (London: SCM, 1976); E. P. Sanders, *Paul and Palestinian Judaism* (London: SCM, 1977); Sanders, *Paul, the Law, and the Jewish People* (Philadelphia: Fortress, 1983). For an example of a reading of Romans in the framework of late Hellenistic philosophy and rhetoric, see Stanley K. Stowers, *A Rereading of Romans* (New Haven: Yale University Press, 1994).

5. See especially Rudolf Bultmann, *Jesus and the Word* (London: Nicholson & Watson, 1935). For an appreciation of this book and its influence, see C. K. Barrett, "Jesus and the Word," in *Jesus and the Word, and Other Essays* (Edinburgh: T&T Clark, 1995), 213-23.

who the real sinner is — namely, the one who does not see the serious-ness, the radicalness of God's demand; who supposes that he is able to stand in God's presence because of his correctness and accomplish-ments, and does not understand that God demands the *entire* man.[6]

In this sense, Bultmann's Jesus induces terror rather than relief, liber-ation but absolute demand. And it is precisely this individualized and exis-tentialist message of a radically new self-understanding that Bultmann finds in Paul's superficially rather different discussions of the law and of the message of the cross.[7] At this deeper level, even if Paul hardly ever quotes Jesus and has no interest in Jesus as teacher, they each confront their contemporaries with the radical address of God. Thus in Bultmann's famous phrase, which I echo in my title, "whoever finds Paul offensive and uncanny *(widerwärtig und unheimlich)* must find Jesus equally so."[8]

E. P. Sanders reads both Jesus and Paul in utterly different terms. His Jesus, who calls the twelve disciples to reconstitute the tribes of Israel and threatens the destruction of the temple, certainly constitutes some sort of threat to the priests, but hardly to Jews or Judaism as such, and certainly not in the terms of Bultmann's existentialism.[9] On the whole, Sanders' Je-sus is law-observant, with the possible exception of the call to discipleship and the duty to bury one's family; there is no schema of religious antithe-ses, such as Bultmann advanced. As we shall see, Sanders recognizes some offensiveness in Jesus' notorious meals with "sinners," but the scope of this offense is limited: "sinners" are a small and very particular segment of the population, and Jesus' offense lies not in promoting a different conception of God or of divine forgiveness (which is always available in Judaism) but, perhaps, in his failure to demand repentance as it was normally under-stood.[10] As for Paul, the standard picture of Paul's stance for grace against Jewish legalism is utterly dismissed. The Judaism of Paul's day, with its pat-

6. Rudolf Bultmann, "Jesus and Paul," in *Existence and Faith* (London: Hodder & Stoughton, 1961), 183-201 (on 190). Cf. Bultmann, "The Significance of the Historical Jesus for the Theology of Paul," in *Faith and Understanding* (New York: Harper & Row, 1966), 220-46.

7. Rudolf Bultmann, *The Theology of the New Testament* (London: SCM, 1952), 187-352.

8. Bultmann, "Jesus and Paul," 194.

9. Sanders, *Jesus and Judaism;* cf. Sanders, *The Historical Figure of Jesus* (London: Pen-guin, 1993).

10. Sanders, *Jesus and Judaism*, 174-211; cf. *The Historical Figure of Jesus*, 232-37.

tern of covenantal nomism, had precisely the same balance of "grace" and "works" as one finds in Paul's theology: the real difference between them lies in Paul's understanding of salvation through participation in Christ, a largely different "pattern of religion" which implicitly undercuts the validity of the covenant, as understood in Judaism.[11]

This is hardly the place for a full discussion of the strengths and weaknesses of these large-scale hypotheses. Let me call attention to just one point. Bultmann's analysis of the offensiveness of Jesus and Paul may be conducted in terms which, with the waning of existentialism and a better understanding of Judaism, we can no longer support. But at least he is struggling with a question which needs to be answered, and that is why both Jesus and Paul considered their message (whether concerning the kingdom of God or the gospel of Christ) a *skandalon* to their contemporaries. Although numerous historical answers can be given to this question, I venture to suggest a thesis which is radical in placing center-stage a factor which Sanders has persuaded a generation of scholars to be completely irrelevant: that is, the enactment of the deeply subversive and sharply caustic grace of God. I hope to show that this *can* be re-entered into the discussion without falling back into old caricatures of a graceless Judaism, or grossly simple antitheses between religions of grace and religions of works.

Jesus, Sinners, and the Discomfort of the Elder Son

Among the very few things about which practically *all* Jesus-questers agree is that Jesus was infamous for consorting with "sinners." The varied evidence for this conclusion, multiply attested, and clearly reflecting something of a scandal in Jesus' day, convinced Sanders that this was one of the facets of Jesus' life which can be judged historically secure, though he also performed a great service to scholarship by clarifying what might and might not be meant by the term "sinner" and how this term was *not* synonymous with the phrase "the people of the land" (*'amme ha-aretz).*[12] "Sinners," in the context of Jesus' controversies, were notorious or persistent law-breakers, Jews whose manner of life brought dishonor or hardship on their fellow Jews through sexual, financial, or political compromise of Is-

11. Sanders, *Paul and Palestinian Judaism,* 431-556.
12. Sanders, *Jesus and Judaism,* 176-99.

rael's ancestral customs. Prostitutes and tax collectors are the two cases named in the Gospels, of course, but not the only ones who could be characterized as "sinners" or "wicked." Now, clarifying the identity of these people with whom Jesus shared meals and an apparently high level of intimacy is one thing, but assessing why his behavior was shocking and why Jesus would take this risk — even court this negative reputation — is another matter altogether. Sanders wrestles mightily with the question of why Jesus' behavior might have caused offense. He dismisses as unrealistic a common view that Jesus simply offers forgiveness and grace: this, he insists, would hardly have been shocking to his contemporaries, who all believed in the efficacy of repentance and forgiveness. Somewhat exasperated with the theological tone of the discussion of this topic, Sanders asks:

> Did [sinners] not know that if they renounced those aspects of their lives which were an affront to God's law, they would have been accepted with open arms? Is it a serious proposal that tax collectors and the wicked longed for forgiveness, but could not find it within ordinary Judaism? . . . [T]here was a universal view that forgiveness is *always* available to those who return to the way of the Lord. . . . If Jesus, by eating with tax collectors, led them to repent, repay those whom they had robbed, and leave off practising their profession, he would have been a national hero.[13]

Sanders concludes that the nature of Jesus' offense must have been something else, and something quite specific: perhaps he "admitted the wicked into *his* community without making the normal demand of restitution and commitment to the law."[14] Perhaps Jesus offered forgiveness to "sinners" *before* they showed signs of repentance; perhaps he also promised inclusion in the kingdom "*without* requiring repentance as normally understood."[15]

Recent discussion about the historical Jesus indicates that there was enough provocation in this claim by Sanders, and enough ambiguity, to spawn considerable further debate, which I cannot enter into here.[16] We could go back and forth on the question whether Jesus issued calls to re-

---

13. Sanders, *Jesus and Judaism*, 202-3.
14. Sanders, *Jesus and Judaism*, 203.
15. Sanders, *Jesus and Judaism*, 206 (italics original).
16. See, e.g., Bruce Chilton, "Jesus and the Repentance of E. P. Sanders," *TynBul* 39 (1988): 1-18; Dale C. Allison, "Jesus and the Covenant: A Response to E. P. Sanders," *JSNT* 29 (1987): 57-78; Wright, *Jesus and the Victory of God*, 264-74.

pentance and what might be meant by this notion in practice. Wright's emphasis on the fact that it was *Jesus* who offered forgiveness and that this was a part of his claim that Israel's final restoration was taking place *now* and *through him* certainly helps us grasp the larger picture into which this provocative action is best placed.[17] But Sanders rightly pointed out that Jesus caused offense by eating precisely with *sinners* (the wicked in Israel, not just, as Wright has it, "the wrong sort of people"), and, in my view, the question is still unresolved as to why Jesus apparently prioritized, or made the focus of special celebration, precisely *these* people and in what respects he thereby scandalized other Jews.

We cannot here rehearse all the texts that touch on this topic, such as the claim that Jesus came to call the righteous, not sinners (Mark 2:15-17; Matt. 9:11-13; Luke 5:30-32), or the complaint that Jesus was a friend of "tax collectors and sinners" (Matt. 11:16-19; Luke 7:31-35; cf. Matt. 21:28-32). I will focus here on only one text, the Parable of the Prodigal Son (Luke 15:11-32), which encapsulates the issue by expressing the offense caused by Jesus' welcome of "sinners." While some attribute the artistry of this parable more to Luke than to Jesus, many scholars find good reason to trace its general tenor to Jesus, whatever one might say about the details of its present literary form. In recent discussion of this parable, N. T. Wright has drawn attention to the way the younger son's return echoes larger themes in Israel's accounts of her own experiences of exile and return, but he is incorrect, I think, to read the text through a particular historical grid, taking the prodigal as sinful Israel as a whole, now returning from metaphorical exile, while jealous figures take Samaritan-roles in resenting her appearance.[18] Similarly, Kenneth Bailey has emphasized the many echoes in this parable of the Esau-Jacob saga in Genesis 27–36, another tale of rival brothers and a father, with an awkward moment of return.[19] But he over-

---

17. Wright, *Jesus and the Victory of God*, 274: "Jesus was replacing adherence or allegiance to the Temple and Torah with allegiance to himself." But the alternative Wright proposes is unnecessary and should be resisted: "The question was not about the sinners, or the moral or theological niceties of whether they had repented, and, if so, in what sense. It was about the scandalous implied redefinition of the kingdom itself" (274).

18. Wright, *Jesus and the Victory of God*, 125-31.

19. Kenneth Bailey, *Jacob and the Prodigal* (Downers Grove: InterVarsity, 2003). For an analysis of the resonances between the story and Hellenistic ideals of liberality, see David A. Holgate, *Prodigality, Liberality and Meanness: The Prodigal Son in Greco-Roman Perspective*, JSNTSup 187 (Sheffield: Sheffield Academic Press, 1999).

does the parallels, as if the parable is simply modeled on the Genesis narrative, curtailing its complexity in intertextual reference. Both, however, rightly require that we ask what Jesus is saying here about Israel and her God — rather than, for instance, about the human soul and salvation, abstractly or individualistically conceived. For my purposes, and in place of a full-dress analysis of this parable, I wish to emphasize just three features:

First, we should note the *irretrievable* damage caused by the younger son's behavior. His scandalous behavior starts at the very beginning of the story when he asks for his share of the family property; as Bailey has noted, this is tantamount to wishing his father dead, and would be considered grossly insulting in an ancient rural environment.[20] Insults like this are never purely private affairs, and his request, granted by the father, his alarming liquidation of the family's assets, and his departure over the horizon would all be noted, resented, and condemned by the community as a whole. Once abroad, his greatest crime is simply the squandering of the family wealth, and the cycle of degradation is given symbolic cultural significance by his eventual occupation, and near starvation, as a keeper of unclean pigs. "And no one would give him anything" (Luke 15:16): so worthless has he become in the eyes of all that he is not even of sufficient significance to be a recipient of benefaction. Faced with starvation, the prodigal has only one possibility for survival. Whether in real repentance or, as Bailey claims, in a cunning scheme, the son decides to return, but now on a wholly different footing. Since he has asked for and lost his share of the family property, he cannot be treated now as a son, drawing off family resources; he can ask only to be *hired* and thus to support himself from his wages, to live as a subordinate and alienated member of the household, subject to permanent communal shame, but at least with food in his stomach.

The details here are true to first-century social reality, and this scenario is surely more realistic than Sanders' image of notorious sinners expecting that if they renounced those aspects of their lives which broke Israel's laws, they would be "accepted with open arms." A prostitute who had brought deep and permanent shame on her family — her parents, her siblings, her cousins, and her village community — would hardly be received back gladly as soon as she abandoned her trade. The tax collector who had ruined families and businesses, whose sharp practice had kept many struggling in debt and driven some to ruin, was hardly going to find everything

---

20. Kenneth Bailey, *Poet and Peasant* (Grand Rapids: Eerdmans, 1976), 161-69.

forgiven and forgotten when he apologized and paid back some of his ill-gotten gains.[21] As the parable indicates, Jesus is dealing with people who can never expect to find social acceptance, the irretrievably wicked, who are permanently subject to hostility or suspicion.

Hence, secondly, the shock, and the huge display of emotion, in the father's welcome of his prodigal son. That the father runs through the village to embrace the son is, as Bailey shows, a sign that he cares little in this situation for common dignity, such is the exuberance of his delight at seeing his son.[22] That he falls on his neck and kisses him is a near verbal echo of Esau's welcome of his alienated brother, Jacob (Gen. 33:4); only here, because it is the father who takes this action, we are already made to wonder, by this intertextual sign, what will be the reaction of *this* boy's elder brother. Everything here is extravagance, expense, surfeit — after the prodigal's extreme lack, in which no one deigned to give him anything, he is now judged worthy to receive the very best and to receive it from the people he has wounded most, his own family. His prepared speech is cut short because, by his father's reckoning, he *can* only be a son, not a hired worker. The party that begins at once is a symbol not just of relief, but of delight, celebration, and overflowing joy: proudly owning his offspring, the father declares, "This, my son, was dead and is alive, was lost and has been found" (15:24).

The party here, like the parties that complete the companion parables of the lost sheep and the lost coin, is a mirror of the real-life celebrations of Jesus, his meal-fellowship with "sinners and tax collectors" in which he welcomed these most unlikely people and perhaps enacted a foretaste of the messianic banquet (cf. 15:1-2, following the banquet parables of Luke 14). Jesus' delight is in reclaiming those apparently lost to Israel, the "lost sheep of the house of Israel" (Matt. 15:24; cf. 9:26), drawing into the promise of the kingdom those most in danger of forfeiting their place. Just as his healings released and reclaimed those "bound by Satan" (Mark 3:27; Luke 13:16), Jesus here made special effort, and derived special joy, in retrieving the hopeless. Both the manner and the object of his celebration were remarkable: that he was announcing the presence, or near presence, of the kingdom precisely in *his* meal-company (not in the temple and not through scribal authority) was striking in itself; that this king-

---

21. As a contemporary social parallel, we may consider the difficulty of communities, even churches, in accepting reformed pedophiles into their midst.

22. Bailey, *Poet and Peasant,* 181-82.

dom's presence constituted not condemnation of the wicked (as one would expect) but their welcome was truly extraordinary. As we can sense in the criticism that Jesus was "a glutton and a drunkard" (Luke 7:34), the exuberance of his company was apparently as noticeable as the joy of the banquet described in our parable.

But then, thirdly, we must account for the offense that this celebration might cause. The elder brother is "in the field" (Luke 15:25), an ominous echo of the story of Jacob and Esau (Gen. 25:27, 29), and we wonder how *this* saga will end. The elder son is angry and resentful, levels lurid accusations against his brother, and refuses to come into the party, thus insulting his father. Why? Is he just mean-spirited? The parable could hardly work if he were an *exceptional* case whose conduct was inexplicably rude; it must follow a recognizable logic. Part of that logic could be a sense of financial injustice: since the younger brother has already received, at the beginning of the parable, his share of the property, his treatment now as a son (and not as a hired laborer) means he will continue to drain the family resources, eating into the *elder brother's* portion through the generosity of the father. But his logic also goes deeper than that. As a dutiful son, who has labored faithfully for his father, he has upheld the interests and honor of the family, an honor built on a publicly recognized system of just reward for fair compliance with social rules. Now he confronts a father, the figurehead and sustainer of that system, who indeed recognizes its fairness and freely acknowledges his son's just privileges and worth: "You are always with me," he assures him, "and all that I have is yours" (Luke 15:31). But this father *also* recognizes a *necessity* in that system, an element it contains but can never fully bound, which is the necessity of unconditional welcome to a lost son. "It was necessary," asserts the father (not "it was fitting," as in many translations, but ἔδει), "to make merry and be glad" (15:32). The elder son is thus faced with an urgent question: will he comply with his father's construal of family justice and necessity and thus also himself welcome back this prodigal, or will he insist on *his own* construal of family rights and thus alienate himself not only from his brother but also from his father? In other words, if he persists in his present refusal to recognize the prodigal as his brother (he calls him only "this son of yours"), he will repudiate his inner congruence with the interests of his father, who has declared that "all that I have [including my found son] is also yours." The father's generosity has created this crisis for the son precisely by unsettling his sense of what it means to belong to this family: but since the father's behavior is what constitutes the ethos of the family, the elder son must either comply with this extravagant and norm-breaking gesture or alienate himself from the family to which he has been so dutiful as an exemplary son!

What might this indicate about Jesus' challenge to Israel? Within the setting of Luke 15, the elder brother clearly corresponds to those who "grumble" at Jesus' table-fellowship with tax-collectors and sinners (15:1-2), the grumblers identified as "Pharisees and scribes." It is hard to be sure exactly who took offense at Jesus' practice, but if this parable goes back to Jesus at all, it suggests that he knew his behavior would gain disapproval, but still thought he had good reason to pursue it — based on his under-standing of God's action in present history. It is important to be clear here on what is *not* being claimed. I am *not* suggesting that Jesus introduced to his contemporary Jews a new concept of God, in some sense a "purer" no-tion of God's grace than what they had learned before. That God's costly grace forgives wayward Israel as well as the wayward *in* Israel is deeply es-tablished in Israel's scriptural traditions and is precisely what Jesus is drawing off, not least in the allusions to Jacob, the wayward younger son. Nor is it the case that Jesus is simply pressing for the boundaries of that grace to be extended a little to include a few people on the edge who might otherwise have missed out. Rather, in this dramatic and critical moment in Israel's history he is asking her to identify with a striking dynamic in divine forgiveness, enacted and symbolized by his meal-fellowship. The offense is partly that it is *Jesus* who is interpreting the times and the will of God in this way and partly that the will of God with which they must identify is one that strains the stability of their own sense of covenant and law. In the name of the Father, Jesus stages a party of welcome to the irretrievably wicked and invites other Jews to join in. What this implies is that more is required of them than keeping the commandments, though those are never attacked. What is required is that the older son join the party be-cause it is here that the Father is enacting and progressing his kingdom. This dramatic act of generosity emerges out of the ethos of Israel's tradi-tions and scriptures, but simultaneously threatens to destabilize the cate-gories and norms by which righteousness is defined and covenant main-tained. The elder son senses injustice where the father spontaneously presses beyond justice in an act of forgiveness — he senses that something within the family ethos is here operating in a way that makes his own posi-tion less predictable and less secure. This is not, as is sometimes said, the operation of an *alternative* economy of gift, in direct opposition to an economy of deserts. The father's appreciation of his elder son's work and his welcome of the prodigal are not two utterly opposed systems of operation as father, but the recognition that within the economy of right and justice, work and its appreciation in reward, there lies an uncontainable element of generosity, unjustifiable and unquantifiable, which threatens to unsettle the whole economy, without thereby sweeping it away or replacing it with something completely different. And the crisis that Jesus' ministry represents for Israel is not just the claim that the eschatological moment of salvation and judgment is breaking in through him, but that this outrageous dynamic of salvation forces Israel to choose if she will join the celebration of welcome to the wicked — or alternatively find herself alienated from God and under judgment. In this sense, the grace which Jesus speaks about and enacts is subversive, both liberating and caustic, both welcoming and threatening (cf. Luke 7:29-30). The parable does not write the elder son off, but it requires that he submit to the understanding of family enacted by his father or find himself unwittingly alienated, as "far off" as was once his prodigal younger brother.

Paul, the Gentiles, and the Unsettling Function of Grace

The theme of grace, or gift, is written so large across Paul's letters that our problem is here not whether Paul said anything on this topic, but what we can select within the confines of this essay. I have elected to begin where Paul began, with his account of his call/conversion, and to end with his most provocative statement on our theme, in Romans 9–11. I can do justice to neither passage, but if I can show how unsettling to his Jewish traditions is his very Jewish understanding of grace I will have succeeded at least in broaching a subject that deserves much fuller consideration.

In his autobiographical account in Galatians 1, Paul recounts his call/conversion in a form which juxtaposes in effect two narratives, one of his former life "in Judaism," the other initiated by the grace of God. In the first, in which he, Paul, is the subject of the verbs, he recounts his former life in terms which entirely conform to our expectations of historical discourse.[23]

---

23. See further my "Paul's Story: Theology as Testimony," in *Narrative Dynamics in Paul: A Critical Assessment*, ed. Bruce W. Longenecker (Louisville: Westminster/John Knox, 2002), 133-56.

Placing himself within his familial and ethnic context, Paul measures his "progress" by comparison with his contemporaries and by the measuring rod of the social norms characterized as "the traditions of our ancestors" (Gal. 1:14). It is a story of success and zeal — and zeal is a positive quality — except for one thing: precisely in making progress Paul was actually persecuting the church of God, and trying to destroy it (Gal. 1:13). As he puts it in Philippians 3, his conscience was entirely clear and his compliance with the law complete: but, as he discovered in or near Damascus, that led paradoxically not to serving God, but to opposing God's will and God's church!

The moment when he realizes this fissure in his understanding of "righteousness" is, he says, the moment when God was pleased to reveal his Son "in me" (Gal. 1:16). This "apocalypse" is the topic of the second narrative, which cuts across the first, whose subject is God and whose theme is grace: "When God who had set me apart from my mother's womb and called me through his grace was pleased to reveal his Son in me. . . ." This revelation and commission to preach Christ among the Gentiles is not the next step along the same path of progress, but first and foremost a divine step which enters and interrupts a human narrative. Although the "I"-narrative will begin again when the subordinate clause is over, it is an "I" that will neither be the same, nor see the same, again (Gal. 2:19-20).[24]

Now it is striking and important that the language which Paul here uses for his call-experience derives from those very Jewish Scriptures in which he was socialized: being set apart from his mother's womb is precisely the way the call of Isaiah, and of Jeremiah, is understood (Isa. 49:1; Jer. 1:5). He is speaking, in other words, from within his tradition, but at the same time describing an event which interrupted and destabilized the normalized progress of that tradition. The language of grace and calling is classic Jewish discourse, but it here operates not to confirm but to subvert the straightforward assumptions of his Jewish socialization. The oddity of Paul's life-story, which appears to haunt him in every retelling, is that the acme of his zeal for the law set him precisely against the church of God. Thus, he experiences the grace of God not as a relief but as a judgment, or rather as a relief entangled with judgment, a shaking of his previously stable system by the uncontainable element he calls the grace of God.

Closely associated with this alarming shifting of the terrain is Paul's

---

24. Cf. J. Louis Martyn, "Epistemology at the Turn of the Ages," in *Theological Issues in the Letters of Paul* (Edinburgh: T&T Clark, 1997), 89-110.

mission to the Gentiles. We cannot know whether his sense of call to the Gentiles emerged as immediately after his Damascus experience as he and Luke suggest, but there is clearly an inner connection between them. There were in Paul's day plenty of proselytes whose induction into the laws of Moses and the ancestral traditions of the Jews was facilitated by Jewish instructors.[25] But Paul could hardly be another such teacher. For him the ancestral traditions had become a problematical entity — not to be rejected tout court, but neither the secure ground on which he could take his stand. With the shaking of his cultural coordinates there collapsed the boundary-fence that previously separated Jew from Gentile. The grace he had experienced, and which Gentiles now experienced in their full receipt of the Spirit, did not simply extend across the border reaching out to bring others within its stable frontier: it destabilized the border itself.

Once again I must insist that the grace of God is not a new theme within Judaism, and Paul does not understand it to *revoke* his ancestral traditions, but to break them open in unexpected and unsettling ways. He can make sense of what has happened to him by reference to the prophetic call-narratives, and he can comprehend the Gentile mission by reference to the radical Abrahamic traditions of faith and promise to the nations. In this respect it makes sense to affirm that Paul stands within the Jewish tradition: he has not moved into a different discourse or introduced an alien conceptuality.[26] Nonetheless, his new making of sense involved a radical reconfiguration of that shared ancestral heritage, in which the grace of God brought it into both judgment and fulfillment.

Nowhere is the operation of that caustic yet redemptive grace more evident than in the complex and ever-fascinating discourse of Romans 9–11. Let me highlight just three samples of that operation in each of the three steps Paul takes through this argument (9:6-29; 9:30–10:21; 11:1-32). The first is perhaps the most basic and the most threatening. As soon as he has listed Israel's privileges in 9:4-5, privileges that he never denies in the chapters that follow, Paul immediately unsettles the category "Israel," to

---

25. As Martin Goodman has argued (in *Mission and Conversion* [Oxford: Clarendon, 1994]), there did not exist in Paul's day a Jewish "mission" to Gentiles comparable to later Christian understandings and practices of mission. But our primary sources reveal a number of proselytes, whose assimilation in Judaism must have been facilitated by instruction (see, e.g., Josephus, *Ant.* 20.17-96).

26. For Paul as a Jew, among other Jews, making (new) sense of his scriptural tradition, see Francis Watson, *Paul and the Hermeneutics of Faith* (London: T&T Clark, 2004).

whom these privileges are accorded. In Romans 9:6-29 Paul calls attention to the pattern by which God has called this Israel, all down her history from Abraham onwards: a pattern of grace or mercy, which both establishes a people to bear his promises and confounds the normal patterns of genealogy and performance, birth and worth, by which one would expect to identify who is a member of the righteous and the elect. If God's grace operates not by human will or exertion, but by God's own compassion, then perhaps "Israel" might constitute a much smaller subset within the ethnic entity called Israel (9:27-29), or it might include a much wider range of people, including, that is, Gentiles who would normally be considered not God's people (9:24-26). One has a strong sense here that something is subverting the normal parameters of Jewish discourse, and that something is the very Jewish notion of divine election and divine grace.

In the second step of his argument (9:30–10:21), Paul expresses this paradoxical reality by speaking of a "stone of stumbling," associated with the fact that Israel pursued but did not attain the law of righteousness, while Gentiles, who never pursued it, achieved the goal they did not set out to attain. What is shocking and deeply uncanny about this stone is that it has been laid by God: "Behold, I am laying in Zion a stone that will make men stumble, a rock that will make them fall" (Rom. 9:33). In due course it becomes clear that this rock is one way of speaking of the Messiah-event (10:11-13), and what Paul emphasizes in this context is that this event is by nature boundary-breaking: there is no distinction between Jew and Gentile because in this event God is rich (in grace and mercy) to *all* who call upon him. But this grace is itself a challenge, even a threat: it represents the imprint on history of the "righteousness of God," which is not wholly opposite to but certainly exceeds Israel's own righteousness. There is no problem with Israel's zeal, as there was none with Paul's (10:2; cf. Phil. 3:6): the problem is in her not knowing, recognizing, or submitting to the operation of God's righteousness in the Messiah-event (10:3), which is in complex ways both the goal and the terminus of the law (10:4). Unless this grace is known and embraced by faith, it stands against Israel, paradoxically, as her rock of stumbling.

And thus to the third and most traumatic step in the argument (11:1-32). Now Paul reveals both the devastating effect of the Messiah-event — the reduction of Israel to a remnant, saved by grace, her stumbling and her spirit of stupor (11:1-10) — and the redemptive purpose of God, which has confined all (even Israel) to disobedience, in order that he might have mercy on all (11:32). Although this extraordinary story involves the grafting in of the wild-olive Gentiles and the promise of the re-grafting of the natural olive Israel (11:16-24), it remains a story in which grace and judgment intertwine. Both Jew and Gentile receive mercy only on the other side of judgment, after condemnation for their disobedience (11:11-16). And both stand, as it were, on the precipice, always capable of toppling over again into disobedience: Paul reminds Gentiles, as much as Jews, of the severity and the kindness of God, since if they do not continue in his kindness, they too can be cut off (11:22). No one is secure here, except by the sole and single thread of divine grace; every other support is cut away. Romans 9–11 is about the bonfire of the vanities, when every social, legal, ethnic, and political support is stripped away by the acerbic, but ultimately redemptive, grace of God. We have hardly understood it if we do not come away deeply unsettled and more than a little scared.

Once again, let us note that Paul is not bringing to bear on his ancestral tradition some external criterion, some alien system of evaluation like the Hellenistic (or European liberal) demand for "universal" and non-particular understandings of God.[27] On the contrary, his central thematic, the grace of God, is deeply embedded in Israel's traditions, and perhaps more characteristic of Judaism than of any other ancient religious tradition. But what is embedded and contained is also uncontainable: it resides within the system always ready to emerge from it and stand over it, not as its polar opposite, but as the excess which reveals the inadequacy of the system in which it cannot be bound. Paul's and Israel's legal rectitude, their utter compliance with the law and its demands, is shown by the Messiah-event to be inadequate, because the grace of God in Christ exceeds that righteousness of the law, and in exceeding it makes it impossible simply to reestablish the law as the continuing norm for the future. Emerging uncontainably from the system, it demands submission to *God's* way of righteousness, which will establish new forms of community, and thus a new system of church polity, but then in turn challenge every human form that calls itself "church."

If the parable of the Prodigal Son emanates (perhaps at a little re-

---

27. See Daniel Boyarin, *Paul: A Radical Jew* (Berkeley: University of California Press, 1994), who understands Paul as an exponent of modern European "universalism" (with its roots in Hellenism). His reading is much influenced by F. C. Baur and the work of the "new perspective," whose conceptual framework lends itself all too well to this reading.

move) from Jesus as Paul's letters emanate from Paul, what can we say in conclusion about "Jesus and Paul"? They clearly operate in different genres and different social contexts, and on this topic we can trace, as far as I can see, no direct lines of continuity in tradition from Jesus to Paul: neither in Romans 9–11 nor in his other discussions of grace does Paul make mention of Jesus' teaching on this matter! Jesus was dealing with sinful Israelites, the wicked who had become irretrievably alienated from Israel's traditions, Paul with sinful Gentiles, who were alienated, as it were, from without. Historians may be able to trace some genetic connection via the medium of the Hellenists, whose receipt of Gentile converts might have been inspired by Jesus' table-fellowship with "sinners," and, in turn, have inspired Paul's mission to Gentiles.[28] But whatever one says about the *connection,* one cannot help being struck by the *congruity* between Jesus and Paul on this issue. Both enact and express a paradigm of God's grace that is simultaneously welcoming to the lost outsider and deeply challenging to the insider — challenging to the point of scorching away the secure marks of a bounded system. Both the elder brother in the parable and the people of Israel in Romans have their familiar coordinates upset, not because God/the Father acts less justly than they might have expected, but because he acts in an excess of gift or forgiveness that dramatically loosens their stable moorings. In both cases it can be claimed that this is precisely how one should expect God to act — with the spontaneous compassion of a Father and the sovereign grace of the one who chose Isaac, not Ishmael, and Jacob, not Esau. In both cases scriptural traditions are activated to make sense of the present drama, but in the full realization that this will unsettle and offend those whose compliance is exemplary and loyalty secure. Neither Jesus nor Paul are appealing to a "different system of religion" or a new concept of God; but nor do they represent some homogenized entity we have created and labeled "covenantal nomism." Both radicalize, intensify, emphasize, and enact the divine impetus of grace, an impetus which emerges fully from Israel's own traditions, but in the teaching of Jesus and the Christology of Paul cannot rest comfortably within that tradition. The result is the paradox I call subversive or caustic grace with which both Jesus and Paul announce their harshest words of divine judgment and their strongest affirmations of divine compassion.

---

28. See A. J. M. Wedderburn, "Paul and Jesus: Similarity and Continuity," in *Paul and Jesus,* 117-43.

Chapter 2

Law and Gospel in Jesus and Paul

STEPHEN WESTERHOLM

N either Jesus nor Paul could avoid addressing issues related to the Torah; yet for neither Jesus nor Paul was Torah the focus of his mission.
That place, we may say, in both cases was occupied by the "gospel." "The
kingdom of God is at hand," proclaims the Markan Jesus; "repent, and believe in the gospel."[1] For Paul, the "gospel" that he preached could be
summed up in the words "Christ died for our sins . . . , he was buried, and
. . . he was raised on the third day in accordance with the scriptures."[2] My
concern in this paper is not to add a few inches to the already imposing
mountains of scholarly literature on Jesus' or Paul's "view of the law" per
se; nor do I intend to address their respective understandings of "the gospel."[3] To be explored here is rather the relationship *between* law and gospel,
as that relationship is seen by Jesus and Paul. Why (we may well wonder)
did God give the law to Moses — as both Jesus and Paul believe he did — if

---

1. Mark 1:15 (RSV); cf. Matt. 4:17; 10:7; Luke 10:9, 11. Matthew sums up Jesus' message
as the "gospel of the kingdom" (Matt. 4:23; 9:35 [RSV]). See also Luke 4:43; 7:22; 8:1. Unless
otherwise indicated, biblical quotations in this paper are taken from the New Revised Standard Version.

2. See 1 Cor. 15:1-4.

3. I am thus not concerned here to compare the *substance* of Jesus' "gospel" of the
dawning kingdom of God with that of Paul's "gospel" of the crucified and resurrected
Christ.

This paper was prepared for oral presentation at the symposium. In revising it for publication, I have chosen to retain the style of the paper as originally given; documentation has
been added only where it seemed essential.

the gospel was to follow? What role is the Mosaic Law thought to play in preparation for, or in the proclamation of, the gospel? Conversely, why is the gospel needed where God has already given the law? What role does the gospel play that the law could not play in the divine scheme of things? These are the types of questions that I wish to address in this paper.

To address them here in even the most preliminary way will require a strict limitation of the sources at which we will look. In the case of Paul, our subject is discussed primarily in his letters to the Romans and the Galatians. For purposes of this paper, I will focus on the argument of Galatians (particularly ch. 3), drawing only occasionally on other parts of Paul's writings. In the case of Jesus, our attention is naturally drawn to the *Matthean* Jesus: of all the Gospels, it is certainly Matthew's that is most suggestive for our topic.[4] (Matthew's Gospel has added interest in that it offers what is, in a number of ways, a different perspective from that of Paul.) As a framework for the discussion of Matthew, I will use the encounter related in each of the Synoptic Gospels between Jesus and an unnamed inquirer now universally known as the "rich young ruler." In Matthew the story begins in 19:16.

The Gospel Supersedes the Law?

"Teacher," the young man asks, "what good deed must I do to have eternal life?" Perhaps we are not as surprised as we ought to be that the young man even raised such a question. Did not every right-thinking Jew already know the answer? God had chosen Israel as his people. He had given them his law. He had told them, "Do this and you will live."[5] Admittedly, the words were initially taken as prescribing the path to blessing for God's people. But the prescription would hardly change for Jews of Jesus' day who believed in life beyond the grave as well: Keep what God has commanded you to keep and you will enjoy God's blessing — in this life *and* the next. Perfection, moreover, was not required: God had ordained ways to atone for sin for those who repented of their wrongdoing. Why, then, would an informed, religious Jew wonder what he had to do to "inherit eternal life"?

---

4. Note that whenever "Jesus" is used in the discussion that follows, it is Matthew's portrait of Jesus that is intended.

5. So we may paraphrase Lev. 18:5. See also, e.g., Deut. 30:15-20.

For our purposes, it will be convenient to assume that our young man's concern about entrance into "life" was stimulated by the teaching of Jesus. As well it might be: after all, much that Jesus says in Matthew's Gospel seems designed to provoke the kind of question raised by our rich young man. "The kingdom of heaven is like treasure hidden in a field, which someone found and hid; then in his joy he goes and sells all that he has and buys that field" (13:44). This is a parable, to be sure, but it is hard to see what in the parable would stand for "Show faithfulness to God by keeping God's commandments!" Entering the kingdom seems rather to be a matter of wise investing — surely an approach that would pique the interest of our "rich young ruler"! But what, the young man might well want to know, would it mean in real life for him to "sell all that he has and buy the field"?

"Again, the kingdom of heaven is like a merchant in search of fine pearls; on finding one pearl of great value, he went and sold all that he had and bought it" (13:45-46). The merchant is undoubtedly portrayed as doing in *his* situation what Jesus' listeners ought to do in *theirs*. But again, our young man might well wonder what it would mean for him to exchange his present possessions for a goodly pearl. What, in real life, should be done to have a part in God's kingdom? Jesus' teaching in these parables appears designed to provoke the young man's question. And the intended answer appears to be something quite different from keeping the law. But what, specifically, does Jesus have in mind?

We may suppose that our young man knows even more about Jesus. Much that Jesus says in Matthew's Gospel suggests that a new and decisive stage in history is about to dawn, or has already begun to dawn, and that a fresh response is required. "The kingdom of heaven has come near," Jesus announces (4:17). Of course in one sense God's kingdom,[6] God's rule, is always with us: "[God's] kingdom is an everlasting kingdom, and [his] dominion endures throughout all generations" (Ps. 145:13). God's rule is eternal in the sense that God is always in control.[7] Still, in Jesus' day (as in our own) not everyone can be said to acknowledge or submit to God's rule;

6. Occasionally Matthew uses the expression "kingdom of God" (Matt. 12:28; 19:24; 21:31, 43; it is found consistently in the Gospels of Mark and Luke), but he prefers "kingdom of heaven." In Jewish circles "heaven" was at times substituted for "God" as a sign of reverence for the deity; the phrases are equivalent in meaning. See Gustaf Dalman, *The Words of Jesus* (Edinburgh: T&T Clark, 1902), 91-96, 217-19.

7. See Dan. 4:34-35.

God's righteous demands are widely ignored or flouted. And as a result, God's creation is marred by human idolatry, immorality, injustice, and violence. "The kingdom of heaven has come near" can only mean that God is about to put things right, to deal decisively with all that is evil, to establish his rule in a way that none can ignore. But how, our young man might well wonder, is one to prepare for this pending development? New times demand new measures: what measures should he take to ensure his part in the coming kingdom?

Jesus goes even further. It is not simply that the kingdom of God is *about* to break in; its day is already dawning. The law and the prophets lasted until John, but their day has now past; "from the days of John the Baptist until now the kingdom of heaven has suffered violence, and the violent take it by force" (Matt. 11:12-13). To his disciples Jesus says, "Blessed are your eyes, for they see, and your ears, for they hear. Truly I tell you, many prophets and righteous people longed to see what you see, but did not see it, and to hear what you hear, but did not hear it" (13:16-17). Not even optimistically can we suppose that our rich young ruler will have overheard these latter words, directed to the inner circle of Jesus' disciples. But perhaps with a little good will we can picture him hearing Jesus denounce his contemporaries for failing to repent when something greater than Jonah, something greater than Solomon, is here in their midst, right now (12:41-42). Yet again, the demand for repentance on Jesus' lips never seems to mean returning to an ever more faithful observance of Torah. The crowd attracted to Jesus included people notoriously negligent in attending to the law;[8] but Jesus does not direct them back to its statutes. Indeed, Jesus' own reputation, at least in certain matters of law-observance, seems dubious.[9] And to at least one challenge he responds that new wine demands new wineskins (9:17).

In short, however strange it might seem that a right-thinking religious Jew like our rich young ruler would wonder what he had to do to inherit eternal life, it is not strange at all that the issue became urgent, and its answer uncertain, for one who listened to the teaching of Jesus. In the texts we have looked at so far Jesus seems to be saying, "The day of the law and the prophets has passed. Now the kingdom of God is upon you, and it is to that kingdom that you must declare your allegiance. Leave behind the old

8. See, e.g., Matt. 9:10; 11:19.
9. See, e.g., Matt. 12:1-8, 9-13; and note 15:1-2.

wineskins; prepare for new wine. Buy the field in which the treasure of the kingdom is found. Purchase that goodly pearl." To all of which a young man might well respond, "Parables are fine for stimulating interest and provoking reflection. But tell me now, in plain text, what I must do to have a part in the kingdom of God!"

The Law Accompanies the Gospel?

And so Jesus responds, in plain text: "If you wish to enter into life, keep the commandments. . . . You shall not murder; You shall not commit adultery; You shall not steal; You shall not bear false witness; Honor your father and your mother; also, You shall love your neighbor as yourself" (Matt. 19:17-19). "If you wish to enter into life, keep the commandments." The kingdom of God and the age to come are open to those who show themselves in *this* life submissive to God's rule; and you show your submission to God by obeying God's commandments in the Law of Moses.

If our young man was not perplexed before, he has every reason to be so now. Jesus' answer sounds suspiciously like getting out the old wineskins. But before we pursue further our young man's quandary, let's pause and ask whether, if he had listened carefully to other things that Jesus says in Matthew's Gospel, he might not have been somewhat prepared for Jesus' answer here.

After all, Matthew does insist repeatedly that the coming of Jesus is simply the climactic conclusion of what has gone before. In his editorial comments, Matthew is frequently concerned to have us understand that Jesus fulfills the expectations announced within the Scriptures of Israel.[10] The same point is repeatedly made by the chief protagonist in his gospel. To say, as Matthew's Jesus says, that the day that God's people have longed for has now come[11] is certainly to indicate that something new and decisive is taking place; but it is also to say that what is now happening is the climax of all that God *has* been doing for centuries with the people of Israel. When disciples of John the Baptist ask Jesus whether he is the one for whom everyone is waiting, Jesus replies: "Go and tell John what you hear and see: the blind receive their sight, the lame walk, the lepers are cleansed,

---

10. Matt. 1:17, 22-23; 2:15, 17-18, 23, etc.
11. Matt. 13:16-17.

the deaf hear, the dead are raised, and the poor have good news brought to them" (11:4-5). What Jesus is doing is just what Isaiah said would happen in the glorious future.[12] What is now taking place is simply what the prophets foretold.

Now if Jesus represents the climactic fulfillment of all that God has been doing with Israel, there is no reason to expect God's will for his people to be any different in the time of Jesus from what it has always been. Jesus says, "Do not think that I have come to abolish the law or the prophets; I have come not to abolish but to fulfill" (5:17). When Jesus sums up human ethical responsibilities in the so-called "Golden Rule" — "Do to others as you would have them do to you" — he adds, "For this is the law and the prophets" (7:12). In other words, what the law and the prophets required in the past is still required today, and it can be summed up in the Golden Rule. When Jesus is asked what the greatest commandment is, he replies with not one, but two: "You shall love the Lord your God with all your heart, and with all your soul, and with all your mind," and "You shall love your neighbor as yourself." And then he adds again, "On these two commandments hang all the law and the prophets" (22:37-40). That is, the message of the law and the prophets retains its force today, and it can be summed up in the commandments to love God and love one's neighbor. God's demands remain today what they were when the law was given to Moses.

Taken by itself, all of this seems straightforward enough. And it need not be contradicted by the stories in which Jesus himself is thought to be lax in certain matters of law observance or by his failure to insist on scrupulous law observance by his followers. Jesus' point could well be (indeed, Jesus' point seems to have been) that his contemporaries had obscured the weightier matters of the law (justice, mercy, and faith) by their punctilious observance of lesser matters, the laws of tithing and ritual purity (23:23-24). The law of Moses is still the law of God, but we must put the emphasis where God put the emphasis when he said in Hosea, "I desire mercy, not sacrifice" (9:13).[13] True submission to God's will is not measured by one's conformity with such external measures as tithing one's produce and maintaining standards of ritual purity. True submission to God's will is found in the attitude of one's heart and in deeds of love and mercy. Even in our story, when Jesus says to the young man, "Keep the commandments,"

---

12. See Isa. 35:5-6; 61:1.
13. See also Matt. 12:7; the reference is to Hos. 6:6.

he repeats exclusively the moral commandments: "You shall not murder; You shall not commit adultery," and so on. The coming of the kingdom, in short, requires a truly radical observance of God's law, and one must focus on its essentials; but the law of God still states what God requires even when the gospel of the kingdom is proclaimed.

So we might think if we simply focused on these latter texts; but these texts, as we have seen, are not alone. The relationship between the law and the gospel seems differently portrayed in different texts. Has the day of the law passed so that something else is required today? Or, does the Law of Moses remain the statement of God's will even now when the gospel of the kingdom is being proclaimed? Before we resort to speculation on the matter, let us return to our story.

The Gospel Overshadows the Law?

Our young man, let us remember, is a right-thinking, well brought up, religious Jew who has known and observed the commandments from his youth; and he says as much to Jesus (19:20). To which Jesus replies, "If you wish to be perfect, go, sell your possessions, and give the money to the poor, and you will have treasure in heaven; then come, follow me" (19:21). The young man thinks that an impossible price for him to pay, and he goes away sorrowfully (19:22).

Jesus' response as found in Mark and Luke[14] leaves no doubt that the young man must sell his possessions and follow Jesus if he is to enter God's kingdom. Matthew's version seems more ambiguous: if the young man wishes to be *perfect*, he must sell what he owns and follow Jesus; perhaps, however, something less might be sufficient if he is content with gaining eternal life. But the sequel appears to rule out the more relaxed interpretation:[15] in Matthew, as in Mark and Luke, Jesus makes it clear that entry into eternal life is very much the issue and that those like our rich young ruler with many possessions find it no easier to follow the path to life than camels find squeezing through the eye of a needle (19:23-26).

---

14. Mark 10:21; Luke 18:22.

15. See the discussion in W. D. Davies and Dale C. Allison, *A Critical and Exegetical Commentary on the Gospel according to Saint Matthew*, 3 vols., ICC (Edinburgh: T&T Clark, 1988, 1991, 1997), 3:49; Ulrich Luz, *Matthew 8–20* (Minneapolis: Fortress, 2001), 513-14.

If Jesus' first response — "Keep the commandments" — insisted on submission to God by observing the commandments given to Moses, the second response insists on a radical commitment to Jesus, with whom God's kingdom comes. What this in effect means is that the answer to our question about the relationship between the law and the gospel lies in the relationship between Jesus' first response to the rich young ruler and his second. Why would Jesus tell the young man that, in order to inherit eternal life, he needed to obey the Mosaic commandments, as though that were an adequate answer, only to add later on, "Oh, yes, one more thing: Sell all you own, give to the poor, and come, follow me!"

One answer, superficially plausible, we may rule out at once. We are surely not to think that admission to the kingdom is granted to those who meet two quite distinct stipulations — "Obey Moses!" *and* "Follow Jesus!" — as though Jesus thought initially only of the first requirement but later recalled and added the second. Unless the first response was hopelessly misleading, the second response must in some way restate or follow from the first. Jesus might then be saying, "You may *think* you have kept the law of Moses, but you have not really loved God with all your heart, soul, and strength as Moses requires. You love your possessions more than you love God. So I will prove to you that you are not really keeping Moses' law by asking whether you are willing to part with your possessions and be my disciple." On this interpretation, the path to life remains to keep the Law of Moses. Jesus' second response, that the young man should forsake all he owns and follow him, is the test that will show whether the young man has really done what Jesus required in his first (and fundamental) response, observe the Law of Moses. Discipleship of Jesus, on this understanding, is demanded as a contemporary expression of the love of God required in the Mosaic Law.

Another way of looking at it would be to say that behind both the Law of Moses and the words of Jesus lies the same fundamental requirement, that human beings give themselves fully to God and to doing God's will. That same submission to God which has hitherto been expressed in radical obedience to the Law of Moses must now, in the presence of God's kingdom, be expressed by recognizing, welcoming, and devoting oneself to the cause of the kingdom of God that is present in Jesus' activity. On this interpretation, Jesus' second response, that the young man should forsake all he owns and come and follow Jesus, is what submission to God's will requires now in the light of recent developments, though up till now it has meant what Jesus stated in the first response, observing the Law of Moses.

In fact, of course, these two interpretations share much in common. On either reading the God of Moses is seen to be the same God whose kingdom breaks in with Jesus' appearance. And on either reading one who truly submits to the God of Moses will now be prepared to follow Jesus.

What can we conclude about the relationship between the law and the gospel from this brief survey of Matthew's Gospel? At least, I would suggest, the following points.

1. The first observation is self-evident but so fundamental to be worth repeating. Underlying everything said about the law *and* the gospel are the convictions that God is God, that humans live in God's world, and that it is appropriate, right, and the path to life and blessing in this world and the next for human beings to acknowledge God and submit to God's will.

2. It is also self-evident in Matthew's Gospel that the God of Moses is the God of Jesus Christ. But perhaps we should begin the other way around. Because the God of Jesus Christ is also the God of Moses, Jesus affirms the Law of Moses as a statement of God's will. Humans who submit to God's will, as they ought, will obey the commandments God gave to Moses. To be sure, those commandments must be interpreted aright, with primary focus given to the commandments to love God and one's neighbor. Indeed, so central in Jesus' teaching are the commandments to love God and neighbor that requirements of tithing, ritual purity, and Sabbath observance are virtually displaced. They turn up in the gospel almost exclusively in contexts where Jesus is defending apparent laxity in these areas because of the overriding demands of love.[16] Mark goes further still, concluding from one of Jesus' sayings that Jesus declared all foods clean, thus in effect doing away with whole chapters of Pentateuchal law (Mark 7:19). Paul appears to be familiar with precisely this tradition when he writes, "I know and am persuaded in the Lord Jesus that nothing is unclean in itself" (Rom. 14:14).[17] But these are conclusions drawn from sayings of Jesus by later interpreters. Jesus himself seems content, in principle at least, to affirm the Law of Moses, though stressing its central commandments. Indeed, the Jesus of Matthew insists explicitly that he did not come to abolish the law (Matt 5:17); and a saying preserved somewhat differently in Mat-

---

16. For a fine statement of the point, see Birger Gerhardsson, *The Ethos of the Bible* (Philadelphia: Fortress, 1981), 41-45.

17. See my *Jesus and Scribal Authority* (Lund: C. W. K. Gleerup, 1978), 81-82.

thew and Luke proclaims that not one smidgeon of the law could ever pass away.[18] So the God of Jesus Christ is also the God of Moses, and Jesus affirms the Mosaic Law. We may also note — it will become significant shortly — that Matthew (like the other Synoptic Gospels) remains faithful to the activities of the historical Jesus by not even raising the issue of Gentile observance of the law.

3. If the God of Jesus Christ is the God of Moses, the God of Moses is also the God of Jesus Christ. True faithfulness to Moses will thus necessarily show itself in the welcome one gives to, and the devotion one shows for, Jesus' message of the kingdom. The giving of God's law on Mount Sinai was an important stage in God's dealings with Israel. But the climax of God's dealings with Israel and with humankind as a whole is the inauguration of God's kingdom in the ministry of Jesus. The giving of the law, when rightly understood, makes clear how God's people are to live in submission to God. But sin, sickness, demonic powers, and death remain realities in the world, even among the people to whom the law was given. Both human deliverance from sin and its consequences and the transformation of God's sin-scarred creation as a whole require a divine intervention beyond the giving of the law. In the activity of Jesus, God — yes, the God *of Moses* — is decisively at work, overcoming sickness, death, and the powers of evil,[19] forgiving sins and showing his love for sinners,[20] and summoning all to a place in the kingdom whose powers are now already on display, though its consummation remains a future expectation.[21] In this transition period, whoever receives Jesus receives the one who sent him (10:40). And since the one who sent Jesus is the God of Moses, one cannot be truly loyal to Moses without showing devotion to Christ.

Indeed, so present is God in the person of his Son, Jesus Christ, that Jesus can command a kind of allegiance that neither Moses nor any other man of God who is not God's Son could ever require. Jesus summons people (like our rich young ruler) to be *his* disciples, to take up their cross and follow *him* (10:38; 16:24), to be willing to lose their life for *his* sake (10:39; 16:25), to love *him* more than one loves father or mother, son or daughter (10:37). The only OT parallel to these demands for devotion is the "first"

18. Matt. 5:18 (Matthew adds "until all is accomplished"); Luke 16:17.
19. Matt. 4:23-24; 8:16; 12:15; etc.
20. Matt. 9:2, 10-13, etc.
21. See Matt. 22:1-10.

commandment[22] of the Law of Moses: Love the Lord your God with all your heart, soul, and strength.[23] Love for God — the God of Moses — is thus to be shown by discipleship of Jesus Christ. Put differently, those committed to obeying the Law of Moses as an expression of their submission to God will now, at the decisive moment in history when God's kingdom dawns, take up their cross and follow Jesus.

4. Though the Law of Moses makes clear how God's people are to live in submission to him, they inevitably fall short. It is axiomatic for Jesus that people, in contrast with God, are evil, and that the human heart is bent on evil.[24] It follows that those whom Jesus invites into his kingdom are sinful human beings, and Jesus includes the most notorious of their number in his invitation. By God's love and grace, forgiveness is offered to the greatest of sinners.[25] Nor did Jesus only communicate in words the offer of forgiveness. He lived a life of forgiveness; and he died a death of forgiveness as well, giving his life as a ransom for many (20:28), offering his life's blood for the forgiveness of sins (26:28). The life of discipleship is built upon grace, from beginning to end. But the reverse is also true: the forgiving and sustaining grace of God is experienced only by those who submit to the rule of God and to discipleship of Jesus Christ.

Perhaps we could sum up the relationship between the law and the gospel in Matthew's Gospel by saying that while the coming of the kingdom does not affect the validity of the law as a statement of God's will, the law's importance is relativized. Correctly understood, with due emphasis given to its central commands, the law is still to be observed even among the followers of Jesus. But the giving of the law itself did nothing to end the rule of sin or to overthrow the powers of darkness; and as the coming of the kingdom represents the decisive stage in God's dealings with beleaguered humanity, so one's response to the message of the kingdom proves decisive if one is to participate in the dawning age of righteousness. We may add that Matthew (and the Matthean Jesus) attributes forgiveness of sins, and deliverance from sins, to the work and death of Jesus, not to the rites of atonement prescribed in the law (1:21; 20:28; 26:28).

---

22. Matt. 22:38.
23. Deut. 6:5.
24. See Matt. 7:11; 15:18-19.
25. See Matt. 9:10-13.

Redemption from the Law

The surface of our topic has scarcely been scratched, but we must move on (much more briefly) to Paul. The Galatian churches to which Paul wrote his epistle were ones that he himself had founded. After his departure, however, they had been visited by others, presumably messianic Jews, who insisted that the Galatians' faith in Jesus as Messiah was fine, but they must also submit to Moses and be circumcised. There can be no question how these outsiders envisaged the relationship between law and gospel. For them, the gospel of Jesus Christ functions within the framework established by the Mosaic Law. The law God gave on Sinai, patently including the requirement of circumcision, must be obeyed by all who would claim to be God's people. The gospel that God's messiah has come in no way alters the basic structure of the covenant given on Mount Sinai. In Paul's mind, however, these people were preaching a distorted gospel — or, rather, no gospel at all (Gal. 1:6-7).

For the Paul of Galatians, the law must not be thought to provide the framework within which the gospel functions; nor can it be said to retain its validity, though relativized in importance. Rather, the law simply gives place to the gospel. Jesus himself was born under the law (Gal. 4:4), but with Jesus the law's validity came to an end. The law was no more than a temporary measure imposed 430 years after God made a promise to Abraham and was binding only until Christ came in fulfillment of that promise (Gal. 3:17-19). To impose its requirements now is to overlook the progression that has taken place in salvation history. Those who have been declared righteous through faith in Christ are no longer under the law (Gal. 3:24-25).

That the coming of the gospel follows the era of the law and marks the end of the law's hegemony by no means exhausts what Paul has to say about the relationship between law and gospel. Christ *redeems* those under the law (Gal. 4:5). More specifically, he redeems them from the curse of the law (3:13). Presupposed in these claims are notions as axiomatic for Paul as they are for Jesus. Human beings live in God's world. As God's creatures they live rightly only when they acknowledge God and obey his will. The Mosaic Law spells out the good path in which humans are to walk[26] if they

---

26. Though given to Israel, the Mosaic Law (at least in its moral demands) spells out the good required of all human beings. Jews, possessing the law, are therefore in a position to

would enjoy life and divine blessing in this world and the next. The law's demands are holy, righteous, and good, to use Paul's language in Rom. 7:12. The same notion underlies Galatians as well, where, according to 3:12, the one who carries out what Moses commands will live; where, according to 5:14, the whole law is summed up in the demand to love one's neighbor as oneself; and where, according to 5:22-23, the law has no objection to raise against one whose life is marked by the fruit of the Spirit. What the law commands is certainly good, and those who practice it will find life; on the other hand, divine judgment awaits those who flout its demands. Here Paul quotes Deuteronomy: "Cursed is everyone who does not observe and obey all the things written in the book of the law" (3:10, citing Deut. 27:26). The problem, as Paul sees it, is that all human beings are thus cursed and in need of redemption from the curse of the law. They belong to the present evil age (1:4). They live in the "flesh" and inevitably practice the sinful "works of the flesh" (5:19-21). It is impossible that "flesh" could be approved by God on the basis of its observance of the works of the law (2:16), for all — Jews as well as Gentiles — are found to be sinners (2:17). The law is by no means opposed to God's promise and purposes, but it has no power to give life to the dead (3:21). All it can do with sinful human beings is consign them to imprisonment under the power of sin; there they await redemption in Jesus Christ from sin's power and the law's curse (3:13, 21-24). They are both redeemed and declared righteous by God apart from the works of the law, by faith in Jesus Christ (2:16).

Let me sum up what we have seen so far about the relationship between law and gospel in Galatians. The law prescribes a path to life that human beings, subject to the power of sin, inhabitants of the present evil age, prove unwilling and unable to follow. On incompliant humanity, the law can only pronounce its curse. The death of Christ sets believers free from the present evil age (Gal. 1:4), redeems them from the curse of the law (3:13; 4:5), and inaugurates an era in which God is served by people who are no longer under the law (3:23-26; 5:18).

---

instruct Gentiles in their moral obligations (so Rom. 2:17-21). See my *Perspectives Old and New on Paul: The "Lutheran" Paul and His Critics* (Grand Rapids: Eerdmans, 2004), 266-71; cf. my "The Righteousness of the Law and the Righteousness of Faith in Romans," *Int* 58 (2004): 257-59.

Law and Gospel in Jesus and Paul

All of this sounds very different from the Jesus of Matthew, for whom (as I argued above) the law retains its validity, though its importance is relativized. The nature of the differences as well as areas of overlap will emerge more clearly if we bring the two positions into closer comparison.

For both Jesus and Paul, the Law of Moses is the law of God and a statement of how God's people are to live. For the Matthean Jesus, it is an abiding statement of God's will; yet it is clear that the giving of the law suffices neither to establish God's rule on earth nor to produce subjects fit to participate in its blessings; for that, the gospel of the coming, activity, death, and resurrection of the Messiah is needed. For Paul, too, the demands of the law are the demands of God. But Paul locates the law's demands within the Sinaitic covenant; and by the terms of that covenant only the obedient enjoy God's blessing, while those who violate the covenant's stipulations become subject to its curse. Since all human beings are sinners, the law and the covenant to which it belongs prove to be institutions of condemnation and death from which only Christ can deliver (cf. 2 Cor. 3:7, 9).

We may thus say that Paul shares with the Matthean Jesus the conviction that the giving of the law does not suffice to bring salvation to sinful human beings and that salvation is only made possible through the gospel of Jesus Christ. The Pauline emphasis that we do not find in Matthew is the negative role played by the law in the drama of human redemption: the notion that the disobedient are subject specifically to the sanctions of the law, and thus that sinful human beings are in need of deliverance from the very law of God. Nowhere in the Gospels is redemption from God's law envisaged. The difference is real enough, though perhaps the reminder that divine judgment and the human need for forgiveness figure largely in the Gospels will keep us from exaggerating their distance from Pauline thought at this point.

If salvation requires the gospel, what can we say about the law as guide for the behavior of those saved through the gospel? For purposes of comparison it will be useful to distinguish the law's ritual or ceremonial demands on the one hand from its moral demands on the other — though we should recognize that neither the Gospels nor the Pauline Epistles make such a distinction explicitly.

We noted some ambiguity in the Jesus tradition about the validity, or at least the importance, of parts of the Mosaic Law: areas such as tithing, ritual purity, Sabbath, and food laws. The whole law is in places affirmed; but elsewhere the essence of the law is said to lie in the Golden Rule or the love commandments, and Jesus never suggests that his followers need to take up careful observance of the laws traditionally labeled "ritual" or "ceremonial." The point, in the Jesus' tradition, is not that these parts of the law were once valid and binding though they are now no longer so,[27] but rather that these areas pertain to the peripheral rather than the central concerns of the law — and attention ought to be focused on the latter. It seems most unlikely that Jesus would have pressed their adoption by Gentiles when he makes no issue of their observance among his Jewish followers, but the Gentile question does not arise in the context of Jesus' activities.

With Paul the Gentile question is precisely what occasions the Epistle to the Galatians: as we have seen, messianic Jews were insisting that Paul's Gentile converts submit to the laws traditionally labeled "ritual" or "ceremonial," beginning with circumcision. We might, indeed, be tempted to explain the difference between Jesus' relative indifference toward these areas of the law and Paul's vehement opposition to their adoption by his converts by pointing to the differences in their audience and situation: Paul wrote to Gentiles for whom the imposition of the law would be both novel and difficult, whereas Jesus lived among Jews accustomed to its practice. But as we have noted, Paul sees something more fundamental at stake than the impracticability of imposing Jewish ritual observances on Gentiles. Neither Jews nor Gentiles are able to meet the law's righteous requirements; therefore a righteousness different from that of the law must be found if "sinners" — whether Jewish or Gentile — are to be declared righteous by God. Paul finds this different, extraordinary righteousness in the righteousness of faith:[28] those declared righteous by faith are redeemed from the law and its curse. If those thus delivered should then submit to the rite of circumcision, they would be reverting to the Sinaitic covenant and obligating themselves to live by its terms once more (5:3). They would be returning to a life of slavery, falling from grace, cutting themselves off from Christ (5:1-4). The peripheral concerns of the law in which Jesus

---

27. Unless, of course, the "all" that must be "accomplished" before the law (or some part of the law?) "passes away" (Matt. 5:18) refers to an event in the past (the death of Jesus?); but what then would be the point of the temporal indicator "until heaven and earth pass away"? On this interpretation, see Davies and Allison, *Matthew,* 1:494-95; Ulrich Luz, *Matthew 1–7* (Minneapolis: Augsburg, 1989), 266-67.

28. See my *Perspectives,* 273-84; "Righteousness," 262-64.

shows little interest are for Paul a part of the covenant of condemnation and death from which Christians have been delivered.

Interestingly enough, the practical upshot of Jesus' and Paul's different perspectives on the "ritual" or "ceremonial" aspects of the law is virtually identical if we agree that Jesus would not have thought that Gentiles need adopt the practice of these laws, thus approximating the position of Paul, and once we recognize that Paul considered their continued observance by Jews a matter of indifference, thus approximating the position of Jesus: "in Christ Jesus neither circumcision nor uncircumcision counts for anything" (5:6; cf. 6:15). But, as we have seen, that practical upshot is reached by different routes. Jesus distinguishes the law's weighty commands from its peripheral ones and concerns himself only with the former; Paul links together the ritual and the moral demands of the law, seeing both as belonging to an obsolete covenant that can only condemn sinners.

And what of the law's moral demands? The Matthean Jesus interprets them radically in the Sermon on the Mount, sums them up in the Golden Rule and the two love commandments, and impresses the importance of observing them on his disciples. Paul, having linked the ritual and the moral demands of the law as both belonging to the Sinaitic covenant, and having declared believers free from its hegemony, is left to construct a Christian ethic independent of the law. Believers are to "live by the Spirit" (5:16, 25); those who do so are not "subject to the law" (5:18). The evil they are to avoid is defined as the "works of the flesh" rather than transgression of the law (5:19). In the lives of believers the "fruit of the Spirit" is to be evident; where it is, the law can find nothing to condemn (5:22-23).

So much is clear. It remains true, however, that for Paul the Law of Moses is the law of God, and the moral demands of the law represent the good that all human beings are to do. Furthermore, like Jesus, and perhaps in dependence on the Jesus tradition, Paul sees the whole law summed up in the commandment to love one's neighbor as oneself (Gal. 5:14; cf. Rom. 8:4; 13:10). While he can hardly define Christian duty in terms of carrying out the law, he must believe that the righteous behavior required in the law is in effect shown in lives where God's Spirit bears its fruit. Though believers are not themselves under the law, the love they are to show represents the fulfillment of what the law demands (Gal. 5:14).[29] Once again we may say that the practical upshot of what Paul says about Christian moral be-

---

29. See my *Perspectives*, 433-38.

havior corresponds closely to Jesus' insistence on observance of the weightier matters of the law. But the route by which that upshot is reached is different.

Christian theologians of a later age attempted to do justice to the NT data by saying that believers are subject to the moral demands of the Mosaic Law, though they have been freed from its "ceremonial" or "ritual" commands.[30] To repeat what was said earlier: such a distinction is not native to the NT itself. On the other hand it seems fair to say that the distinction can serve as a rough and ready guide to the substance of NT ethics, remarkably bridging the positions of Matthew and Paul. For Matthew, the distinction between "weighty" and peripheral commands differs little, one suspects, from the later terminology of moral and ceremonial. For Paul, the "works of the law" that he insists must not be imposed upon Gentiles amount in the first place to its ritual demands, while the good that even believers are to practice amounts to the law's moral commands. What must not be lost to view, however, are, in Matthew's case, the radical interpretations that Jesus gives to the law's moral commands and the decisive requirement of following Jesus; in Paul's case, the inability and disinclination of "flesh" to meet God's demands; the necessity of salvation by grace, through faith, apart from the "works of the law"; and the decisive role played by the Spirit in Christian ethics.

Let me conclude by returning to my four summary points about Jesus and seeing to what extent they can be said of Paul.

On the first there is wholehearted agreement: humans live as God's creatures in God's world and can only enjoy life and divine blessing as they acknowledge God and submit to God's will.

Second, for Paul, as for Jesus, the God of Jesus Christ is also the God of Moses, and the Law of Moses remains a statement of God's will. But for Paul, the law as such belongs to a bygone era in salvation history, its demands representing a path to life that sinful human beings have neither the will nor the capacity to pursue, its sanctions representing the curse from which human beings need redemption.

Third, for Paul, as for Jesus, the God of Moses is also the God of Jesus Christ; the climax of salvation history is reached with Christ's coming, and allegiance to God requires allegiance to his Son. In the Gospels, such alle-

---

30. See, e.g., Augustine, *Contra Faustum Manichaeum* 6.2; 10.2; John Calvin, *Institutes of the Christian Religion* 2.7.12-17.

giance is shown in a life of discipleship: a literal following of Jesus in some cases,[31] but in all cases obedience to his words and a willingness to confess him before others, at whatever cost.[32] In Paul's letters, sinners are found righteous only through faith in Christ; but those so found righteous are thereafter bound to live in the service of righteousness, their faith being active in love.[33]

Finally, as Jesus, expressing God's love and grace, welcomes even the most notorious sinners who respond to the message of the kingdom, so Paul's gospel is a gospel of divine grace for sinful human beings. Paul himself had once persecuted the church of God, but he had been called by God's grace (Gal. 1:13, 15). His converts, too, had been called by God into the grace of Christ (1:6), and in grace they must stand (5:4). Paul's prayer for his spiritual children was that the "grace of our Lord Jesus Christ" should be with them (6:18). For Jesus and Paul, the Law of Moses states God's righteous demands, but God's approval and blessing, and entrance into God's kingdom, are all granted to sinners who respond in faith to the good news of God's grace in Jesus Christ. And it is by God's grace that they are now to live a life in Christ's service.

---

31. Matt. 4:18-22; 9:9.
32. Matt. 7:24-27; 10:32-33, 37-39.
33. Rom. 6:12-19; Gal. 5:6.

Chapter 3

Good News to the Poor: Jesus, Paul, and Jerusalem

BRUCE W. LONGENECKER

I n Jesus' day, the majority of people throughout the Mediterranean basin found themselves trapped in economically vulnerable situations. The vastness of destitution and impoverishment was advertised in both urban and rural contexts, as the needy and expendable populated virtually every corner of society.

The Greco-Roman cultures that were untouched by Jewish Scripture and tradition generally demonstrate little concern for the poor.[1] In times of famine the elite, who were small in number but great in resources, may have opened their storehouses to benefit the poor and needy, but their motivation on such occasions would have been driven less by altruistic, humanitarian concern than by selfish expediency. Their donations in times of extreme famine served to maintain the status quo rather than face a desperate uprising by the masses and the plundering of those same storehouses. Emperors may have distributed bread to those gathered in the Colosseum, but not out of concern for their well-being so much as to enhance their own reputation among the populace gathered there and to receive their adulation. Outside contexts of this sort, there is little evidence of an entrenched concern for the poor and needy in the ancient world.

Such was not the case, however, for those influenced by Jewish Scripture and tradition. In case after case, Jewish literature demonstrates that

---

1. The evidence is collected in A. R. Hands, *Charity and Social Aid in Greece and Rome* (London: Thames & Hudson, 1968).

concern for the poor and needy was a deeply entrenched marker of Jewish social responsibility.

This point cannot be stressed enough in relation to Jesus research, which has repeatedly emphasized both Jesus' Jewishness and his concern for the poor.[2] But what of that other NT figure who was "a member of the people of Israel, of the tribe of Benjamin, a Hebrew born of Hebrews" (Phil. 3:5; cf. 2 Cor. 11:22)? What of Paul who, prior to his encounter with the risen Christ, had prided himself on being "a Pharisee" who was "blameless" in his performance of the law (Phil. 3:5-6) and who claimed to have "advanced . . . beyond many among my people of the same age, for I was far more zealous for the traditions of my ancestors" (Gal. 1:14)? What effect did the revelation of God's Son have on Paul, who found himself called to "proclaim him [Jesus Christ] among the Gentiles" (Gal. 1:16)?

Surprisingly, the attitudes of Jesus and Paul toward the poor have been notably neglected in scholarly comparison of these two first-century Jews. In this essay, however, concern for the poor will take pride of place as the point of our comparison of Jesus and Paul.

Concern for the Poor in Jesus' Proclamation of the Empire of God

One of the most historically secure traditions regarding Jesus of Nazareth is contained in both Matt. 11:2-6 and Luke 7:18-23 — passages that recount one of the most critically defining moments in Jesus' public career. In the Matthean account, for instance, the imprisoned John the Baptist sends a query to Jesus: "Are you he who is to come, or shall we look for another?" (11:3). Jesus' reply in 11:4-5 outlines his actions in Matthew 8–9, with six entries listed as his credentials:

Go and tell John what you hear and see:

1. the blind receive their sight,
2. the lame walk,
3. lepers are cleansed,
4. the deaf hear,

---

2. It might not be stretching the point to say that, in fact, Jesus' concern for the poor is part and parcel of his Jewishness, so that the two should not be examined independently of each other.

5. the dead are raised up, and
6. the poor have good news preached to them.

John the Baptist seems to have expected "the coming one" to bring the fire of judgment down from heaven against a wicked world (cf. Matt. 3:7-12). Instead, what he found in Jesus was one who ate with tax collectors and sinners (cf. Mark 2:18-20; Matt. 11:18-19; Luke 7:33-34), associating intimately with those that "the coming one" was expected to condemn.

Most of the components of Jesus' response to the Baptist's query resonate with Isaianic depictions of God's acts of eschatological liberation:

1. the healing of the blind (Isa. 29:18; 35:5; 42:7; 61:1);
2. the curing of the lame (35:6);
3. the restoration of the deaf (29:18; 35:5);
4. the raising of the dead (26:19; 29:18-19); and
5. the good news being preached to the poor (61:1).

Jesus' reply to John, then, enlists in subtle fashion the Isaianic narrative of divine triumph and places Jesus centrally within that narrative.[3]

So much is standard interpretation. But what is somewhat more controversial is the interpretation of the phrase that closes Jesus' reply to John the Baptist: "and the poor have good news preached to them." Why is preaching to the poor placed in a list of what otherwise consists wholly of dramatic miracles? And why is it placed in the final position of the list?

For some, its position as the final entry in Jesus' overview of his min-

---

3. The exception to this is the reference to the healing of lepers. Note James D. G. Dunn's comment (*Jesus Remembered* [Grand Rapids: Eerdmans, 2003], 450): "There is nothing in Isaiah which might have inspired the inclusion of that item. Nor . . . is there any record of leprosy/skin diseases being healed in the records of the earliest churches. The item can be here only because it was generally believed (by Jesus too!) that he had also cleansed lepers."

Similarly, Jesus' reply is fashioned to do more than simply assure John of Jesus' messianic identity. It challenges the ideological basis on which John's query was founded. The very passages that act as Isaianic precursors to Jesus' list of activities occasionally contain references to divine judgment (29:20-21; 35:4; 61:2). But this feature is not mentioned in Jesus' overview of the main contours of his ministry. Instead, each aspect of Jesus' overview highlights the merciful and restorative power of God at work in Jesus, rather than highlighting any judgmental dimension (although Jesus retained a place for that as well). So in this case, at least, the reply is both an assurance of Jesus' messianic identity and a corrective to John's understanding of that identity.

istry might appear to be anticlimactic unless the term "the poor" (οἱ πτωχοί) is interpreted not as depicting a deprived economic group but, instead, "those who are completely dependent upon God for help."[4] Support for this interpretation of "the poor" can be mustered from the term "the poor in spirit" of Matt. 5:3. Along these lines, the term "the poor" might not signify material deprivation but could potentially refer to needs of a variety of kinds, irrespective of economic factors. This interpretation has some attraction. But the two terms — "the poor in spirit" (5:3) and "poor" (11:5) — are not synonymous and cannot be conflated: "the poor in spirit" has a broader reference than simply economic depravity, while "the poor" generally has an economic reference as its primary reference, unless the context suggests otherwise.[5] And in this case the context is such that a non-economic reading of "the poor" is difficult to sustain. This is because, as we have seen, Jesus' words seem intended to resonate with the Isaianic narrative of divine triumph, and in Isa. 61:1 "the poor" (πτωχοῖς [LXX]) are most likely the economically deprived, and perhaps even the economically "oppressed" (cf. NRSV; Isa. 61:6-9).

So it seems that the term "the poor" has an economic meaning when Jesus uses it in the list that he compiles to outline his credentials to an uncertain John the Baptist. The preaching of good news to the economically insecure should not, however, be seen as an anticlimax in a list that otherwise features dramatic miracles of divine power. It is the culmination of Jesus' list, not as an exception to what the others are about, but as their capstone.[6] Jesus' reply depicts a world in which healing blindness, curing disease, restoring hearing, and raising the dead were as exceptional as encouraging the poor. The astonishment that would have attended Jesus' miracles is, we are led to think, comparable to the aston-

---

4. David E. Garland, *Reading Matthew: A Literary and Theological Commentary on the First Gospel* (London: SPCK, 1993), 125.

5. The converse strategy is to read the "poor in spirit" of 5:3 in relation to the materially poor; e.g., Warren Carter, *Matthew and the Margins: A Sociopolitical and Religious Reading*, JSNTSup 204 (Sheffield: Sheffield Academic Press, 2000), 131: "The poor in spirit . . . are those who are economically poor and whose spirits or being are crushed by economic injustice." But while the terms "poor in spirit" of Matt. 5:3 and "poor" of Matt. 11:5 overlap, they nonetheless have distinct referents.

6. Cf. James D. G. Dunn (*Jesus and the Spirit* [London: SCM Press, 1975], 60-61): The proclamation of the good news to the poor is "more important as an indication of the eschatological Now" than "the miracle of resurrection."

ishment that would have attended Jesus' pronouncement of blessing to the poor.

In the agrarian context of first-century Palestine, this is not wholly surprising. In that context, the economic systems were deeply entrenched in ways that promoted the interests of the elite and secure, to the inevitable disadvantage of the poor and economically insecure. It is not simply radical scholars who have recognized the point. The harsh economic realities of Jesus' day have impressed themselves on the most mainstream of interpreters. So, for instance, James Dunn writes:[7]

> Poverty . . . was a social condition, with social causes, often the result of greed and manipulation on the part of others. The poor were vulnerable before those members of society who controlled economic and political power, and who were willing to use that power ruthlessly. Consequently, the poor were also the downtrodden and oppressed, often pushed by circumstances to the margin of society.

Accordingly, it seems that Jesus' reply to John the Baptist takes account of the full force of the systemic injustice that was inherent within the economic structures of his day. As evidence of his place within the narrative of divine triumph, Jesus highlighted not only pyrotechnic displays of divine power but also the blessing of the poor. If the structures of health and disease, life and death, are prone to inversion before God's invading power, the same power proved to be a threat to the unshakable economic structures that had ingrained themselves in the empires of this world. The empire of God that Jesus announced offered to the poor the opposite of what the empires of the world offered them, precisely because God's is an empire of justice and mercy, as indicated within Isaiah 61 itself: "For I the LORD love justice, I hate robbery and wrongdoing" (v. 8).

For Jesus, then, the encouragement of the poor was itself part and parcel of the unleashing of eschatological divine power against which no worldly structures could stand. Just as his miraculous healings were signs that the house of Satan was being plundered, so too the encouragement of the poor was an indication of God's impending overthrow of the economic exploitation that is systemically built into the very structures of this world. Clearly this was good news for those who found themselves to be despised within the ancient system of honor and shame that had en-

7. Dunn, *Jesus Remembered*, 518.

trenched much of the Greco-Roman world, including much of life within Palestine. As a consequence of Jesus' Spirit-filled ministry, however, those who were thought to be deficient in honor were becoming honorable citizens of God's sovereign and eternal empire, whatever their standing might be within the empires of this world.

This general interpretation of Jesus' words coincides wholly with the Lukan interpretation of the significance of Jesus' ministry found in the account of Jesus' preaching at Nazareth (Luke 4:17-21), as we will see momentarily. But it also coheres perfectly with Jesus' pronouncement of blessings, or "beatitudes," as recounted in Matt. 5:3-12 and Luke 6:20-23. These accounts of Jesus' blessings have probably been refracted through the theological lenses of the Matthean and Lukan evangelists somewhat. So, for instance, twice we see the Matthean interest in "righteousness" reflected in the Matthean beatitudes (5:6, 10), without correspondence in Luke; and in Luke the pronouncement of fourfold blessings corresponds with the pronouncement of fourfold curses (Luke 6:24-26), without correspondence in Matthew. But, nonetheless, as most scholars think, the pronouncement of such eschatological blessings is most likely to be traced back to Jesus himself. This is especially the case with Jesus' blessings on "the poor,"[8] on those that "weep," and on those that "mourn."[9] And it is precisely these groups who are highlighted in Isaiah 61: the poor (πτωχοί, 61:1 [LXX]), those who are broken-hearted (τοὺς συντετριμμένους τῇ καρδίᾳ, 61:1 [LXX]), and those who mourn (τοὺς πενθοῦντας = τοῖς πενθοῦσιν, 61:2-3 [LXX]). These beatitudes, then, add to the pool of evidence suggesting that Jesus saw his ministry as falling within the narrative of divine sovereignty and triumph as highlighted in Isaiah 61. And furthermore, they testify to Jesus' conviction that the needy and downtrodden are primary targets of blessing within the empire of God that was being inaugurated in Jesus' own ministry.

It may well be significant that the first public words of Jesus in the Matthean narrative (that is, those cited above from Matthew 5) are words indebted to the narrative of Isaiah 61. The same is true for the Lukan narrative, as is evident from Luke 4:17-21. There Luke depicts Jesus as reading

---

8. "The poor" (οἱ πτωχοί, Luke 6:20); "poor in spirit" (οἱ πτωχοὶ τῷ πνεύματι, Matt. 5:3).

9. "Those that weep" (οἱ κλαίοντες, Luke 6:21); "those that mourn" (οἱ πενθοῦντες, Matt. 5:4).

the outline of his ministry right off the pages of Isaiah 61. Having been given the scroll of Isaiah to read before the synagogue, Jesus "found the place where it is written" in Isaiah:

> The Spirit of the Lord is upon me, because he has anointed me to bring good news to the poor. He has sent me to proclaim release to the captives and recovery of sight to the blind, to let the oppressed go free, to proclaim the year of the Lord's favor.

Luke tells us that Jesus then said to those in the synagogue: "Today this Scripture has been fulfilled even as you heard it being read." The fulfillment of Scripture lies in Jesus' proclamation and enactment of merciful divine favor — including as the starting point of this list the proclamation of good news to the poor.

The Nazareth incident is depicted in Luke's Gospel as a defining moment, and as such, as a moment characteristic of Jesus' mission. In his construction of the story of God's activity in Jesus, Luke has moved the incident from the middle of Jesus' public ministry, where it falls in the Markan and Matthean Gospels (cf. Mark 6:1-6; Matt. 13:53-58), to the beginning of Jesus' public ministry, taking place immediately after the account of Jesus' temptation. For Luke, then, this episode informs the audience as to the essential features of Jesus' identity and mission, serving as the frontispiece to the narrative that follows. Like the other maiden speeches in Luke's work, this one is likely to function as a kind of "speech in character," indicating the sort of thing Jesus would generally have said in a variety of situations. And there, the proclamation of good news to the poor takes central position.

It needs to be recognized, of course, that Luke's depiction of the Nazareth incident in Luke 4 is frequently considered to be a largely Lukan construct, at least in terms of the specific content of Jesus' words in that episode. This issue need not detain us here, since the Lukan version of the Nazareth incident falls well within the boundaries of Jesus tradition as we know it from other sources, not least the more secure traditions regarding (1) John the Baptist's questioning of Jesus, and (2) Jesus' pronouncement of blessings in the beatitude traditions of Matthew and Luke.[10] In each of

---

10. See, for instance, Dunn, *Jesus Remembered*, 447-48, a position defended at length in his *Jesus and the Spirit*, 54-60. There he concludes (p. 60): "[John's] question and [Jesus'] answer fit so neatly within the life-situation of Jesus and lack coherence if either or both were first prompted by a post-Easter situation, that the substance . . . of the account must be

these traditions, as in the narrative of Luke 4, the Isaianic narrative of divine triumph (particularly as articulated in Isaiah 61) serves as the foundation for Jesus' pronouncement of good news and blessings to the poor.

So too, with Isaiah 61 serving as its narrative substructure, the poor referred to in the Nazareth incident of Luke 4 are those who were insecurely placed within the severe socioeconomic systems of Jesus' day. Although the term "the poor" may take on broader connotations than straightforward economic ones in Luke's perspective,[11] the material sense of the term nonetheless maintains a high profile throughout the Lukan narrative. That Luke has his eye on the materially impoverished is clear from the manner in which he highlights their plight repeatedly through Jesus' words about them and interaction with them. From the Lukan Gospel alone, such features would include:

1. Jesus' parable of the Good Samaritan, who cared for a stranger from his own resources despite significant inconvenience and danger to himself (10:25-28);
2. the Lukan version of the Lord's Prayer, with its petition that the Father "keep giving" (δίδου) the necessity of bread on a daily basis (11:3);
3. Jesus' parable of the rich fool, who hoards his possessions rather than sharing them with those in need (so the implication seems to be; 12:13-21);
4. Jesus' command to the rich man, "Sell your possessions and give to the poor (δότε ἐλεημοσύνην)" (12:33);
5. Jesus' parable of the Great Banquet, in which the invited guests include "the poor, the maimed, the blind and the lame" (14:15-24);

---

regarded as historical." Cf. also Graham N. Stanton, *Jesus and Gospel* (Cambridge: Cambridge University Press, 2004), 13-18.

11. Luke occasionally seems to understand "the poor" in relation to wider categories than economic ones. He seems to include in their number not only those who had been overcome by the severity of the economic system but also those with illness and physical disabilities, those who had entered into despised professions, those excluded from the normal definition of the "people of God," those possessed by evil spirits, and any others who found themselves marginalized, the object of derision, or simply in need (not least, needing forgiveness). They are among those that Luke considered "poor," the blessed ones to whom the empire of God belongs (6:20). So Joel B. Green, "Good News to Whom? Jesus and the 'Poor' in the Gospel of Luke," in *Jesus of Nazareth: Lord and Christ*, ed. Joel B. Green and Max Turner (Carlisle: Paternoster Press, 1994), 59-74.

6. Jesus' parable of the rich man and Lazarus, in which the rich man finds himself in Hades as a consequence (it seems) of his failure to recognize the needy around him (Luke 16:19-31). In this parable, Jesus seems to suggest that "Moses and the prophets" are properly interpreted only in contexts where the needs of the poor are not overlooked (16:29);

7. Jesus' words to the elite ruler of Luke 18, who is commanded to "sell all that you have and distribute it to the poor" (18:22); and

8. Zacchaeus' act of obedience to Jesus in giving half of his goods to the poor and ensuring that the rest of his resources could be claimed by those whom he had defrauded, to which Jesus responds, "Today salvation has come to this house" (Luke 19:8-9).

In light of such overall evidence, it seems fair to say that the materially poor and vulnerable were of special significance and concern to Jesus. As Dunn well writes: "For whom did Jesus intend his message? At or near the top of any list which Jesus himself might have drawn up were clearly 'the poor.'"[12]

Concern for the Indigenous Poor in Pauline Communities

When the investigation moves from Jesus to Paul, we might be excused for thinking that any comparison of Jesus and Paul on the issue of the poor would reveal more of a diversity of interest than an overlap. If the poor had a central place in the proclamation and ministry of Jesus, nowhere in Paul's letters are the poor so extensively featured and so notably cherished. Paul was commissioned to preach to the Gentiles — commissioned both by God (Gal. 1:16) and by the leaders of the Jerusalem community (Gal. 2:7-9). His primary concern as a follower of Christ was to establish communities of Christ followers throughout the Mediterranean basin, consisting of Jew and Greek, slave and free, male and female (to rework Gal. 3:28 slightly). There is little in these well-known features to suggest that the materially poor were of special significance in Paul's theological horizons.[13]

12. Dunn, *Jesus Remembered*, 517.
13. This is true even of the entry "slave" in Gal. 3:28 and 1 Cor. 12:13, where it is not an economic category. Barring the elite strata, slaves were evident throughout the economic spectrum of the time and could often be in positions of relative material security.

The same impression would be gleaned from scholarly work on the relationship between Jesus and Paul. In books and articles given to comparing Jesus and Paul, attention is most frequently given to questions about Christology, soteriology, theology, Israel, the temple, the law, ethical particulars (e.g., divorce, loving others, taking oaths), women, the coming of the Lord, and the extent to which Paul was familiar with Jesus tradition (e.g., sayings, infancy narratives, etc.).[14] But rarely have the economically vulnerable, who took pride of place in Jesus' ministry, been used as a point of comparison between Jesus and Paul.

Occasionally, however, scholars do entertain such comparisons, but usually with rather paltry outcomes. So, for instance, in his extensive attempt to demonstrate the common interests of Jesus and Paul, David Wenham struggles to make a significant connection between the two on the matter of a declared concern for the poor. The best he is able to suggest is that Jesus' command in Matt. 19:21 to "sell your possessions and give to the poor" compares favorably to Paul's statement in 1 Cor. 13:3: "If I give away all my possessions . . . but do not have love, I gain nothing." Since the Greek expression for "possessions" is the same in each text (τὰ ὑπάρχοντα), Wenham makes the optimistic proposal that "this difficult teaching of Jesus was well known in the church, including Pauline circles."[15] I must confess that I am relatively unimpressed by this rather tenuous link between the mission of Jesus and that of Paul.[16] It may well be, of

14. See, for instance, Victor Paul Furnish's overview of scholarly interest in Jesus and Paul in previous generations, "The Jesus-Paul Debate: From Baur to Bultmann," in *Paul and Jesus: Collected Essays,* ed. A. J. M. Wedderburn, JSNTSup 37 (Sheffield: Sheffield Academic Press, 1989), 17-50. His overview reveals that "the poor" is a neglected topic in the early debate, and the same could be shown in the debates of successive generations.

15. David Wenham, *Paul: Follower of Jesus or Founder of Christianity?* (Grand Rapids: Eerdmans, 1995), 84. Wenham is clearly a "maximalist" in finding as many bridges between Jesus and Paul as possible, sometimes at the expense of persuasive force, as in this case. In his little booklet on the subject (*Paul and the Historical Jesus* [Cambridge: Grove Books, 1998]), Wenham discusses Paul's theology and ethics, but never discusses the issue of "the poor." Under ethics, he focuses simply on matters of "divorce" and "women."

16. Not least, only the Matthean Gospel includes τὰ ὑπάρχοντα ("possessions"). In their versions of the saying (Mark 10:21; Luke 18:22), neither the Markan nor the Lukan Gospels include this expression. So even if Wenham is right to think that the saying circulated widely, it is far from evident that the term ὑπάρχοντα ever circulated widely or that it had currency prior to the mid-80s when Matthew's Gospel seems to have been completed. Attempts to establish parallels between Matt. 19:21 and 1 Cor. 13:3 inevitably are unsuccessful.

course, that Jesus' difficult teaching about giving to the poor was, in fact, remembered in this form in Pauline communities, but we seem to have no evidence to confirm that.

Sometimes we can almost sense the need to apologize on behalf of Paul when it comes to this perceived lack of interest in the poor in his letters. So, for instance, in her recent work on the poor in the Bible, Leslie J. Hoppe writes:[17]

> Paul's attitude toward the poor was probably colored by his expectations regarding the imminent return of Christ. The apostle's belief that Christ's return was near made dealing with socioeconomic problems at any great length unnecessary.

But Paul's belief that Christ's return was near can play both ways. If Christ's return was thought to be near, then why not start establishing communities that resemble the eschatological age in as many respects as possible, even in the present overlap of the ages? Paul was seeking to do precisely this in other respects, so why should concern for the poor have been any different? Moreover, some have maintained that Jesus' own ministry was marked by the same expectation of the imminence of the end (e.g., Mark 9:1; Matt. 16:28; Luke 9:27),[18] in which case the differences between Paul and Jesus with regard to the poor remain as pronounced as ever, despite the well-intentioned attempt to let Paul "off the hook," so to speak. If, in fact, Paul had an underdeveloped sense of concern for the poor, then his attitude simply must be contrasted with the great traditions of Judaism in general and with the attitude of Jesus in particular. Perhaps such a scenario would cause us to conclude that the revelation of God's resurrected Son to Paul on the Damascus Road had the effect of denuding Paul of any concern for the poor that he might have had prior to that christophany.

One way to remove the sting of such a conclusion would be to broaden our categories of comparison somewhat and to compare Jesus and Paul in terms of their shared interest in reaching out to those usually thought to be unworthy of such incentives.

---

17. Leslie J. Hoppe, *There Shall Be No Poor among You: Poverty in the Bible* (Nashville: Abingdon, 2004), 158.

18. See the recent overview in Dunn, *Jesus Remembered*, 431-37.

1. So, for Jesus, the grace and sovereignty of God broke down the deeply engrained structures of honor and shame that permeated and were perpetuated in many cultures throughout the ancient Mediterranean basin, and for Jesus this resulted in good news for the frequently despised poor.

2. Similarly, for Paul, the grace and sovereignty of God broke down the deeply engrained structures of ethnocentric covenantalism that permeated and were perpetuated by many Jewish communities throughout the Mediterranean basin, and for Paul this resulted in good news for the frequently despised Gentiles.[19]

In this broader context of comparison, a common pattern would seem to be shared by Jesus and Paul, even if differences are perceptible in Jesus' and Paul's application of that pattern.

But while such a comparison would be profitable, it would also mask a more direct line of favorable comparison. For when comparing Jesus and Paul on the matter of "the poor," a mutual concern *is* in fact evident, although it has for too long been neglected in scholars' comparisons of the two figures. According to John Knox, there is "plenty of evidence in Paul's letters that the churches were expected to care for their poor."[20] This claim is, perhaps, overstated. Although Paul could depict himself as one who had himself many times been "hungry and thirsty, often without food, cold and naked" (2 Cor. 11:27), concern for the poor is not a primary feature of Paul's explicit rhetoric in his letters.[21] But more significant than statistical counts of situational letters is the way that references to caring for the needy show Paul to have been uncompromising in promoting care for the poor as integral to Christian practice. Occasionally the Pauline corpus tes-

---

19. Luke seems to do something similar within his gospel, where discussion of the materially poor moves into discussion of the "spiritually" poor — i.e., the outsiders to the traditions of Israel. This is evident, most clearly in Luke 4:18-30, where concern for the poor progressively embraces concern for the Gentiles.

20. John Knox, *Chapters in a Life of Paul,* rev. ed. (London: SCM Press, 1989), 38.

21. In private conversation, John Barclay raised the prospect that Paul may not have used the term "poor" to speak of members of his own communities because (almost) all members of his communities were likely to have been relatively poor; in that context one's terminological options include things like "bear one another's burdens" and "serve one another in love," and the like. The terminology of "the poor" is peripheralized in communities populated primarily by the poor.

tifies to the fact that such care was a well-established practice within Pauline communities.

One way of demonstrating that caring for the needy was a regular practice within Pauline Christianity is to examine how the first interpreters of Paul depict his attitude towards the poor. In this, evidence from Acts and from letters frequently thought to be pseudonymous needs to be highlighted, especially because that evidence is so frequently overlooked in discussions of Paul's social ethic.

Two passages from texts whose authorship is disputed indicate that Pauline Christianity regularly established common treasuries for the poor, from which the poor and needy were offered assistance. So 2 Thess. 3:6-12 testifies to the way in which one of Paul's communities was having difficulty managing its treasury for the poor. Some idle members were receiving food supplies from other members, presumably illegitimately so, since the idle members were of sufficient age and health to have provided for themselves without diminishing the resources of the community.[22] Virtually the same picture emerges from 1 Tim. 5:3-16, where the common treasury for the support of widows was, in the eyes of the author, being abused by some who should not have been eligible for support of this kind.[23] The same text comes to a close with an emphasis on doing good works, in which context it is clear that an "economic" dimension is to the fore in the author's mind: the rich are "to do good, to be rich in good works, generous, and ready to share" (1 Tim. 6:18).

It is certainly significant that both 2 Thessalonians and 1 Timothy depict the existence of a treasury for the poor within Pauline communities, and the significance does not diminish if one or both of these texts prove to have been written pseudonymously sometime after Paul's death. In fact, if these texts were written by authors other than Paul in an effort to apply his voice in new situations, it is highly noteworthy that their authors simply presumed that communal treasuries for the poor were hallmarks of Christian communities founded by Paul. So these disputed texts are clearly significant testaments to a concern for the poor and needy within Pauline communities, regardless of one's view about the identity of their author(s).

22. See, for instance, Justin J. Meggitt, *Paul, Poverty, and Survival,* SNTW (Edinburgh: T&T Clark, 1998), 162.

23. For more on this, see esp. Bruce W. Winter, *Seek the Welfare of the City: Christians as Benefactors and Citizens* (Grand Rapids: Eerdmans, 1994), 62-78.

A very similar picture emerges in Luke's depiction of Paul in the Acts of the Apostles (written ca. 95 c.e.), demonstrating the extent to which Paul's own concern for the poor was deeply ingrained and was to be replicated in the corporate lives of other followers of Christ.[24] In Acts 20:18-35, Paul gives what are essentially his final words to the "gathered church" of communities that he has founded (represented by the entourage from Ephesus who had joined Paul in Miletus).[25] That farewell speech of exhortation closes with the words: "We must support the weak (δεῖ ἀντιλαμβάνεσθαι τῶν ἀσθενούντων), remembering the words of the Lord Jesus, for he himself said, 'It is more blessed to give than to receive'" (20:35). The context makes it clear that the term "the weak" indicates those who are poor and economically vulnerable. It is also clear from the context that "supporting the weak" is not meant to involve simply praying for them or wishing them well. For the Paul of Acts 20, supporting the weak involves using one's own resources to offset the needs of others (as is clear from 20:33-34, where Paul himself appears as an example of precisely this behavior).

It cannot be overemphasized, then, that the Paul of Acts 20:

1. includes exhortations about the necessity of caring for the poor within the speech that serves as his farewell speech to the Christian communities that he founded and towards which had felt parental responsibility;
2. highlights concern for the poor and needy at the point of culmination in his words of exhortation; and
3. embeds "support for the weak" firmly within his talk about "the message of his [God's] grace which is able to build you up and to give you an inheritance among all those that are sanctified" (20:32).

Although it is unlikely that Luke has recounted Paul's precise words in Acts 20:18-35, it is likely nonetheless that Luke has done his best to re-

24. Luke's portrait of Paul has at times been subject to criticism by scholars who imagine that Luke completely misrepresented Paul's theology and mission. Although there is reason to be cautious about some aspects of Luke's portraits in Acts, the more extreme versions of criticism on this score arise more from scholarly exaggeration and carelessness than Lukan exaggeration and carelessness.

25. So Acts 20:25: "And now I know that none of you, among whom I have gone about proclaiming the kingdom, will ever see my face again."

construct the sort of thing that Paul might have said on just such an occasion. Orators, historians, and storytellers of the ancient world were trained in precisely this skill of reconstructing a person's "speech in character" (or *prosopopoeia*). Consequently, even though Luke probably has not recorded Paul's precise words, it is far more significant that Luke thought that this "speech in character" was precisely the sort of thing that Paul would have said on an occasion like this. Luke "remembers" Paul as one whose own practice and Christian exhortation showcased concern for the poor, and Luke wanted those who heard the story of Paul to remember Paul in precisely the same fashion.[26]

In this regard, Luke's attempt at "speech in character" in Acts 20:18-35 seems well-informed, at least in relation to the pattern of mentioning the needs of the poor towards the close of Paul's exhortation to other followers of Christ. So, for instance, at the very close of his letter to the Galatian communities, just prior to picking up the "pen" himself in 6:11-18 to write his concluding summary, Paul writes in 6:9-10: "Let us not grow weary in doing good. . . . Therefore, then, as often as God gives the opportunity, let us work the good for all people, especially for those of the household of faith." The double particle "therefore then" (Ἄρα οὖν) that stands at the beginning of 6:10 seems intended to draw attention to the point that is being made, as if to signal that the flow of Paul's thought is coming to a culminating point. And, that point involves the doing of "the good" to others — clearly others within Christian communities especially, but not exclusively so.

Although some have suggested that Paul's reference to doing "the good" refers simply "to beneficent deeds, whether the benefit be spiritual or material,"[27] the primary referent of doing good must certainly involve the giving of material aid to those in need. This is strengthened by Bruce Winter's observation that the phrase "to do the good" (ἐργαζώμεθα τὸ

---

26. This may be all the more significant in view of the fact that Luke has chosen not to recount the delivery of Paul's collection "for the poor among the saints in Jerusalem" (in Paul's words of Rom. 15:26) in the narrative of Paul's final trip to Jerusalem (Acts 20–21). If Luke omitted reference to the Pauline collection because the collection was not favorably received, as most think, Luke seems constrained nonetheless to document Paul's deeply ingrained concern for the poor in other ways, taking opportunity to emphasize the point in Acts 20:35 (a prime location, structurally speaking).

27. Ronald Y. K. Fung, *The Epistle to the Galatians*, NICNT (Grand Rapids: Eerdmans, 1988), 298.

ἀγαθὸν) that appears in 6:10 is (virtually) technical terminology in the ancient world for bestowing material benefits on others.[28] By extension, this material beneficence is probably what Paul has in mind in 6:9 as well, since "the good" (τὸ καλὸν) referred to there is likely to be virtually synonymous with "the good" (τὸ ἀγαθὸν) referred to in 6:10.[29] Prior to Paul's own summarizing conclusion in Gal. 6:11-18, Gal. 6:9-10 holds a key structural position in the unfolding of Paul's Galatian letter, representing the end result or ultimate outcome of his theological reflections. In this way, Paul reserves key structural terrain for his admonition to care for others, among whom the economically insecure would have taken pride of place.[30]

A similar phenomenon is evident in the structure of 1 Thessalonians. Just prior to registering his final farewells in 1 Thess. 5:23-28, Paul includes a list of admonitions in 5:12-22. Included within that list is the charge to "encourage the faint-hearted, help the weak (ἀντέχεσθε τῶν ἀσθενῶν), be patient with all of them" (5:14). Here the "faint-hearted" and the "weak" would seem to include those who were vulnerable to and oppressed by the harsh economic realities of the ancient world.[31] This, at least, is the impression that Luke wants to give in Acts 20:35 where, as we have seen, Paul highlights the needs of "the weak" ("we must support the weak" [δεῖ ἀντιλαμβάνεσθαι τῶν ἀσθενούντων]) and where "the weak" are clearly those in positions of economic insecurity. And the same identification of the weak as the economically insecure makes the most sense within the context of 1 Thessalonians 5. Immersed in a culture that proclaimed all to be well under Rome's oversight, the Thessalonian Christian communities were not to lose sight of the poor who continued to populate their city and its neighboring countryside. They were to work for the establishment of

---

28. Winter, *Seek the Welfare*, 11-40. Although the phrase "to do good" had strong significance within patterns of ancient patronage, there is little indication that Paul intends to replicate the full system of Greco-Roman patronage within Christian communities.

29. Cf. H. D. Betz, *Galatians* (Hermeneia; Philadelphia: Fortress Press, 1979), 309: "τὸ καλὸν and τὸ ἀγαθὸν mean the same thing ('the good')."

30. Meggitt (*Paul*, 156) identifies these verses as "clear evidence that almsgiving was practised (or at least prescribed) in the Pauline communities."

31. This seems far more likely to me than to take the weak as being those who are "morally" weak, with Paul involved in the act of psychagogy. For this reading, see Abraham J. Malherbe, *The Letters to the Thessalonians*, AB 32B (New York: Doubleday, 2000), 318-20. Malherbe lists other possibilities as well, and rightly rejects them (p. 318), but never explores the option of the weak being those who are economically insecure, due perhaps to actual physical weaknesses and vulnerabilities.

the "good news" of peace and security in communities of Christ followers empowered by the Holy Spirit, where the needs of the faint-hearted and weak were to be met. And just as in Gal. 6:10 (cf. 1 Tim. 6:18), so also in 1 Thess. 5:14, when Paul comes to the letter's final exhortations, he focuses on "pursuing the good" (τὸ ἀγαθὸν διώκετε), both in relation to the corporate community (εἰς ἀλλήλους) and to broader society in general (εἰς πάντας), with the poor and needy having a high profile in both categories.

Thus far, a coherent picture has emerged from the Pauline Letters and Acts revealing that care for the poor was an integral part of Paul's instructions to members of his own Christian communities. Evidence from Romans suggests that Paul followed this same practice even when addressing followers of Christ in communities founded by others. So, in Rom. 12:13 Paul encourages the Roman Christians, whom he had never visited, to "contribute to the needs [χρείαις] of the saints." While some have understood the word "needs" to have a non-material point of reference, Douglas Moo is right to maintain that the "needs" mentioned here "are material ones: food, clothing, and shelter."[32] This is because, as he notes, the NT consistently uses the Greek term χρεία to refer exclusively to material needs. Here, then, we see Paul calling the Roman Christians to ensure that they make provision for others — "widows, orphans, strangers, and the community's poor in general."[33] This is highlighted again in Rom. 12:16, where Paul concludes his instruction about intra-Christian concerns, and where his final exhortation is to forsake pride and conceit by "associating with the lowly" (τοῖς ταπεινοῖς συναπαγόμενοι).[34]

32. Douglas J. Moo, *The Epistle to the Romans,* NICNT (Grand Rapids: Eerdmans, 1996), 779. Cf. James D. G. Dunn, *Romans,* 2 vols., WBC 38A-38B (Dallas: Word Publishers, 1988), 2:743: "here personal difficulties, particularly financial and daily necessities are probably in view."

33. Dunn, *Romans,* 743. Cf. Moo, *Romans,* 779-80: "Therefore the fellowship we are called to here is the sharing of our material goods with Christians who are less well-off." Moo continues, rightly in my view, "Some scholars think that Paul might be thinking specifically of the Jewish Christians in Jerusalem (cf. 15:25, 26) to whom Paul was bringing money collected from the Gentile churches (cf. 15:30-33). But, while we should not of course exclude these Christians from Paul's reference, there is nothing to suggest that he has them particularly in mind here."

34. Elsewhere, I seek to demonstrate that a cross-over "chain-link interlock" exists in Rom. 12:14-16, so that 12:14 introduces the issue of Christian relationships with non-Christians (12:14, 17-21) and 12:15-16 concludes the issue of Christian relationships with other Christians (12:10-13, 16). Structurally speaking, then, Rom. 12:16 is "just next door" to 12:13

If Paul wrote Romans from Corinth, it was to the Corinthians that he had earlier written "do not seek your own advantage, but that of the other" (10:24). And to that same community Paul speaks harsh words in 1 Cor. 11 when he hears that some of those who are economically insecure are being disadvantaged in the corporate gatherings of the community. His extreme indignation is clearly evident. His strategy to overcome the injustice is to impose the narrative of the self-giving Jesus onto Corinthian corporate practice, expecting the Corinthians to follow in the narrative's wake. Suzanne Watts Henderson is not too far from the mark when she glosses Jesus' command to "do this in remembrance of me" (11:24-25) as, "Do this, that is, give yourselves (and your resources) up for others, just as I am doing for you."[35] In doing precisely that (i.e., giving of themselves and their resources), the Corinthians will be "proclaiming the Lord's death." In Paul's view, the Lord's Supper involved a meal in which the poor are not disadvantaged and where basic material needs are met. For Paul, a supper of this kind conforms to the cruciform narrative of the self-giving Lord and, consequently, is itself an embodiment and proclamation of the Christian gospel. It is little wonder, then, that Paul's ire towards Corinthian abuse of the poor spills so boldly onto the "pages" of 1 Corinthians 11. Much like a true prophet of Israel, Paul links the serious offenses against the poor within Corinthian communities to the harsh realities of divine judgment, noting: "For this reason [i.e., offending the Lord's Supper in your treatment of the poor], many of you are weak and ill, and some have died" (1 Cor. 11:30). For Paul, caring for the poor lays at the heart of Christian identity, because it lies at the heart of the story of the Jesus who is proclaimed as Lord and at the heart of the story of the sovereign God who judges all.

---

and concludes the first section that amplifies 12:9, before beginning the second section in 12:14, 17-21. See my *Rhetoric at the Boundaries: The Art and Theology of New Testament Chain-Link Transitions* (Waco: Baylor University Press, 2005), 95-99.

35. Suzanne Watts Henderson, "'If Anyone Hungers . . .': An Integrated Reading of 1 Cor 11.17-34," *NTS* 48 (2002): 195-208, 202. She may even be right in reinterpreting Paul's charge in 11:34 so that it means not "let those (rich) who are hungry eat at home (before coming to the community meal)" but instead means "let those (poor) who are hungry eat in the house (of public gathering)."

Paul's Concern for the Jerusalem Poor and His Death

The same Christological narrative that underlies Paul's concern for the poor in 1 Corinthians 11 is also evident in other Pauline texts, frequently in the service of a practical exhortation to support others in need. So, for instance, Paul's admonition to do good to all in Gal. 6:10 is ultimately derived from the narrative of "the Son of God, who loved me and gave himself for me" recounted in Gal. 2:20, a narrative now refracted through other paraenetic passages in Galatians, such as 5:13 ("through love be servants of one another") and 6:2 ("bear one another's burdens, and so fulfill the law of Christ").[36]

Paul's strategy of using the narrative of the self-giving Christ to foster concern for the needy was applied late in his public ministry to one particular project that was of special importance to him: his sponsorship of a collection of money from Gentile Christians to help alleviate the poverty of some needy Jewish Christians in Jerusalem. In 2 Cor. 8:9 Paul writes: "Although he [our Lord Jesus Christ] was rich, yet for your sake he became poor, so that by his poverty you might become rich." This "rich" Christological statement falls within two extended chapters dedicated to the issue of the collection that Paul was administering. For Paul, the Christological narrative should inform the narrative of the Christian communities in Corinth and in the regions of Macedonia and Achaia, so that they too should give of themselves and their "riches" (relatively speaking, perhaps) to assist "the poor among the saints in Jerusalem," as Paul calls them in Rom. 15:26. Indeed, Paul congratulates the Macedonian churches for having given generously to the cause, and more than they could afford, as an expression of their concern for Christian brothers and sisters in need (2 Cor. 8:1-4).

This collection seems to have been of considerable concern to Paul from about 53 c.e. (or so)[37] to about 57 c.e. (or so), when he finally took

36. On this and other instances within the Pauline corpus, see Bruce W. Longenecker, *The Triumph of Abraham's God: Transformation and Identity in Galatians* (Edinburgh: T&T Clark, 1998), 69-88.

37. Since Paul resided with the Corinthians for eighteen months in the years 50-51 and in 54 is giving the same Christians basic instructions about the collection (1 Cor. 16:1-4), it seems that Paul did not put any energy into the collection that he delivered to Jerusalem until the year 52 at the very earliest. With 2 Cor. 8:6-10 in view, it would seem that the first that the Corinthians heard of Paul's collection was in the autumn of 53 (assuming that 2 Corinthians 8 was written in 54 c.e.).

the collection personally to the needy among the Jerusalem Christians. The collection seems to have been a controversial development in Paul's mission, even among his own Gentile communities. Some of the Corinthian Christians seemingly suspected that Paul had orchestrated it in order to plunder their resources for his own personal gain (reading between the lines of 2 Cor. 12:14-18). And it may even be that Paul lost the support of the Galatian communities in the course of his collection efforts.[38]

But setbacks of this kind were of an altogether different order than the prospects that awaited him in Jerusalem, in which life-threatening dynamics were in play. Even before Paul undertook his journey to deliver the collection to its destination, Paul was keenly aware of the personal dangers that would face him when he arrived in Jerusalem — dangers having nothing to do with his collection for the poor itself, but with his controversial reputation regarding observance of the law. That Paul was aware of this danger is clear from his Letter to the Romans, written about 57 c.e. Towards the end of that letter, Paul encourages his addressees "to join me in earnest prayer to God on my behalf, that I may be rescued from the unbelievers in Judea, and that my ministry to Jerusalem may be acceptable to the saints" (Rom. 15:30-31). It seems that Paul was right to suspect trouble from non-Christians, and perhaps even fellow Christians, who awaited him in Jerusalem. As we read in Acts, his return to Jerusalem precipitated an outcry against him, leading to his arrest in Jerusalem[39] and, ultimately, to his death in Rome.[40]

38. It is possible that Paul's controversial reputation lost him the support of the Galatian communities in his collection efforts. Although we hear in 1 Corinthians (written in 54 c.e.) of Galatian involvement in Paul's collection (16:1), Paul does not mention their participation when he writes Romans (in 57 c.e.) (15:26). This reconstruction might be qualified by the observation that in neither his Corinthian nor his Roman letters does Paul mention Ephesian involvement in his collection, whereas presumably Christians in that major Pauline foothold would have also been involved in such a significant undertaking. It is likely that Paul's meeting with the leaders of the Ephesian church while Paul was en route to Jerusalem, as described in Acts 20:17-25, involved the handing over of resources from the Ephesian Christian communities to be included in Paul's collection for the "poor among the saints in Jerusalem." This would combine with the impression that Paul's traveling companions identified in 20:4 were representatives of Pauline communities (in Berea, Thessalonica, Derbe, and "Asia") who were charged with accompanying Paul as he delivered the collection to Jerusalem.

39. For Luke's version of the event, see Acts 21:18-36.

40. This is the most likely outcome of Paul's journey under arrest to Rome, where the Acts narrative leaves off in Acts 28. The alternative, that Paul was released and went on to evangelize for a few more years, is less likely.

If we were to draw lines of connection from Paul's ministry to his eventual death, those lines would need to include his concern for the poor. There would also need to be other lines of connection as well, of course. High on the list of connections would be Paul's controversial reputation among those who saw his mission to be a corruption of fidelity to the God of Israel. Additionally, his final trip to Jerusalem cannot have been motivated simply by his desire to help out needy Christians, for obviously there were needy Christians spread throughout the Mediterranean basin. Scholars have debated what other motivations might have been present,[41] but no clear consensus has emerged except, perhaps, that whatever other motivations Paul might have had are not clear. But in the assemblage of possible motivations for Paul's trip to Jerusalem, one motive stands out as relatively non-controversial: that is, Paul's desire "to be of service to them" (ἐν τοῖς σαρκικοῖς λειτουργῆσαι αὐτοῖς, Rom. 15:27), with the "them" being identified as "the poor among the saints in Jerusalem" (15:26). Although this motive cannot explain everything about Paul's collection, neither can everything about Paul's collection be explained without this motive. And since the delivery of his collection seems to have been the trigger of Paul's arrest and eventual death, it would be irresponsible not to draw lines of connection between Paul's concern for the poor and his death.

We have seen that throughout the early to mid 50s Paul unfailingly put his own energies and the resources of his communities into an effort designed to help offset the material destitution of a specific group of needy people. And we have seen that he did so despite opposition from within his own communities and despite the risk to his own reputation and, ultimately, his own life. This scenario provides a helpful background to similar concerns expressed by Paul in the late 40s — an issue to which we now turn.

---

41. Tried options include: (1) Paul sought to fulfill prophecy about the Gentiles bringing gifts to Zion (although Paul never quite says so much); (2) Paul sought to provoke Jews to jealousy and thereby place their faith in Jesus Christ (a view developed on the basis of Rom. 11:13-14); (3) Paul was attempting to replicate the half-shekel Temple tax paid by Jews (although the comparison does not work in certain respects); (4) Paul wanted to demonstrate, right in the heart of the city/community where opposition to him was sometimes evident, the validity of his Gentile mission, and thereby his own apostolic legitimacy, by demonstrating how God was working graciously among the Gentiles. The last seems to me to be a strong candidate for inclusion among the motives for Paul's collection, especially when placed against the backdrop of the widespread lack of concern for the poor within the pagan world untouched by Jewish Scripture and traditions.

Apostolic Concern for the Poor (Gal. 2:10)

The one piece of the Pauline puzzle yet to be considered is Gal. 2:10. There Paul depicts the leaders of the Jerusalem church (i.e., James, Peter, and John) as stipulating that Paul and Barnabas, when taking the gospel to the Gentiles, should "remember the poor," which, says Paul, "was the very thing that I was committed to."

The standard interpretation of this verse is that, at the meeting described in Gal. 2:1-10 and dated to around the year of 48 c.e. (or so), the Jerusalem leaders requested that Pauline churches (or the Antiochene church in particular) should send financial support to Christians in Jerusalem, not least in view of the extensive famines that plagued Judea in the late 40s.

This interpretation has merit, although I personally am more inclined to another view, in which the term "the poor" has no implied reference to Jerusalem. That is, the leaders were *not* requesting financial assistance for "the *Jerusalem* poor." Instead, their stipulation was that Paul should ensure that Gentile Christians should care for the poor and needy within their own local contexts. After all, prior to their conversion to Jesus Christ, many of the Gentile Christians in Paul's communities had been pagans untouched by Jewish Scripture and tradition concerning the need to care for the poor and needy. James and the other leaders of the Jerusalem church were sure that the Jews to whom Peter was to take the gospel of Christ would exhibit concern for the poor and needy, as stipulated in Jewish Scripture and tradition. What those leaders also wanted to ensure was that the Gentiles to whom Paul was to take the gospel of Christ would similarly be involved in caring for the poor and needy wherever they found them, in conformity to the will of God expressed in Jewish Scripture. In other words, the assumption would have been that Jewish Christians, immersed in Jewish traditions regarding the necessity of caring for the vulnerable, would be unfailing in their attempts to remember the poor, just as the *worry* might have been that Gentile Christians might not have been so interested in remembering the poor, since their previous practices had not been regulated by Jewish Scripture and traditions.

But whether the standard interpretation or the one postulated here has the most merit, it is clear that Paul was committed to give assistance to those in need on this occasion in the late 40s. This should not surprise us, in light of what we have seen about the place of the poor within Paul's communities and interests. It is also clear that among the early followers of Jesus, Paul was not distinctive in his concern for the poor. A further look into life in Jerusalem Christianity demonstrates this, as do the interests of James, the brother of Jesus. It is to these matters that we now turn, lest our comparison of Jesus and Paul should give the impression that these two figures are the only significant figures for our historical and theological consideration.

Concern for the Poor in Earliest Christianity

We have seen above that care for the poor was a key component of Jesus' concerns. The same concern is evident in the earliest days of Jerusalem Christianity, at least as Luke depicts those days. The early chapters of Acts depict the earliest community of followers of the resurrected Christ to be concerned with the material well-being of their members. Luke depicts individuals making substantial donations to a common fund that was used to offset people's needs. Acts 2:44-47a reads:

> All who believed were together and had all things in common; they would sell their possessions and goods and distribute the proceeds to all, as any had need. Day by day . . . they broke bread from house to house and ate their food with glad and generous hearts, praising God and having the goodwill of all the people.

To this Luke adds the note, "And day by day the Lord added to their number those who were being saved" (2:47b). In his telling of these accounts, Luke might be implying that the explosion in the community's membership (as described in 2:47) was a direct consequence of the community's provision of resources for those in need (as described in 2:44-47).

This is at least the implication given by Acts 4:32-37. There Luke notes that the early Christians did not make any personal claims to their possessions but shared everything between them. Acts 4:32 reports that "everything they owned was held in common." This point is then elaborated upon in 4:34-37, being punctuated by claims such as "there was not a needy person among them" (4:34), and the common fund "was distributed to each as any had need" (4:35). But between the introduction of this scenario in 4:32 and its elaboration in 4:34-37, we find in 4:33 what might appear to be a stray comment: "With great power the apostles gave their testimony to the resurrection of the Lord Jesus, and great grace was upon them all." Evidently Luke intends his readers to imagine that the evangelistic power of the apostles corresponded to, or was in direct relationship with, the integrity of the community to which the apostles belonged, being a community in which care for the needy was a marker of corporate identity.

Of course some scholars suspect that Luke has painted a somewhat idealized portrait of communal sharing among the earliest Jerusalem Christians.[42] While this might well be the case, he is probably drawing on generally reliable traditions nonetheless, traditions that demonstrate the practice of radical discipleship in the earliest stratum of the Christian movement in Jerusalem. As in other eras in the church's history, caring for the needy proved to be a powerful evangelistic tool for the earliest Christians precisely because radical social practice marked out their corporate identity.[43] It is little wonder, then, that the Jerusalem leaders may have stipulated (as I have suggested above) that the Gentile Christian communities founded by Paul should be encouraged to remember the poor in their own localized contexts (Gal. 2:10), not least in order to assist in the spreading of the Christian gospel.

This interrelationship of social concern and evangelistic respectability leads to the consideration of one further figure in particular. As the recognized leader of the Jerusalem church from the early 40s[44] to his death in

42. Luke's own narrative seems to suggest as much. In Acts 21:16, for instance, we hear of Mnason of Cyprus offering hospitality to other Christians within his own home. Mnason is depicted as "a disciple from the beginning" (ἀρχαίῳ μαθητῇ, trans. mine), and this early disciple continued to own his own home well in the late 50s, when the account of Acts 21 took place. Here, then, is one who seems not to have contributed (the whole of) his resources to the Christian community in Jerusalem but retained (a significant portion of) his material resources within his own control. And here, then, is a Lukan exception to the Lukan claim that "as many as were possessors of lands or houses sold them, and brought the proceeds of what was sold and laid it at the apostles' feet" (4:35).

43. See esp. Rodney Stark, *The Rise of Christianity: A Sociologist Reconsiders History* (Princeton: Princeton University Press, 1996).

44. This is implied, for instance, (1) in the order of apostolic names in Gal. 2:9, with James in the place of precedence, (2) in the term "men from James" in Gal. 2:12, and (3) in the Lukan record of events in the second half of the Acts narrative, where James is clearly the figure of primary authority in Jerusalem. In Acts 15 it is he who speaks last in order to summarize the discussion and point the way forward.

62 C.E., it was probably James, the brother of Jesus, who initiated the stipulation of Gal. 2:10 that Paul (and his communities) should remember the poor as part of the spreading of the Christian gospel. And so the focus of this survey comes to rest finally on James.

Jacobite Concern for the Poor

Just as the poor held a central place in Jesus' proclamation and embodiment of the empire of God, so too the poor seem to have held a central place in the concerns of Jesus' brother, James. Himself a formidable figure, James became the recognized leader of the Jerusalem church at least by the early or mid 40s. The Letter of James demonstrates a "deep concern for and sympathy with the poor and persecuted."[45] Of course, the authorship of the Jacobite letter is disputed, with some thinking it to have been written by James himself from Jerusalem sometime in the 40s or 50s and others thinking it to have been written at a later date by an unknown author who deemed it best to attribute the text to James. The issue is of no real significance for our purposes. Even if the Letter of James is pseudonymous, it is significant that the unknown author thought the letter to be representative of the kind of things that concerned James the brother of Jesus. So the issue of actual authorship need not detain us further.

What is significant is that the letter written by, or attributed to, James has the poor and oppressed in the forefront of its interests repeatedly. As Ralph Martin rightly notes:

> No NT document — not even Luke-Acts — has such a socially sensitized conscience and so explicitly champions the cause of the economically disadvantaged, the victims of oppression or unjust wage agreements, and the poor who are seen in the widows and orphans who have no legal defender to speak up for their rights (1:27). . . . In a day when economic and social wrongs cried out for redress, James directed attention to ways in which the poor and victimized could be helped (1:27) as a sign of a living faith.[46]

---

45. Ralph P. Martin, *James*, WBC 48 (Waco: Word Books, 1988), lxvii, where this concern and sympathy are cited as "the chief theme" of the letter.
46. Martin, *James*, lxvii, lxviii.

The evidence for this view hardly needs reviewing. It is there in living color in James 2:1-17, for instance, in which three phenomena are assembled and combined in triangulated fashion to bolster the author's conviction regarding the indispensability of caring for the poor. Those three phenomena are: (1) "the faithfulness of our Lord Jesus Christ" (τὴν πίστιν τοῦ κυρίου ἡμῶν Ἰησοῦ Χριστοῦ, 2:1); (2) the "royal law," the "law of liberty" (2:8, 12); and (3) the outworking of faith (πίστις, 2:14-17). Whenever partiality is shown to the rich or the poor are dishonored, these three are repudiated. By implication, whenever the needs of the poor are met, the faithfulness of Christ is extended into the life of the person of faith, in fulfillment of the royal law of liberty. Evidence for the same concern for the poor is obvious in James 5:1-6, with its rigorous denunciation of the rich (cf. 1:9-11), in view of their oppression of the poor. By contrast, the author upholds caring for the needy (i.e., the visitation of "orphans and widows in their affliction") as the embodiment of "religion that is pure and undefiled before God" (1:17).

We need also to note the dynamics surrounding the death of James, the brother of Jesus. We learn from Josephus (*Ant.* 20.200-202) that James was stoned to death as a lawbreaker after an unjust trial had been rigged by the high priest Ananias II (ca. 62 C.E.). Moreover, Josephus tells us that Ananias's actions offended "those in the city who were most fair-minded." Sometimes scholars deduce that "those who were most fair-minded" must have been opposed to Ananias's view that James had transgressed the law. But Josephus does not explicitly say that much. Instead, he focuses on Ananias's *trial procedures* as the point objected to by the "fair-minded" (i.e., it was not lawful for Ananias to assemble a Sanhedrin without the consent of King Agrippa). Josephus does not explicitly say that the fair-minded opposed the view that James was a transgressor, simply that they opposed the rigged trial procedures. Nonetheless, it is not too much to think that "fair-minded" opposition to Ananias's procedures was, in fact, driven by sympathy for James and opposition to Ananias's negative view of him.[47] The "fair-minded" point of view probably contended that James was a righteous man, rather than being a transgressor of the law, and that a properly orchestrated trial would have revealed as much.

Why, then, would Ananias have needed to rig James's trial? The best solutions to this conundrum place James's situation within the context of Ananias's larger power struggle, positioning James as a potential threat to

47. Compare Luke's depiction of Joseph of Arimathea in Luke 23:50-54.

Ananias's authority in some manner. In my view, the most plausible reconstructions of events leading up to James's death envisage James as highly critical of Ananias and some of the powerful Jewish aristocracy in Jerusalem. Ralph Martin, for instance, argues that James was probably disparaging of "Sadducean priests and their associates who despised and exploited the poor," with Ananias "react[ing] violently to James's eschatological denunciations of the rich and influential."[48] If there is a primary reason for Ananias's animosity against James, it might well be found in the same concern for the poor and chastisement of the rich that we find enunciated in the letter bearing James's name.[49]

Concluding Reflections

In this survey of the place of the poor in the ministries of Jesus and Paul, we have needed to broaden out our terms of reference to include the earliest Christian community in Jerusalem and James the brother of Jesus. The following eight points have emerged from our study:

1. Concern for the poor was at the forefront of the good news proclaimed by Jesus. He seems to have considered the blessings of the poor to be one of the most obvious indications of the arrival of the empire of God in a world where the poor generally had little about which to be happy.

2. Radical patterns of discipleship were practiced among the earliest followers of Jesus in Jerusalem, with a common fund having been established in order to offset the needs of the poor (Acts 2; 4).

3. Like the Jerusalem Christian community, Pauline communities seem to have set up common funds for the same reason as their fellow Christians in Jerusalem — that is, to offset the needs of the economically vulnerable (2 Thess. 3:6-12; 1 Tim. 5:3-16; Rom. 12:13-16).

48. Martin, *James,* lxix.

49. Cf. also Pierre-Antoine Bernheim, *James, Brother of Jesus,* trans. John Bowden (London: SCM Press, 1997), 252: "there is nothing to prevent our thinking that James criticized the greed of the priestly aristocracy, thus drawing its wrath upon himself." Note also the argument by D. Seccombe ("Was There Organised Charity in Jerusalem before the Christians," *JTS* 29 [1978]: 140-43), undermining the view of Joachim Jeremias that the Jewish leaders in Jerusalem organized relief efforts for the poor at the time of Jesus.

4. James, the brother of Jesus, while representing the Jerusalem follow-ers of Christ, stipulated along with Peter and John that Paul should enhance concern for the poor among Gentile Christian communities (although it is disputed whether those poor are the Jerusalem poor or the indigenous poor throughout the Mediterranean basin). Paul notes that inculcation of remembrance for the poor was precisely what he was committed to in conducting his ministry (Gal. 2:10).

5. Paul emphasized the need for Christians to care for the poor (e.g., Gal. 6:9-10; 1 Thess. 5:14). The abuse of the needy within the Corin-thian community resulted in extreme agitation on Paul's part, not least since it represented a compromise of the proclamation of "the Lord's death until he comes" (1 Cor. 11:26) and had called down God's eschatological judgment on the community (11:30).

6. Paul initiated a collection for the poor among the Christians in Jeru-salem, and this collection was the source of controversy even within his own communities (e.g., 2 Cor. 12:14-18; contrast 1 Cor. 16:1-4 with Rom. 15:26 [see n. 38 above]).

7. A line of cause-and-effect can be drawn from Paul's concern from the Jerusalem poor to his eventual death, via his delivery of the col-lection to Jerusalem, despite his awareness of the grave personal dan-gers involved (Rom. 15:30-31; cf. Acts 21:18-36).

8. A cause-and-effect connection might also lie between the death of James and his concern for the poor. This concern is clearly evident in the letter bearing his name (James 2; 4) and might have set him at odds with the powerful aristocracy among the Jewish priesthood.

To these eight conclusions might be added another, although I have not been able to demonstrate the point here. That is, it would not be diffi-cult to demonstrate that (1) Jesus' own concern for the poor went hand in hand with his opposition to those in the halls of power, both in Jerusalem and in Rome, whose use of the codes of honor and shame resulted in dra-matic abuses of the poor, and that (2) this opposition to those in power was one of the historical causes leading to his death. If this could be dem-onstrated, then it is likely that the deaths of Jesus, Paul, and James can all be connected to a shared concern for the disadvantaged and needy.

But since this ninth point cannot be demonstrated here, the other eight conclusions must suffice in our comparison of attitudes to the poor in the ministries of Jesus and Paul. But if we who are Christians are satisfied to leave the issue as one of historical interest, we would be guilty of overlooking the point that presses itself down on us most obviously and practically. That is, we have seen the considerable concern for the poor that was evidenced by those who lay the earliest foundations of Christian identity and practice. This point should not be dulled by the valid search for historical comparisons between Jesus and Paul. And its challenge is as clear as it is sobering. The overwhelming evidence of concern for the poor in the founders of the early Christian movement might be indicative of an indispensable feature of Christian practice for the generations that follow.[50] But those generations would also be advised to recognize the corporate and communal context out of which such concern for the poor usually emerged. Paul might be speaking as much for Jesus as for himself when he instructed the Galatian Christians to establish themselves as communities in which members "bear each others' burdens" (Gal. 6:2). As a manifestation of the work of the Holy Spirit, this corporate dimension of service is the best hope for Christians today who seek to follow the example of their Lord and his earliest followers in the challenging work of caring for the poor and needy in a world awaiting the full manifestation of the empire of God.

50. See Philip F. Esler, *Community and Gospel in Luke-Acts* (SNTSMS 57; Cambridge: Cambridge University Press, 1987), 164-200, for a convincing articulation of the view that, for Luke at least, Jesus' promise of "good news for the poor" was not merely a promise about a future eschatological time but included a "this-worldly" dimension that was both an appealing prospect for the poor and a poignant challenge for the rich.

Chapter 4

Peter between Jesus and Paul:
The "Third Quest" and the "New Perspective"
on the First Disciple

Markus Bockmuehl

Introduction

Has recent scholarship on Jesus and on Paul taught us anything new about the relationship between them, beyond the classic treatments of the past century?[1] My approach to this question will be somewhat oblique and arises out of a longer-term interest in the Apostle Peter: I wish to ask what role Simon Peter might play as a kind of index or litmus test for the way "New Perspective" Pauline scholarship relates to the Jesus of the so-called

---

1. Key twentieth-century contributions included Josef Blank, *Paulus und Jesus: Eine theologische Grundlegung*, SANT 18 (München: Kösel-Verlag, 1968); Adolf Jülicher, *Paulus und Jesus*, Religionsgeschichtliche Volksbücher für die deutsche christliche Gegenwart 1:14 (Tübingen: Mohr, 1907); Eberhard Jüngel, *Paulus und Jesus: Eine Untersuchung zur Präzisierung der Frage nach dem Ursprung der Christologie*, HUT 2, 2d ed. (Tübingen: Mohr [Siebeck], 1964); Johannes Weiss, *Paul and Jesus*, trans. H. J. Chaytor (New York: Harper, 1909); E. Earle Ellis and Erich Grässer, eds., *Jesus und Paulus: Festschrift für Werner Georg Kümmel zum 70. Geburtstag* (Göttingen: Vandenhoeck & Ruprecht, 1975); cf. Joseph Klausner, *From Jesus to Paul*, trans. W. F. Stinespring (New York: Macmillan, 1943); David Wenham, *Paul: Follower of Jesus or Founder of Christianity?* (Grand Rapids: Eerdmans, 1995), and *Paul and Jesus: The True Story* (London: SPCK, 2002); Victor Paul Furnish, "The Jesus-Paul Debate: From Baur to Bultmann," in *Paul and Jesus: Collected Essays*, ed. A. J. M. Wedderburn, JSNTSup 37 (Sheffield: Sheffield Academic Press, 1989), 17-50, and *Jesus according to Paul*, Understanding Jesus Today (Cambridge: Cambridge University Press, 1993).

I am grateful for comments and suggestions on this paper from fellow participants in the 2004 Drumwright Colloquium at Baylor University's Truett Theological Seminary and from other colleagues, including C. Kavin Rowe and Michael B. Thompson.

"Third Quest." In order to focus this inquiry, Peter's profile will be traced in the work of leading scholars who have been active in *both* projects. As I hope to show, this oblique approach to an old problem entails one or two promising suggestions about the way forward.

Simon Peter is arguably the only major player to feature in the ministries of both Jesus and Paul; and on any reckoning he provides a vital personal continuity between them both. What writers of books on both Paul and Jesus say about this man ought by rights to have some bearing on how their work in these two areas coheres — or does not, as the case may be. The image of Peter lends itself to being examined without obvious prejudice to some of the key questions driving the traditional Jesus-Paul debate: he is important to both Paul and the Jesus tradition and yet he also comes in for significant criticism in both. Conversely, the *contrast* between the Jesus tradition's virtually exclusive mission to Israel and the Pauline mission to Gentiles suggests there could be some analytical benefit in reflecting on Simon Peter's connection with *both* these endeavors.

Classically, nineteenth- and twentieth-century critical scholarship tended to see Peter as a vacillating but ultimately reactionary figure who failed to understand either Jesus or Paul. Here my aim is not to propose a historical reassessment of that picture but to offer a kind of Petrine cross-section through some of the newer scholarship, in order to discover how it conceives of the vexed conundrum that is the interface between a Jewish Jesus and a (rather differently) Jewish Paul. One of the implications of this recent work is to suggest that the figure of Peter may hold potential to mediate some of the continuities as well as discontinuities between them.

The Elusive "Third Quest"

Turning first to recent Jesus research, we find ourselves immediately confronted with the reality of twenty years of trench warfare between two irreconcilable schools of thought. On the one side are those whose historical reconstruction departs from a minimal stock of sayings, largely culled from the apocryphal *Gospel of Thomas* and an early version of the hypothetical sayings source Q. Opposed to them are scholars who, while differing widely on questions of historicity, take a more sanguine estimation of the value of certain *narrative* episodes alongside teachings, sometimes even prioritizing certain *acts* of Jesus over his words (as E. P. Sanders in

1985 famously did) and placing particular emphasis on the Jewish contexts of Jesus' ministry and the reasons for his death.

Chronicles, analyses, and typologies of the last quarter-century's lively Jesus scholarship are widely available and need not detain us here. Suffice it to say that a number of observers and even participants in the debate have begun to doubt that N. T. Wright's astonishingly influential declaration of an identifiable "Third Quest" for the Historical Jesus two decades ago[2] really captures the rather more polymorphous reality on the ground either at that time or since then. There have indeed been fresh points of departure, but at least some of the most popularly influential work since that time has been somewhat continuous with the earlier Synoptic criticism of Rudolf Bultmann's students and their successors. Even the "Third Quest" nomenclature's implicit characterization of the preceding research has been questioned because it seems to distort or sideline too much of what in fact transpired, for instance between 1920 and 1950, or in subsequent work like that of Jeremias, Gerhardsson, and the Scandinavian school. Some critics find themselves unable to recognize three distinct phases of Jesus research, while others have identified as many as nine.[3]

So in seeking to engage with the Jesus — let alone the Peter — of the so-called Third Quest we are evidently dealing with a moving target, or even a phantom, which may in fact not be altogether identifiable. A further problem is that so much of the debate seems to have been an Anglo-American or indeed an internal American pastime: the Jesus Seminar's star, which is perhaps now waning, never in fact rose in the scholarly firmament of continental Europe; similar observations might be made about other high-profile positions within the so-called Third Quest. Indeed, with the exception of Gerd Theissen and perhaps Gerd Lüdemann, German scholarship has been virtually absent from this enterprise.

---

2. Stephen Neill and N. T. Wright, *The Interpretation of the New Testament: 1861-1986* (Oxford: Oxford University Press, 1988), 379-403 and *passim*.

3. See, e.g., the critique of Clive Marsh, "Quests of the Historical Jesus in New Historicist Perspective," *BibInt* 5 (1997): 403-37; similarly Dale C. Allison, "The Contemporary Quest for the Historical Jesus," *IBS* 18 (1996): 174-94; Stanley E. Porter, *The Criteria for Authenticity in Historical-Jesus Research: Previous Discussion and New Proposals,* JSNTSup 191 (Sheffield: Sheffield Academic Press, 2000); Mark Allan Powell, *The Jesus Debate: Modern Historians Investigate the Life of Christ* (Oxford: Lion, 1998), and the important analysis of James Carleton Paget, "Quests for the Historical Jesus," in *The Cambridge Companion to Jesus,* ed. Markus Bockmuehl (Cambridge: Cambridge University Press, 2001), 138-55.

Even to many sympathetic observers it still seems unclear what, if anything, is the bottom-line gain of these two extraordinarily prolific decades of Jesus research. We continue to be deeply divided about such issues as the balance of sapiential and apocalyptic elements in the earliest Jesus tradition or about its concern for a deliberate abrogation or supersession of a common, Temple and Torah-centered Judaism. Perhaps at the end of the day the one main upshot of the Third Quest is, as John P. Meier has suggested, its "ringing affirmation of the Jewishness of the flesh the Word assumed."[4] Even in his original identification of a Third Quest, N. T. Wright already regarded this as the "central" agreement uniting its diverse practitioners: "the determination to set Jesus in the context of Judaism on the one hand and of the early Church on the other."[5] If true, that would indeed be a gain well worth celebrating. The only problem, of course, is that this conclusion is far from unanimously held among the makers of recent books on Jesus — and even where it is, the Jewishness of Jesus is so disparately rendered that one may still be permitted to wonder what is really meant by it.

The degree of dissonance on this subject was brought home to me by a recent review in the *Catholic Biblical Quarterly,* which slated a Scandinavian dissertation on prayer in the Jesus tradition for failing to do justice to "several important third-quest elements."[6] To begin with, the work under review had not in any case sought to position itself in these terms. Even beyond that, however, it was telling to note the supposed lacunae for which it was criticized: they included an emphasis on extracanonical traditions, especially the *Gospel of Thomas;* comparative social-science perspectives, including the so-called "horizon of Mediterranean patronage" as delineated by Bruce J. Malina; the recognition that mainstream Jewish prayer texts in fact merely "represent the views of powerful elites," which Jesus as a Galilean peasant did not follow but sought to subvert (citing W. R. Herzog); and an acceptance that the Synoptic scribes suppressed the political dimensions of the original Jesus movement "for obvious ideological reasons," as demonstrated by "third-quest work in the United States." My point here is not to deny that many of these ideas have indeed been prominently asserted in some recent works on Jesus, but merely to

4. John P. Meier, "The Present State of the 'Third Quest' for the Historical Jesus: Loss and Gain," *Bib* 80 (1999): 459-87 (on 486).

5. Neill and Wright, *Interpretation,* 399.

6. Douglas E. Oakman, review of Ville Auvinen, *Jesus' Teaching on Prayer,* CBQ 66 (2004): 470-71.

suggest that several of them are at best peripheral to the work of many *other* leading authors associated with the so-called Third Quest — including every one of those scholars identified in that original discussion by N. T. Wright. It is at this point that one begins to wonder if there is a meaningful designation here at all. Perhaps one simply pays one's SBL dues and takes one's choice from its cafeteria of Quests? Or should one boldly claim the high ground by declaring one's own work to be The New Perspective on Jesus?[7]

What's New in the New Perspective?

On the Pauline side, things appear initially somewhat simpler and clearer. One could justly question whether what writers like Sanders and Dunn offer is a New Perspective on Paul or rather on Paul's Judaism. And it is debatable if they pioneered or merely popularized a less Protestant reading of Judaism: certainly a number of Sanders's most influential insights in this department were previously advanced by writers like C. G. Montefiore, George Foot Moore, Krister Stendahl, and others.

Be that as it may, there clearly is recognizable overlap between Sanders and those like James D. G. Dunn, N. T. Wright, and others who have been linked with the so-called New Perspective on Paul.[8] One shared feature of this approach includes the recognition that Judaism, like early Christianity, overwhelmingly affirmed salvation in the first instance by covenantal gift rather than human merit. As a result, Paul's reaction against an emphasis on "works of law" tends to be seen by Dunn and others in sociological terms as resisting practices used to reinforce a narrow ethnic exclusivity. Another common feature is the rejection of the idea that Paul holds any unmediated dichotomy between Christianity and Judaism, law and grace, faith and works, atonement and participation, or indeed between individual and corporate elements of salvation.

For all its undoubted diversity, in this respect the New Perspective is

---

7. Cf. James D. G. Dunn, *A New Perspective on Jesus: What the Quest for the Historical Jesus Missed* (Grand Rapids: Baker Academic, 2005), and *Jesus Remembered* (Grand Rapids: Eerdmans, 2003), 881-84. See my review of the latter in *JTS* 56 (2005): 140-49.

8. A brief but serviceable and user-friendly assessment of the New Perspective is given in Michael B. Thompson, *The New Perspective on Paul*, Grove Biblical Series 26 (Cambridge: Grove Books, 2002).

rather easier to identify and describe than the Third Quest. Unlike historical Jesus research, it tends characteristically to be more concerned with certain aspects of Pauline soteriology than with a comprehensive description of words and deeds of "the historical Paul of Tarsus." (And to that extent a direct comparison with the Third Quest is in any case difficult.) Perhaps for the same reason, however, this project has also evoked a much stronger backlash in a number of quarters, not least among some traditional Protestant scholars in Germany and America.[9] Even more than the Third Quest, the New Perspective has remained a predominantly Anglophone, North Atlantic, and specifically Protestant pursuit; no major Roman Catholic protagonist has appeared to date.

Throughout all this, it is an unfortunate irony that the New Perspective has failed to advance the discussion precisely in areas where one might have expected it to do so. Three examples may suffice to illustrate this point. First, Pauline scholarship seems no nearer to a consensus about the supposedly all-consuming divisions between Paul and anti-Paulinists in early Christianity. While F. C. Baur's influential position today has relatively few adherents in its undiluted form, especially in his native Germany, a number of Anglophone sympathizers continue to prosper and proliferate both within and without the New Perspective.[10] Secondly, we seem to have few tools to resolve the division between advocates of a narrative, salvation-historical approach to Paul and those who favor the sup-

---

9. In Germany note, e.g., Martin Hengel and Roland Deines, *The Pre-Christian Paul,* trans. John Bowden (London: SCM, 1991); Peter Stuhlmacher and Donald A. Hagner, *Revisiting Paul's Doctrine of Justification: A Challenge to the New Perspective* (Downers Grove: InterVarsity, 2001); Friedrich Avemarie, *Tora und Leben: Untersuchungen zur Heilsbedeutung der Tora in der frühen rabbinischen Literatur,* TSAJ 55 (Tübingen: Mohr Siebeck, 1996); prominent North American objectors include Seyoon Kim, *Paul and the New Perspective: Second Thoughts on the Origin of Paul's Gospel* (Grand Rapids: Eerdmans, 2002); Mark A. Seifrid, *Christ, Our Righteousness: Paul's Theology of Justification* (Downers Grove: InterVarsity, 2000); Stephen Westerholm, *Perspectives Old and New on Paul: The "Lutheran" Paul and His Critics* (Grand Rapids: Eerdmans, 2004); and a number of the contributors to D. A. Carson, Peter T. O'Brien, and Mark A. Seifrid, eds., *Justification and Variegated Nomism: A Fresh Appraisal of Paul and Second Temple Judaism,* 2 vols., WUNT 2/140, 181 (Tübingen: Mohr Siebeck, 2001, 2004). For a very compact and lucid assessment of the current *status quaestionis* see also James D. G. Dunn, "Introduction," in *The Cambridge Companion to St Paul,* ed. James D. G. Dunn (Cambridge: Cambridge University Press, 2003), 9-13.

10. See, e.g., C. K. Barrett, David C. Sim, Douglas A. Campbell, Michael D. Goulder, Marvin C. Pate, and Gerd Lüdemann.

posedly more "apocalyptic" interpretation of Ernst Käsemann or J. Louis Martyn, according to which Paul largely abandons salvation history, especially in Galatians, in favor of a radically innovative Christian gospel.[11] Supporters of the New Perspective are again found on both sides of this debate. Finally, and somewhat paradoxically, the New Perspective in many ways has not managed to achieve consensus on the key question of Paul's Jewishness or apostasy from Judaism, whether in theological or practical terms. Similarly, little of what has been written helps to assuage fundamental Jewish suspicions about Paul: although scholars like Daniel Boyarin or Alan Segal do share a determination to take Paul more seriously on Jewish terms,[12] Pauline hermeneutics and politics vis-à-vis Israel remain deeply suspect to most Jewish readers. Other unresolved questions in this department include the continuing lack of clarity about Paul's interest in Jewish Christianity, in a mission to Israel, or in any abiding moral function of the Mosaic Law. And with respect to the old "Jesus and Paul" problem, even after the New Perspective some scholars have happily returned to a position that is in important respects indistinguishable from that of Rudolf Bultmann: Paul's Christ could have no truck with a Jewish Jesus.[13]

So what is new about the New Perspective? When all is said and done, it may be that progress amounts to rather less than meets the eye. Even supposedly cutting-edge scholarship on Paul, as perhaps on Jesus, involves a greater element of appearance and fashion than its practitioners like to think.

For present purposes it seems right to prioritize E. P. Sanders and James D. G. Dunn, two writers who are widely perceived as having to date

11. On this debate see now Todd A. Wilson, "Wilderness Apostasy and Paul's Portrayal of the Crisis in Galatians," *NTS* 40 (2004): 550-71. Cf. earlier Sylvia C. Keesmaat, *Paul and His Story: (Re)interpreting the Exodus Tradition,* JSNTSup 181 (Sheffield: Sheffield Academic Press, 1999); contrast Bruce W. Longenecker, *The Triumph of Abraham's God: The Transformation of Identity in Galatians* (Edinburgh: T&T Clark, 1998). It is worth noting that the term "apocalyptic" tends to be used rather loosely in this connection.

12. See e.g. Daniel Boyarin, *Border Lines: The Partition of Judaeo-Christianity,* Divinations (Philadelphia: University of Pennsylvania Press, 2004), and Alan F. Segal, *Paul the Convert: The Apostolate and Apostasy of Saul the Pharisee* (New Haven: Yale University Press, 1990).

13. So, e.g., explicitly David Catchpole, "Q's Thesis and Paul's Antithesis," in *Forschungen zum Neuen Testament und seiner Umwelt: Festschrift für Albert Fuchs,* ed. C. Niemand, Linzer Philosophisch-Theologische Beiträge 7 (Frankfurt: Peter Lang, 2002): 347-66 (see esp. 363-64 with 348).

made perhaps the most prominent contributions to *both* the Third Quest and the New Perspective. Placing their works in chronological order, I will interleaf between them a consideration of John Dominic Crossan and of N. T. Wright.

E. P. Sanders

First, then, to Simon Peter in E. P. Sanders's Jesus and Paul, which for chronological reasons are best discussed in reverse order.

Peter and Sanders's Paul

Sanders's work on the Pauline "New Perspective" predates that on the Third Quest. Perhaps partly for that reason, the question of continuity or discontinuity with the Jesus tradition is far from prominent in books like *Paul and Palestinian Judaism* (1977) or *Paul, the Law, and the Jewish People* (1983). For a reflection on Paul informed by his work on both subjects, we must turn to his recently reissued popular title *Paul: A Very Short Introduction* (1991, 2001); and as we shall see, it is indeed in that late work that he turns noticeably less taciturn on the role of Peter (perhaps because the tone of the series encourages him to speak more frankly?).

Sanders used to claim, as also in the subtitle of *Paul and Palestinian Judaism*, that he was interested not in theology but merely in a historical "comparison of patterns of religion." These protestations notwithstanding, the chief concern of his two big books on Paul was an emphatically soteriological one — to wit, the dynamic of grace and merit in human salvation. For all its bluster and overstatement, Jacob Neusner's famously petulant critique of *Paul and Palestinian Judaism* perhaps was right to query the remarkably Protestant theological shape of that question.[14] Indeed, only the final chapter of *Paul, the Law, and the Jewish People* ventures marginally outside that remit to consider some closely related aspects of Paul's view of

---

14. E. P. Sanders, "Puzzling Out Rabbinic Judaism," in *Approaches to Ancient Judaism*, 6 vols., ed. William S. Green (Chico: Scholars Press, 1980), 2:49-50 and *passim*. Cf. Jacob Neusner, "Review Article: Comparing Religions," *HR* 18 (1979): 177-91. See the response in Sanders, "Rabbinic Judaism."

Israel.[15] Although in subsequent publications Sanders considerably expanded his coverage of ancient Judaism, this is not nearly so true for his work on Paul.[16]

Understandably, perhaps, there is therefore little interest in Peter, who remains a somewhat two-dimensional, colorless figure with virtually no personality or teaching of his own. He does seem to function as a figure of continuity in the most general sense of embodying Jewish Christianity, but aside from this most general of connections there are no concrete points of contact with the Jesus tradition. Paul's visit in Jerusalem (Gal. 1:18) and Peter's resurrection appearance (1 Cor. 15:5), for example, which are sometimes adduced in this connection, never surface in either of Sanders's big books on Paul.[17]

At the same time, Peter stands above all as a cipher of *discontinuity* with the Apostle to the Gentiles, whose sharply contrasting relationship with Judaism Sanders famously characterized in the statement, "In short, this is what Paul finds wrong with Judaism: *it is not Christianity*."[18] And thus, in discussing Paul's view of continued law observance, Sanders in 1977 takes sharp exception to the so-called "status quo" theory (proposed by Albert Schweitzer and endorsed by W. D. Davies and others). He explains that Schweitzer fails to explain why in Galatians Paul is so passionately opposed to Gentile law observance and yet so unconcerned about Peter's supposed non-observance at Antioch — rather than insisting, as Schweitzer's theory would demand, that Jewish Christians always keep the law.[19] Instead, Paul had no objection to Peter's keeping of dietary laws per se, but considered it "only wrong because it cut him off from Gentile Christians"[20] and would lead to the wholly unacceptable establishment of

15. E. P. Sanders, *Paul, the Law, and the Jewish People* (Philadelphia: Fortress, 1983), 171-206.

16. On Judaism see the substantial work of E. P. Sanders, *Jewish Law from Jesus to the Mishnah: Five Studies* (London: SCM, 1990); E. P. Sanders, *Judaism: Practice and Belief, 63 BCE–66 CE* (London: SCM; Philadelphia: TPI, 1992); contrast his slim survey volume on Paul: *Paul: A Very Short Introduction* (Oxford: Oxford University Press, 2001).

17. There is one passing reference to Gal. 1:19 and "a private meeting with Peter and James" in Sanders, *Paul, the Law, and the Jewish People*, 186.

18. E. P. Sanders, *Paul and Palestinian Judaism* (London: SCM, 1977), 552 (italics original). Cf. also the more moderate judgment on p. 543: "Paul presents an essentially different type of religiousness from any found in Palestinian Jewish literature."

19. Cf. Sanders, *Paul and Palestinian Judaism*, 478-80.

20. Sanders, *Paul and Palestinian Judaism*, 480-81. N.B. with that ecclesiological pro-

two separate Christian churches.[21] And conversely, in Sanders's view Galatians locates the key difference between Peter and Paul in the fact that while Peter could *tolerate* Gentile Christian non-observance, Paul's "exclusivist soteriology" *required* it.[22] Thus Sanders considers the possibility, which for Daniel Boyarin has become a fundamental principle, that Paul unlike Peter insists on the radical obliteration of *all* distinctions between Jews and Gentiles[23] — indeed it is precisely Peter's continued acceptance of such distinctions that constitutes his "hypocrisy."[24] Sanders even shows moderate sympathy for C. K. Barrett's revived Tübingen theory that the relationship between Paul and Peter was one of lasting enmity not just in Antioch, but also in Corinth and elsewhere: even if Paul generally abided by the terms of the Jerusalem Agreement and concentrated his efforts on Gentiles, Peter may indeed "have meddled in Paul's churches."[25]

At the same time, the Jerusalem Agreement shows that Peter and James "basically . . . agreed with Paul on the question of the Gentiles," including the fact that they did not need to proselytize.[26] The reason for Peter's withdrawal from Gentile fellowship was therefore "probably" his sense of loyalty to the Jewish mission, rather than any disagreement with Paul's Gentile one.[27] Given the likely numbers involved in the first century, it is interesting to note Sanders's untroubled conviction that whereas Paul's mission to the Gentiles has been a success, "the mission of Peter and others to the circumcised (Gal. 2:9) had largely failed."[28]

---

viso, Sanders still affirms "that the evidence is entirely against attributing to Paul a gospel which required Jews not to observe the law" (*Paul, the Law, and the Jewish People*, 187).

21. So Sanders, *Paul, the Law, and the Jewish People*, 188.

22. Sanders, *Paul and Palestinian Judaism*, 519; cf. 497. Citing Johannes Munck, Sanders considers inaccurate Paul's accusation that Peter "compelled" Gentiles to Judaize, since the requirement applied "only if they wished to eat with him."

23. Sanders, *Paul and Palestinian Judaism*, 154. Cf. Daniel Boyarin, *A Radical Jew: Paul and the Politics of Identity* (Berkeley: University of California Press, 1994), *passim*.

24. Sanders, *Paul, the Law, and the Jewish People*, 165 n. 34.

25. Sanders, *Paul, the Law, and the Jewish People*, 190.

26. Sanders, *Paul, the Law, and the Jewish People*, 19; cf. 181.

27. Sanders, *Paul, the Law, and the Jewish People*, 19, 177. Contrast, however, the odd suggestion on p. 192 (and 204 n. 7) that Peter and James "probably" did not admit Gentiles, and for that reason mostly escaped Jewish persecution. Such an interpretation seems patently inaccurate for both apostles, arguably in relation to Gentiles as much as to persecution. On Jewish persecution of the Jerusalem church, see, e.g., my full discussion in "1 Thessalonians 2:14-16 and the Church in Jerusalem," *TynBul* 52 (2001): 1-31.

28. Sanders, *Paul, the Law, and the Jewish People*, 184-85; similarly Sanders, *Paul*, 4, 139.

Peter and Sanders's Jesus

Although his publications on the Gospels date back to the 1960s, Sanders's two main books on Jesus are the programmatic *Jesus and Judaism* (1985) and the more accessible and synthetic work *The Historical Figure of Jesus* (1993). In *Jesus and Judaism* Sanders promotes many of his distinctive methodological principles, including the greater emphasis on certain core narrative assertions within the Jesus tradition and thus the prioritizing of a minimum of "almost indisputable facts." One of these facts, albeit admittedly the least certain on the list, is Jesus' calling of the Twelve.[29] Sanders does not, however, offer any real discussion of individual disciples. This is quite different eight years later, when in *The Historical Figure of Jesus* he presents a much fuller, more rounded picture both of Jesus and of other figures associated with the early Christian movement. Quite possibly because of a greater confidence in the validity of the Third Quest's more sanguine estimation of (some) narratival traditions, now there are extensive discussions of the disciples as a group,[30] and we find repeated comments on Peter in particular. Along with his brother Andrew and the sons of Zebedee, Peter is among the four chief disciples. Basic Gospel outlines of the story of Peter are now explicitly affirmed, including his profession as a poor fisherman who apparently could not afford a boat[31] but who had a house in Capernaum that formed the setting for Jesus' healing of his mother-in-law.[32] Peter made a messianic affirmation about Jesus but was rebuked for his interpretation of it.[33] Sanders also mentions a number of other Petrine episodes, usually taking care not to move beyond descriptive to historical statements. Nevertheless, in analyzing Matthew's account of Peter walking on the water, Sanders does in fact conclude that this is "historicizing legend":[34]

> It is really true, for example, that Peter wavered in faith. He did so first when Jesus was arrested. He followed from afar and denied that he was one of Jesus' followers when he was asked (Mark 14.66-72). Later he

29. E. P. Sanders, *Jesus and Judaism* (London: SCM, 1985), 11, 100-101.
30. E. P. Sanders, *The Historical Figure of Jesus* (London: Penguin, 1993), 118-27; cf. 291.
31. Sanders, *Historical Figure of Jesus,* 103.
32. Sanders, *Historical Figure of Jesus,* 98; cf. 128.
33. Sanders, *Historical Figure of Jesus,* 241, 242.
34. Sanders, *Historical Figure of Jesus,* 158-59; cf. 154.

also wavered on the question of whether or not Gentile converts to the Christian movement should be required to observe the Jewish food laws, and Paul claimed that he acted hypocritically (Gal 2.11-24). Peter's inability to walk on water, according to this explanation, is only a pictorial representation of a character failing. It describes his weakness by narrating a brief legend.

Sanders's apparent willingness to rescue even a minimal historical kernel from this most homiletical of Matthean haggadic discourses is symptomatic of his general willingness, noted above, to take seriously the integrity of the gospel narrative in arriving at a more rounded, flesh-and-blood picture of the historical Jesus.

Here as in other contexts, moreover, we encounter a willingness to link the Peter of the Jesus tradition with the Apostle to the circumcised as he appears in the Pauline Epistles;[35] in one passage Sanders even cites Gal. 2:6-10 as corroborating evidence for the claim that Peter was the leading disciple of Jesus. To be sure, Sanders remains a little more skeptical of Luke's attempt in Acts 10 to depict Peter's vision at Joppa as Jesus' instruction that all foods are clean: had Paul known of such a tale, he would no doubt "have worked this into his argument" in Galatians 2.[36] And it is true that Sanders's earlier work on Paul, like his first book on Jesus, had precious little to say about Peter or for that matter about other connections between Jesus and Paul. Nevertheless, his overall portrait of Jesus here clearly moves beyond the older Jesus scholarship in allowing for Peter as a substantive link between Jesus and Paul.

This view is confirmed in his little book entitled *Paul: A Very Short Introduction,* first published in 1991 but reissued with this new title in 2001. Many of the earlier themes are repeated: Peter and others "had not been very successful" in their mission to Israel,[37] while the difference between the "urbanite," "cosmopolitan" Paul and the Galilean Peter "could hardly have been greater."[38] Yet Sanders now bases his understanding of their relationship not on an *a priori* ideological polarity; instead, he develops a synthetic view of both the Pauline epistles and Acts, which he regards as reliable on the main events even if its consistently harmonious view of the

35. Sanders, *Historical Figure of Jesus,* 107.
36. Sanders, *Historical Figure of Jesus,* 221-22.
37. Sanders, *Paul,* 4.
38. Sanders, *Paul,* 11.

relationship between Peter and Paul masks their sometimes fierce disagreements.[39] Chief among these disagreements is evidently the dispute at Antioch, although Sanders sheds no real light on the motivation for Peter's conduct.[40] At the same time, he does acknowledge that while the sermons attributed to *Peter* in Acts place rather more stress on the life of Jesus and somewhat less on the parousia, otherwise they reflect "fairly closely" what Paul's letters tell us about *his own* "basic missionary message."[41]

Sanders on Peter, Paul, and Jesus

Overall, then, one must say that Sanders does remarkably little to bring his work on the New Perspective into dialogue with that on the Third Quest. On the positive side, he shows no doubt about Peter's historicity in either of these projects. Despite the absence of sustained reflection on how Paul relates to Jesus, Peter does play a modest part in a certain change of tone on that question — from Sanders's early work on Paul toward a more synthetic approach in the books on Jesus and in the later semi-popular guide to Paul.

John Dominic Crossan

Like Sanders, John Dominic Crossan first contributed to NT scholarship in the 1960s, although his more notable impact began with his no less than ten books and numerous articles published in the 1970s and 1980s on matters like parables, narrative, eschatology, canonical, and apocryphal gospel sources. All this prepared him well to burst on the scene in 1991 with his hugely successful work *The Historical Jesus.* This book reflects in part his membership in the so-called Jesus Seminar; the Fellows of that group have at one time or another included other leading Jesus scholars like Robert W. Funk, Marcus J. Borg, and Stephen J. Patterson, whose own books on the subject manifest cognate methods. Crossan's first Jesus book, an instant bestseller, was soon followed by several others, of which his *Jesus: A Revolutionary Biography* (1994) was perhaps the most influential.

---

39. Sanders, *Paul*, 18, 22.
40. Sanders, *Paul*, 61-65.
41. Sanders, *Paul*, 27-29.

Crossan has turned his explicit attention to Paul only in his most recent, co-authored volume entitled *In Search of Paul* (2004). Even his earlier work *The Birth of Christianity* (1998) allows one to conclude that among the Jesus Seminar's most prolific and best-known authors he is certainly the one whose work comes closest to writing about Paul — albeit at first in predominantly deprecating mode, as we shall see.

Peter and Crossan's Jesus

We turn first to the few episodes of Petrine interest in the two cited books on Jesus. In keeping with his minimalist inventory of authentic sayings based on a preference for the hypothetical source "Q^1" and an uncommonly early *Gospel of Thomas,* Crossan regards the entire early Petrine narrative of Mark 1:16-38 as unhistorical, but imbued nonetheless with symbolic value: "Peter's house is becoming a brokerage place for Jesus' healing, and Peter will broker between Jesus and those seeking help."[42] In particular, the episode of Peter's early morning search for Jesus (1:35-38) is the evangelist's creation, which shows Mark "opposing Jesus to Peter and showing their, from Mark's point of view, incompatible visions of mission."[43] The passage serves primarily to demonstrate the opposition between Peter's "brokerage" and Jesus' more radical view of "itinerancy." A similar pattern surfaces in Mark's three passion predictions of chs. 8–10: both the predictions and the reactions of Peter and others form part of Mark's "programmatic denigration" of them.[44]

Although Peter is in practice a largely irrelevant figure for Crossan, this same anti-Petrine spin resurfaces later on in relation to the resurrection. Luke 24, for example, demonstrates how Peter's witness preempts that of others by imposing the primacy of "specific leader" over against "general community."[45] Similarly, John 21 employs "not exactly subtle"

---

42. John Dominic Crossan, *Jesus: A Revolutionary Biography* (San Francisco: HarperSanFrancisco, 1994), 100, and *The Historical Jesus: The Life of a Mediterranean Jewish Peasant* (San Francisco: HarperSanFrancisco, 1991), 346. Cf. more fully John Dominic Crossan and Jonathan L. Reed, *Excavating Jesus: Beneath the Stones, Behind the Texts* (San Francisco: HarperSanFrancisco, 2001), 90-96, 184.

43. Crossan, *Jesus*, 101.

44. Crossan, *Jesus*, 191.

45. Crossan, *Jesus*, 173 (cf. Crossan, *Historical Jesus*, 400).

apologetics to justify the authority of the Petrine individual over the community and the leadership group — although Crossan concedes that this same story occurs previously in Luke's call narrative (5:1-11) where it develops less explicit authority for Peter.[46] The equally fictional tradition about Mary Magdalene in Matthew 28 has in Crossan's view been suppressed by the time we get to her threefold misinterpretation of the resurrection in John 21.[47] As might be expected, the stories of John 20–21 are also seen to raise the classic question of the envisaged conflict of Peter and John in terms of "institutional as against charismatic, hierarchical as against egalitarian, patronal as against servile leadership." This trajectory is grounded in the concluding logion of the *Gospel of Thomas* (114). Although seen by many as a late addition, that saying is here taken to epitomize Peter's misogynistic opposition to female leadership — a stance in which "historically, he succeeds."[48] *The Da Vinci Code* in a nutshell, one might say.[49]

Peter and Crossan's Paul

Version 1: Peter and the Dehumanizing Platonist

In his sequel entitled *The Birth of Christianity,* Crossan deliberately excludes Paul — in order, as he says, to concentrate on the 30s and 40s of the first century.[50] He does so by setting apart these two decades from what he calls "the historical Paul in the 50s." Added to this is his prior belief in a radically dualistic, Platonizing Paul, who has so thoroughly broken with all of Palestinian Jewish Christianity that he is no longer representative of it: "I bracket Paul," writes Crossan, "to concentrate on a Christianity that had

46. Crossan, *Jesus,* 182.

47. Crossan, *Jesus,* 187-88.

48. Crossan, *Historical Jesus,* 411.

49. After the best-selling controversial novel by Dan Brown, *The Da Vinci Code* (New York: Doubleday, 2003). An early review on Amazon.com described John Dominic Crossan and Jonathan L. Reed, *In Search of Paul: How Jesus's Apostle Opposed Rome's Empire with God's Kingdom, A New Vision of Paul's Words and World* (San Francisco: HarperSanFrancisco, 2004) as "*The Da Vinci Code* with pictures" (so Robert Grimm [cited 11 November 2004]), but the similarities with this book seem more remote.

50. John Dominic Crossan, *The Birth of Christianity: Discovering What Happened in the Years Immediately after the Execution of Jesus* (San Francisco: HarperSan Francisco, 1998), xxi.

to be born before he could notice its existence and persecute its pres‑ence."[51] Although he agrees with Daniel Boyarin's view of Paul as attempt‑ing to work out a *compromise* between Judaism and Hellenism,[52] the up‑shot seems from another perspective to cohere with aspects of Sanders's often stark contrast between Paul and Judaism. Crossan also takes consid‑erable exception to what he regards as Paul's persistent failure to apply his compromise on ethnicity to the issues of class and gender.[53] Paul's "funda‑mentally dehumanizing" Platonism is for Crossan most apparent in his supposedly radical, and only rarely compromised, hostility to the body.[54]

To be sure, a difficulty with Crossan's scheme is that a majority of scholars would regard the 30s and 40s as the Christian Paul's key formative period from his conversion around 34 C.E., via his missionary activity in Judea, Arabia, Antioch, Asia Minor, and Greece, to the Jerusalem Confer‑ence and his Galatian and Thessalonian correspondence in 49 or 50. It is hard to see how one can speak of Christianity's birth in these years with extensive reference to the *Gospel of Thomas* and the *Didache*, all the while programmatically excluding Paul.[55] Among other things this requires one to ignore, as Crossan studiously does, the work of those such as Martin Hengel, Rainer Riesner, and others who have written extensively on Paul's life and thought precisely during the 30s and 40s — decades that also in‑volved troubled and sporadic and yet continuing contacts with Jewish Christianity in Jerusalem, Antioch, and elsewhere. But regardless of what one makes of Crossan's attempt to "bracket" Paul, *The Birth of Christianity* does in fact represent a substantial, if perhaps largely oblique (not to say apophatic), verdict on the Apostle of the Gentiles.

If Crossan's 650-page vision of Judea in the 30s and 40s is surprisingly restrained on Paul, it is even more remarkable for having virtually nothing to say on Peter. Unlike numerous other ancient persons, both Christian and non-Christian, Simon Peter does not appear in the Index — though he does

---

51. Crossan, *Birth of Christianity*, xxvii.

52. Cf. Boyarin, *Radical Jew*.

53. Crossan, *Birth of Christianity*, xxvi-xxviii.

54. Crossan, *Birth of Christianity*, xxix-xxx.

55. Cf. e.g. Crossan, *Birth of Christianity*, 364-87 and *passim*. Crossan asserts the source-critical independence of the *Didache* from the Synoptic tradition, 383-87; contrast now the radical (if similarly problematic) claim of Alan J. P. Garrow, *The Gospel of Matthew's Dependence on the Didache*, JSNTSup 254 (London: T&T Clark, 2004) about Matthew's *dependence* on the *Didache*.

surface from time to time, partly as the redactional plaything of Mark or John. Crossan offers a dyadic interpretation of Jerusalem Christianity as simultaneously sustained by a male process of exegesis and a female process of lament.[56] In the absence of a body or a tomb, female "ritual lament is what changed prophetic exegesis into biographical story" of passion and resurrection.[57] Crossan is keenly interested in what he calls "communities of resistance," among whom he includes the Essenes and also the group around James the Just.[58] In this connection he acknowledges that Paul's letters show both James and Simon Peter to have been "important figures" in early Christianity; indeed, he suggests Gal. 1:18 might make one think that "Cephas was more important than James" at the time of Paul's visit.[59] Only James and the community around him, however, merit any sustained discussion — or for that matter an entry in the Index. Peter was, it seems, important — but we never discover how or why. He is largely airbrushed out of both the Jesus tradition and the Jerusalem church of the first two decades. This historical invisibility of Peter (in a book ostensibly concerned with the first two decades of Jewish Christianity) also strikes one in Crossan's remarkably pallid sketch of the Antioch dispute, where Peter's role is that of a soulless functionary without any character or theology of his own:

> Peter and Barnabas presumed that kosher regulations were no longer important, *one way or the other*. It was not important to follow them, but neither was it important to not follow them. Hence, before James's intervention, they ate with pagans like pagans. After it, they wanted everyone, including pagans, to eat like Jews. Paul called that hypocrisy; they probably considered it courtesy. Paul, in any case, refused to give in, found himself isolated, and, in my view, went westward, never to return to Antioch.[60]

Version 2: Peter and the Egalitarian Anti-imperialist

With all this in view, it comes as a surprise to find that six years after *The Birth of Christianity* Crossan did go on to co-author a major book on Paul

56. Crossan, *Birth of Christianity,* 568-73 and *passim.*
57. Crossan, *Birth of Christianity,* 572, 573.
58. Crossan, *Birth of Christianity,* 462-76.
59. Crossan, *Birth of Christianity,* 465.
60. Crossan, *Birth of Christianity,* 466.

(In Search of Paul). This is a passionate, bracing, and highly attractive attempt to place Paul in the wider context of contemporary Greco-Roman imperial culture and ideology. The authors' informative and well-presented discussion is richly illustrated and ranges widely through the textual and archaeological record. Although touching repeatedly on Diaspora Judaism, they mount a trenchant exposé of Greco-Roman values and institutions as expressed in attitudes to sex, patriarchy, slavery, and the imperial ideology. Interestingly, a good deal more time is spent on this cultural framework than on a close reading of Paul's letters. The overall concern of the book is the *tour de force* clearly articulated in the book's subtitle: *How Jesus's Apostle Opposed Rome's Empire with God's Kingdom.* Therein lies an agenda that evokes repeated explicit sideswipes at perceived twenty-first-century analogies with America's "Empire."

In this treatment, ironically, Paul now emerges not so much as a secondary and "fundamentally dehumanizing" figure but as the tireless and radical apostle of Jesus, whose egalitarian gospel of Christ not Caesar makes him "Rome's most dangerous opponent."[61] Paul's "Platonizing" hostility to the body has here been replaced by his robust insistence on a bodily resurrection vis-à-vis the Platonism of Corinth,[62] and on an undiluted equality of the sexes in the family, in the church, and in the apostolate.

Crossan's previously bumbling compromiser on slaves and women in *The Birth of Christianity* has here been comprehensively transformed into the radical egalitarian who "would never accept the idea that they could be equal spiritually, internally, in the assembly, but unequal physically, externally, in the world."[63] The change is striking: the villain of the piece is now no longer Paul but rather certain pseudonymous and "deliberately anti-Pauline" forgers responsible for the inauthentic letters (Ephesians, Colossians, and the Pastorals). They moved the Apostle "in exactly the opposite direction," by "framing" him into either "an ultraconservative position" of a fertile "patriarchal misogyny" subservient to social convention, or else into an "ultraradical" stance of celibacy.[64] Romans, by contrast, seen here as Paul's final piece of writing ("last will and testament"),[65]

---

61. Crossan and Reed, *Paul,* 9 and *passim.*
62. Crossan and Reed, *Paul,* 341-45.
63. Crossan and Reed, *Paul,* 110; cf. 107-16.
64. Crossan and Reed, *Paul,* 106 and *passim.*
65. Crossan and Reed, *Paul,* 409.

shows the apostle as a man with deep insight into the nature of "global sin" and the ideal of a human unity under a global divine justice as incarnated in Christ's death.

As in most other books on Paul, Peter remains distinctly on the sidelines — and he sheds little or no light on the question of "Jesus and Paul." (He does, ironically, merit a dozen entries in the Index — in marked contrast to *The Birth of Christianity,* which ostensibly dealt with the earliest Judean Christians.) Luke's notion of harmony between Paul, James, and Peter is a distinct case of Lukan wishful thinking: the evangelist appears "to care very little" about Paul's real concerns and intentions.[66] Unlike Luke, Paul views himself (and others, including women) as an apostle, even if not part of the group comprising Peter and "the Twelve."[67] The role of Peter is, of course, undeniable in the Antioch episode, which Crossan and Reed present in an unexpectedly nuanced light. Where Luke's assumption of mutual understanding was previously rubbished, here we discover that when confronted with the demand for Gentile circumcision, James and Peter agreed with Barnabas and Paul in resisting this challenge and establishing instead the twin missions of Paul to the Gentiles and Peter to the Jews;[68] Paul and Jerusalem are in agreement. The Antioch dispute concerned not this essential agreement but its practical implications, somewhat implausibly understood to concern "kosher restrictions."[69] Paul calls Peter a hypocrite for abandoning his earlier custom of non-observance and opting instead for a "kosher-for-everyone" policy.[70] Unlike many Protestant commentators, for whom Paul's condemnation of Peter is an open-and-shut case, Crossan here places on Peter's lips the disarmingly Irish-sounding reply, "It's not hypocrisy, Paul. It is simple courtesy."[71] But Crossan's Paul knows it is not theology that divides him from James and

---

66. Crossan and Reed, *Paul,* 28.

67. Crossan and Reed, *Paul,* 29-30.

68. Crossan and Reed, *Paul,* 216.

69. See, e.g., Markus Bockmuehl, *Jewish Law in Gentile Churches: Halakhah and the Beginning of Christian Public Ethics* (Edinburgh: T&T Clark, 2000), 56-61, 71-82, and *passim* for an elucidation of some of the issues affecting Jewish-Gentile relations at Antioch. In light of the text's statement that at James's intervention Jews stopped eating with Gentiles altogether (Gal. 2:12), it is unclear on what basis Crossan and Reed believe James to have demanded merely that "kosher was to be observed by everyone at joint meals" (*Paul,* 219).

70. Crossan and Reed, *Paul,* 219-20; note once again that Gal. 2:12, on the contrary, has Paul assert that Peter stopped eating with Gentiles altogether.

71. Crossan and Reed, *Paul,* 220; cf. Crossan, *Birth of Christianity,* 466.

Peter, not even the notion of justification by faith. He is in agreement with Peter, even about how one experiences the work of the Spirit.[72]

Peter next turns up in the discussion of where the early Christians lived in the city of Rome. Crossan and Reed closely follow Peter Lampe's influential argument that the primary geographic concentrations of Christian catacombs outside the city walls are indicative of where most Christians lived *inside* the city.[73] Since this archaeological record points to a concentration in Trastevere and along the beginning of the Via Appia, this is where the key Christian settlements must be sought.[74] In this connection, Crossan and Reed confirm the plausibility of a Christian memorial for Peter's martyrdom on the Vatican hill — not far from Trastevere and the associated tombs of the Via Aurelia. The identification of this memorial, "presumably Peter's grave," follows along Lampe's largely mainstream position, and the point of mentioning it is simply to confirm the geographic and lower-class social setting of the Roman church, rather than to develop any thesis about Peter. Where Peter's death does resurface, however, is in the final chapter, where it is deliberately placed alongside Paul's in the Neronian persecution of 64 C.E.: despite their "fierce disagreement" at Antioch, in the end these two apostles are "reconciled, at least by later tradition, as martyrs under Nero. . . . Peter and Paul, *weak* Christians and *strong* Christians, united in martyrdom."[75]

72. Crossan, *Birth of Christianity*, 221-22.

73. Crossan and Reed, *Paul*, 369-74, citing Peter Lampe, "The Roman Christians of Romans 16," in *The Romans Debate*, ed. Karl P. Donfried, rev. ed. (Peabody: Hendrickson, 1991), 216-30. The singular emphasis on Christian burials is, however, a somewhat simplistic reduction of Lampe's argument, which in fact also pays attention to evidence from the geographic clustering of local traditions, Jewish quarters, the clustering of ancient titular churches, and contemporary literary evidence of Christian presence. See further Peter Lampe, *From Paul to Valentinus: Christians at Rome in the First Two Centuries*, ed. Marshall D. Johnson, trans. Michael Steinhauser (Minneapolis: Fortress, 2003), 3-47.

74. Lampe, *Christians at Rome*, rightly highlights Trastevere and the Via Appia, but arguably underrates the evidence of the smaller cluster of titular churches (S. Prassede, S. Pudenziana) near Jewish populations around the Viminal Hill (Subura), combined with several catacombs along the Via Nomentana.

75. Crossan and Reed, *Paul*, 402.

Crossan on Peter, Paul, and Jesus

On Crossan's reading we seem to be offered two quite different Peters, depending on which book we read. In the account of the earliest Jerusalem church, he is a flat-footed and unthinking authoritarian peasant whose "brokered" vision of faith shares little with those of either Jesus or Paul, but is opposed to them both — as indeed their visions are to each other. The book on Paul gives us a Peter who is at once less colorful but also, it seems, less drastically opposed to Paul and to Jesus. There is real conflict with Paul, but Peter's Jewish missionary commitment and concern for continuing courtesy to Jerusalem are treated sympathetically — indeed even Paul's collection is construed, combining the Epistles and Acts, in terms of a cognate concern as a "gift to preserve unity."[76] In his latest, co-authored volume, Crossan thus shows some signs of movement towards a more open, "ecumenical" Peter who may, surprisingly, turn out to be not far in essentials from either Jesus or Paul.

N. T. Wright

Like all the authors here under consideration, Tom Wright has produced a mind-boggling volume of literary output. Leaving aside his enormously popular *For Everyone* series of NT expositions, his most definitive scholarly books in our present area of interest have included *Jesus and the Victory of God* and *The Resurrection of the Son of God*. Earlier scholarly books on Paul have included *The Climax of the Covenant* and *What Saint Paul Really Said;* one might also include his commentaries on Colossians and Romans, or for that matter *The New Testament and the People of God*. Wright's major series *Christian Origins and the Question of God* has not yet progressed beyond vols. 2 and 3 to the promised major monograph on Paul. As a result, my study of Peter in Wright's Paul is significantly restrained by the largely topical and theological nature of his scholarly treatment of Paul to date.[77]

---

76. Crossan and Reed, *Paul,* 397-98.

77. Bibliographical details for the aforementioned works by N. T. Wright appear in subsequent notes.

Peter and Wright's Paul

Wright's Paul remains fairly taciturn about Simon Peter, at least in his scholarly publications to date. *What Saint Paul Really Said,* for example, mentions Peter just once, in a quotation of 1 Cor. 15:3-8,[78] while he is entirely absent from *The Climax of the Covenant* and the Colossians commentary.[79] Only the popular volumes on Romans and on Galatians and Thessalonians in the *Paul for Everyone* series refer to Peter in passing, as does the larger Romans commentary.[80] In this commentary there is virtually no discussion of the likely origin of Roman Christianity, beyond explaining that it was "founded by someone other than Paul."[81] At Rom. 15:20 Wright considers, but leaves open, the possibility that the man upon whose apostolic foundation Paul does not want to build could be Peter — a possibility that seems to have strengthened somewhat in the popular *Paul for Everyone* series.[82] Writing on Galatians in that same series, Wright considers that the readership may already know about the dispute in Antioch, possibly from a report that assigned to Peter the stronger arguments.[83] Paul's rebuke of Peter was partly for "masking" and "play-acting" (based on a familiar etymologizing interpretation of the word *hypokrisis*), and partly for compromising his own better knowledge about the essence of Christian identity as transcending the Jew-Gentile distinction.[84] But in the scholarly works on Paul published thus far, it is difficult to find consistent reflection on Peter's motivation at Antioch or on his roles as a bearer of Jesus tradition and a traveling missionary.

78. N. T. Wright, *What Saint Paul Really Said: Was Paul of Tarsus the Real Founder of Christianity?* (Oxford: Lion, 1997), 90.

79. N. T. Wright, *The Climax of the Covenant: Christ and the Law in Pauline Theology* (Edinburgh: T&T Clark, 1991), and *The Epistles of Paul to the Colossians and to Philemon,* TNTC 12 (Grand Rapids: Eerdmans, 1986).

80. N. T. Wright, *Paul for Everyone: Galatians and Thessalonians,* 2d ed. (London: SPCK, 2004), *Paul for Everyone: Romans,* 2 vols., 2d ed. (London: SPCK, 2004), and "The Letter to the Romans: Introduction, Commentary, and Reflections," in *NIB,* 12 vols. (Nashville: Abingdon, 2002), 10:375-793.

81. Wright, "Romans," 422.

82. Wright, "Romans," 755; cf. Wright, *Romans,* 2:123.

83. Wright, *Galatians and Thessalonians,* 22.

84. Wright, *Galatians and Thessalonians,* 22-23.

Peter and Wright's Jesus

Even in Wright's works on Jesus, however, Petrine pickings are surprisingly slim. He has sometimes been accused of paying insufficient attention to questions of authenticity in his Jesus research. This impression is partly confirmed in his handling of Simon Peter, whose five appearances in *Jesus and the Victory of God* all take the form not of analytical judgments but of gospel paraphrase, even in key passages like the confession at Caesarea Philippi.[85] Indeed, although he knows that Jesus' famously controversial response to Peter as the "rock" of the church (Matt. 16:16-17) is frequently regarded as secondary, Wright cites Ben F. Meyer in support of the view that it is a further, evidently historical, affirmation of Jesus' messianic status.[86] Similarly, unlike Crossan, he declares Jesus' call of Peter, Andrew, James, and John to be "an indubitable historical event" without further ado, even if recast "through the different stories" of all four evangelists; no attempt is made to reconcile the Lukan or Johannine narratives of Peter's call with those of Mark or Matthew.[87] Despite the volume's length of over 700 pages, a number of Petrine episodes are entirely absent. These range from Jesus' early visit to the house of Peter to heal his mother-in-law all the way to Peter's drawing his sword at Jesus' arrest.[88] Even Peter's denial is mentioned only in a single passing footnote, as confirming Jesus to be a true prophet.[89]

Rather more attention is paid to Peter in *The Resurrection of the Son of God*. Some of this, to be sure, again consists largely of narrative paraphrase: Peter's speeches and healing miracles in Acts, Peter's escape from prison, the NT resurrection accounts, Paul's knowledge of Peter (as

85. See N. T. Wright, *Jesus and the Victory of God* (London: SPCK, 1996), 298, 462, 478, 529, 651.

86. Wright, *Jesus*, 529 n. 182, citing Ben F. Meyer, *The Aims of Jesus* (London: SCM, 1979), 185-97. Cf. similarly his *The Resurrection of the Son of God* (London: SPCK, 2003), 409, on Peter's rebuke of Jesus. Wright's debating partner Marcus J. Borg, "An Appreciative Disagreement," in *Jesus and the Restoration of Israel: A Critical Assessment of N. T. Wright's Jesus and the Victory of God*, ed. Carey C. Newman (Downers Grove: InterVarsity, 1999), 234-35, questions his confidence on this matter.

87. Wright, *Jesus*, 298.

88. Also noted by Paul R. Eddy, "The (W)Right Jesus: Eschatological Prophet, Israel's Messiah, Yahweh Embodied," in *Jesus and Restoration*, 40-60 (on 46).

89. Wright, *Jesus*, 525 n. 165; similarly Wright, *Resurrection*, 620 n. 16. The denial also surfaces *en passant*, pp. 629, 649, 664, 676.

Cephas) as a traveling missionary, etc.[90] There are brief discussions of extra-canonical traditions about Peter in *1 Clement* and in Ignatius,[91] but neither of these is explored for any significant Petrine implications; the same is true both for 1–2 Peter and for the later Petrine pseudepigrapha. Wright explicitly takes issue with what he calls the "modern consensus" on the resurrection narratives, one part of which is to stress "stories which pit one apostle against another (the women against the men, Peter and John against one another, and so on)."[92] Instead, Wright strongly resists attempts to see any of the resurrection narratives as playing off a particular disciple or form of Christianity against another, whether that be associated with Mary Magdalene, Peter, or someone else.[93] Similarly, the Easter experience of Peter and the others cannot be reduced, with Edward Schillebeeckx, to a conversion-like experience of grace and forgiveness.[94] Elsewhere, in summarizing the points of contact and agreement between the diverse canonical accounts of the resurrection, Wright stresses Luke's and John's agreement that the women's discovery of the empty tomb and encounter with an angel was followed by Peter and one other disciple visiting the tomb "to see for themselves."[95] He also finds it "highly likely" that Mark *intended* to continue his gospel beyond 16:8 with an account somewhat like Matthew's, including Peter and the other disciples meeting Jesus in Galilee and being commissioned to take the gospel to the nations.[96]

Wright on Peter, Paul, and Jesus

Overall, therefore, Wright's Peter remains largely within the confines of the biblical narrative, with no obvious attempt either to inflate Peter's role or to deflate it. Little fresh analysis is introduced, and there is no real discus-

---

90. E.g. Wright, *Resurrection*, 22, 65, 134, 324-25, 454-55, 553, 590, 654, 657, 658, 663-65, and *passim*.

91. *1 Clem.* 5–6 (Wright, *Resurrection*, 481-82); Ign., *Smyrn.* 3.1-3 (Wright, *Resurrection*, 485).

92. Wright, *Resurrection*, 588-89.

93. Wright, *Resurrection*, 677-78 (on John 20–21) and *passim*.

94. Wright, *Resurrection*, 701; cf. 705, 706.

95. Wright, *Resurrection*, 613.

96. Wright, *Resurrection*, 623-24; this outline of Mark's intended ending "may well be secure" (624).

sion of questions such as Peter's role vis-à-vis the Jesus tradition, his potential bridging function between the Jewish and Gentile mission, or for that matter his developing relationship with Paul over the period of the Pauline letter corpus.

James D. G. Dunn

We turn finally to James D. G. Dunn, who invented the nomenclature of a "New Perspective on Paul."[97] Like Sanders, he has been a major voice in scholarship on both Paul and Jesus, with articles and large books amounting to thousands of printed pages. Most recently, he has advanced his work on memory and tradition as a "New Perspective on Jesus." For chronological reasons I shall again proceed from Paul to Jesus.

Peter and Dunn's Paul

James Dunn's work on Paul is earlier, more substantial, and probably more influential than that on Jesus. Not only is it he who first named this school of thought over two decades ago,[98] but he has also contributed numerous significant books and articles both before and since that time. There are major commentaries on several Pauline letters including Romans and Galatians, influential monographs — *Unity and Diversity in the New Testament, Christology in the Making, The Partings of the Ways, Jesus, Paul, and the Law*, and the 800-page *Theology of Paul the Apostle* — not to mention numerous articles and several other edited books on related topics.[99] The sheer volume of

97. James D. G. Dunn, "The New Perspective on Paul," *BJRL* 65 (1983): 95-122.

98. Dunn, "New Perspective."

99. E.g. James D. G. Dunn, *Unity and Diversity in the New Testament: An Inquiry into the Character of Earliest Christianity* (London: SCM, 1977); "New Perspective"; *Christology in the Making: A New Testament Inquiry into the Character of Earliest Christianity*, 2d ed. (London: SCM, 1989); *Jesus, Paul, and the Law: Studies in Mark and Galatians* (Louisville: Westminster/John Knox, 1990); *The Partings of the Ways between Christianity and Judaism and Their Significance for the Character of Christianity* (London: SCM, 1991); *Jews and Christians: The Parting of the Ways, A.D. 70 to 135*, WUNT 66 (Tübingen: Mohr Siebeck, 1989); *The Epistle to the Galatians* (BNTC; London: A&C Black, 1993); "Prolegomena to a Theology of Paul," *NTS* 40 (1994): 407-32; "4QMMT and Galatians," *NTS* 43 (1997): 147-53; *The Theology of Paul the Apostle* (Grand Rapids: Eerdmans, 1998); "Noch einmal 'Works of the Law': The

material dictates that we must once again be eclectic. I will concentrate on his exposition of the dispute between Peter and Paul at Antioch.

In his exposition of Galatians, Dunn affirms that Paul's visit to Jerusalem "to get to know Cephas" (1:18) is the Apostle's way of gingerly wanting "neither to claim too much nor to deny too little." Peter is clearly recognized as a man with a "key position," but he did not commission Paul nor did he instruct Paul on the meaning of the revelation on the Damascus Road. Instead, the substance of this extensive two-week visit within five years of the death of Jesus specifically involved learning about Peter as his leading disciple in Galilee — and thus "a fairly substantive level of 'information content'" about the beginnings of the Jesus movement.[100] Paul's account of the Jerusalem conference in Gal. 2:7-8 establishes a close analogy between Paul's role in the Gentile mission and Peter's apostolic importance and considerable success in the mission to Israel.[101] (It is worth contrasting Sanders's insistence, noted above, that Peter had largely failed. Dunn also plausibly suggests that James the Just's leadership role in Jerusalem may be due primarily to Peter's missionary activities rather than to any usurping of power, as is often suggested.)[102]

Dunn has spelled out his influential interpretation of the Antioch dispute in several publications.[103] Here our primary interest is in the person of Peter. He is described (not unreasonably given 2:9, 11) as having in Paul's view gone back on the Jerusalem agreement about the equivalence of their respective assignments — although Dunn rightly implies that Peter had in fact come to Antioch not to interfere but in pursuit of his own mission to Israel.[104] Like all other interpreters examined in this paper, Dunn views Paul's charge of hypocrisy as attacking Peter for responding to the prompting from James by withdrawing from table fellowship with

---

Dialogue Continues," in *Fair Play: Diversity and Conflicts in Early Christianity: Essays in Honour of Heikki Räisänen,* ed. Ismo Dunderberg, Christopher Tuckett, and Kari Syreeni, NovTSup 103 (Leiden: Brill, 2002); and Dunn., ed., *Paul and the Mosaic Law,* WUNT 89 (Tübingen: Mohr Siebeck, 1996).

100. Dunn, *Galatians,* 73-74; cf. Dunn, *Theology of Paul,* 188.

101. Dunn, *Galatians,* 105-7; also p. 107 on the fact that the apostolicity of Peter is not reaffirmed for Paul.

102. Dunn, *Galatians,* 109.

103. Including Dunn, *Galatians,* 115-31; Dunn, *Jesus, Paul, and the Law,* 129-82; also 108-28; cf. Dunn, *Unity and Diversity,* 130-35; Dunn, "4QMMT and Galatians."

104. Dunn, *Galatians,* 116. On Antioch's large Jewish community and the Jewish perception of the city as part of the Holy Land, see e.g. my discussion in *Jewish Law,* 61-70.

Gentile Christians. (That they were *Christians* rather than unbaptized pagans is here, in keeping with most commentators, regarded as "obvious" without further argument.)[105] The diversity of Jewish contacts with Gentiles is rightly emphasized over against more simplistic viewpoints that Jews never ate with Gentiles.[106]

Peter's change of practice, suggests Professor Dunn, is not from complete non-observance of food laws to observance, but from a position of presuming the acceptability of Gentile food along the lines of 1 Corinthians 10 to a position of insisting on basic food rules[107] — or in other words from a "soft" to a "hard" interpretation of the Jerusalem agreement.[108] Peter's withdrawal and separation (Gal. 2:12) returned him to a pretense of "playing the Pharisee," but it may also reflect a real ambivalence about whether at Antioch the appropriate *modus vivendi* should be keeping with the Jewish or with the Gentile mission.[109] His temporary mode of "living like a Gentile" (Gal. 2:14), as Paul puts it using a slogan of intra-Jewish polemic, meant not his total abandonment of Jewish praxis but rather a mode of life that for the nationalists transgressed what they regarded as specific boundaries of identity.[110] Peter's "hypocrisy" is not a matter of acting against his own best convictions, but his inability to see that his behavior compromises the Jerusalem Agreement as Paul understood it.

As for Peter's "fear of the circumcision," this is for Dunn best understood in terms of nationalist zealots in Jerusalem, probably "believers included."[111] Peter's action, he surmises, was motivated by the desire not to cause scandal to fellow Jewish believers, and he accepted the argument of James's people that the Jerusalem Agreement required Jews to live as Jews rather than as Gentiles.[112] To "compel Gentiles to Judaize" in this context cannot refer to a compulsion to convert to Judaism, but to assimilate one's lifestyle to that of Jews.[113]

---

105. Dunn, *Galatians*, 119.

106. Dunn, *Galatians*, 119-20; cf. Bockmuehl, *Jewish Law*, 56-61 for further discussion of alternative points of view.

107. Dunn, *Galatians*, 121.

108. Thus Dunn, *Galatians*, 123.

109. Dunn, *Galatians*, 122; cf. 125.

110. Dunn, *Galatians*, 127-28.

111. Dunn, *Galatians*, 123.

112. Dunn, *Galatians*, 125-26.

113. Dunn, *Galatians*, 129.

At the root of the Antioch dispute, therefore, is for Dunn a clash of principles that appears to Paul as hypocrisy and to Peter, and to some extent Barnabas, as loyalty to the mother church's concern for the Jewish identity of the mission to Israel. Paul describes the outcome of the argument with Peter as a victory for the gospel, but it is really a defeat. He does not claim that Peter accepted his rebuke and reverted to his former practice; indeed, Paul received no backing from the Antioch church, whether Jews or Gentiles. If anything, Peter's position prevails at Antioch: the more liberal Gentile table fellowship accommodated itself to the more Jewish one.[114] Dunn describes the upshot of the dispute as a Pauline breach with Jerusalem, with Barnabas and with Antioch[115] — though not, it seems, with Peter, who is not mentioned. Although allowing that these breaches may subsequently have been reconciled or mitigated,[116] Dunn says no more about the future of Paul's relationship with Peter.

Peter and Dunn's Jesus

In *Jesus Remembered*, Professor Dunn has surprisingly little to say about individual disciples. Nevertheless, his notion of a living tradition oriented around apostolic memory and diverse performance does involve a category of "apostolic custodians" among whom Peter, James, and John are recognized as leading figures from the first. Indeed, it is seen as significant that in all lists of disciples "Simon Peter is as firmly rooted at the top as Judas Iscariot is at the end,"[117] and Dunn stresses the "essential historicity" of the call of the two pairs of brothers, called as empowered missionaries, despite the fact that John's account shows the Synoptic evangelists to be omitting earlier contacts between Jesus, Andrew, and Simon.[118] Evidence for the early and persistent prominence of these three leading custodians is found not only in Acts, but also confirmed by their continuity with Paul's account in Gal. 2:9. Dunn concludes, "This correlates well with the re-

---

114. Dunn, *Galatians*, 129-30.

115. Dunn, *Galatians*, 130-31.

116. The notion of a threefold breach is found in both Dunn, *Unity and Diversity*, 134-35, and Dunn, *Galatians*, 130-31, but only the latter text allows that "not . . . all these breaches were equally deep or permanent."

117. Dunn, *Jesus Remembered*, 508.

118. Dunn, *Jesus Remembered*, 509 n. 96, 557; cf. John 1:40-42.

membrance of the Jesus tradition that Peter and the brothers Zebedee [*sic*] had been closest to Jesus and thus were accounted principal witnesses to and custodians of Jesus' heritage."[119] This is for Dunn at the core of the Jesus tradition, and he chides John P. Meier for suggesting that the entire apostolic trio might be the product of Mark's redactional creativity: it makes far more sense that their early post-Easter status reflects a prior pre-Easter prominence than vice versa.[120]

Three more specific aspects of the gospel tradition attract Dunn's attention. First, he accepts as a reliable part of the remembered Jesus tradition the Johannine assertion of Peter's birth in Bethsaida (along with Andrew and Philip)[121] and his subsequent settlement in Capernaum; the so-called "house of Peter" discovered at Capernaum may well be Jesus' own residence.[122] Dunn does not say how this is relevant or why, or indeed on what grounds he regards the reference to Bethsaida as reliable.

The second significant Petrine feature is Peter's confession.[123] Although undeniably important to the structure and redaction of Mark's Gospel, the evangelist in fact draws on "a well-rooted memory" whose diverse written expression in the four Gospels is due to oral "performance flexibility" (and confirmed in the independent attestation of John 6:69). The folksy informality of this method surfaces, for example, in Dunn's suggestion that Peter and the early disciples would be "almost certainly" among the first to raise the issue of Jesus' messiahship — and Peter's blurting out the answer (Mark 9:34; 10:37 and par.) is in keeping with his character.[124] Contrary to Bultmann's assertion that this episode is a displaced resurrection story, Dunn insists that it belongs in the ministry of Jesus; a post-Easter origin is further rendered unlikely by the criterion of embarrassment attaching to Peter's being rebuked as "Satan."[125]

119. Dunn, *Jesus Remembered*, 181.

120. Dunn, *Jesus Remembered*, 540 n. 250.

121. Dunn, *Jesus Remembered*, 318.

122. Dunn, *Jesus Remembered*, 317 n. 302.

123. Dunn, *Jesus Remembered*, 644-55.

124. Methodological informality in the handling of an oral "performance flexibility" has been noted by a number of reviewers, including Samuel Byrskog, "A New Perspective on the Jesus Tradition: Reflections on James D. G. Dunn's *Jesus Remembered*," *JSNT* 26 (2004): 459-71; cf. most recently Birger Gerhardsson, "The Secret of the Transmission of the Unwritten Jesus Tradition," *NTS* 51 (2005): 1-18.

125. Dunn, *Jesus Remembered*, 644-45 and n. 147, citing Rudolf Bultmann, *The History of the Synoptic Tradition*, trans. John Marsh, 3d ed. (Oxford: Blackwell, 1972), 259.

Peter also appears, finally, in the complex evidence surrounding the resurrection. The diversity of the empty tomb accounts reflects, in Dunn's view, the retellings of the core tradition that would be characteristic of an oral traditioning process.[126] The Fourth Gospel, we learn, emphasizes the eyewitness testimony of Peter, and it does so without in any way intending to repress the tradition surrounding Mary Magdalene — Dunn here takes an implicit sideswipe at readings like that of Crossan, discussed earlier.[127]

The complex problem of the resurrection appearance to Peter elicits a nimble discussion of Luke 24:34 and 1 Cor. 15:5; Dunn suggests that Luke's reluctance to describe this experience "could possibly reflect Peter's own reticence on the subject" — a possibility deliberately set against the assertion of Gerd Lüdemann and others that all the resurrection stories derive from the modest claim of Luke 24:34.[128] Related to this is the knotty question of what to make of the similarities between Luke's Petrine call narrative (Luke 5:1-11) and the account in John 21 (which the Fourth Gospel calls the "third" rather than, as in 1 Cor. 15:5, the first appearance). Dunn leaves unresolved the possibility that Luke may have come across a post-Easter appearance to Peter in Galilee, but one that had never become a part of "official" tradition:

> One possible pointer towards a solution to the problem of such divergent versions is that throughout Peter's life the appearance to Peter was retained as personal testimony and never allowed to become church tradition as such. In which case, it was only after Peter's death that the testimony could be retold, and only then from a Johannine (beloved disciple) perspective, a perspective, it would appear, for which the issue of both Petrine and Jerusalem priority was not an important factor.[129]

Overall, then, the Peter of Dunn's major Jesus book is a figure of fairly clear definition and significance, whose profile appears largely in keeping with what one might expect from a synoptic reading of the four Gospels.

---

126. Dunn, *Jesus Remembered*, 831.
127. Dunn, *Jesus Remembered*, 831, 833-34.
128. Dunn, *Jesus Remembered*, 843-46, esp. 844 and n. 77.
129. Dunn, *Jesus Remembered*, 846 and nn. 82-83.

Dunn on Peter, Paul, and Jesus

A fuller historical and exegetical assessment of Professor Dunn's interpretation cannot here be our primary concern.[130] Suffice it to note simply that the question of *continuity or discontinuity* between the Peter of Jesus and the Peter of Paul is somewhat obscured by the fact that Dunn's approach significantly underrates certain factors that might facilitate a more explicit conversation between his two big projects. On the Pauline side, Peter's connection with the Jesus tradition is acknowledged more or less in passing, and Dunn firmly rejects the Bultmann school's notorious interpretation of 2 Cor. 5:16 as Paul's rejection of the need to know anything about Jesus.[131] Dunn's own Paul, by contrast, is certainly interested in Jesus tradition — but while the Jesus who emerges has a number of "Synoptic" characteristics, the Apostle's knowledge of him seems to share few immediate links with the "Third Quest's" very Jewish Jesus.[132] So there is little consideration here that the shape of Peter's loyalty to the Jewish mission might reflect some of Jesus' own concerns for the restoration of Israel; Paul's occasional hints that he retained an interest in matters like Jerusalem, a Davidic Christology, or Jesus' conflict with the Jewish authorities are noted but not explored with a view to cognate themes in the Third Quest.

Dunn's work on Jesus is generally later than that on Paul and less reticent to allow that the Peter of Galilee is also the Peter of Antioch. Even here, however, the primary stress lies less on personal continuity than on the anonymous "living tradition" of "performative" communities.[133] By contrast, both Pauline and numerous second-century Christian sources from Papias to Irenaeus suggest that the nature of early Christian "remembering" was often formally tethered to the identity of those apostolic individuals who witnessed and remembered. To be sure, Dunn offers a fleeting reference to "Apostolic Custodians," and we learn that Peter, James, and

---

130. On Dunn, *Jesus Remembered*, see further my review of the volume.

131. E.g. Dunn, *Theology of Paul*, 84-85, 188 and n. 26.

132. Note also the explicit discussion in James D. G. Dunn, "Paul's Knowledge of the Jesus Tradition: The Evidence of Romans," in *Christus bezeugen: Festschrift für Wolfgang Trilling zum 65. Geburtstag*, ed. K. Kertelge, ETS 59 (Freiburg: Herder, 1990), 193-207; and "Jesus Tradition in Paul," in *Studying the Historical Jesus: Evaluations of the State of Current Research*, ed. Bruce Chilton and Craig A. Evans, NTTS 19 (Leiden: Brill, 1994), 155-78, on Paul's knowledge of Jesus tradition in Romans and elsewhere.

133. Note, e.g., Dunn, *Jesus Remembered*, 482-87.

John were indeed among the gospel tradition's "principal witnesses";[134] for Peter and John at any rate that is also the clear testimony of the NT and the early church. What such early Christian preference for the apostolicity of individual tradents and their memory might mean in the case of Simon Peter and others, however, remains insufficiently scrutinized. As a result, the genuine potential to identify connections between his work on Jesus and on Paul is left without clear criteria to distinguish between diverse understandings of the "traditioning process" that Dunn regards as either excessively formal and restrictive[135] or on the other hand excessively flexible and creative.[136]

Conclusion

At one level, the result of our survey remains somewhat disappointing. While all four writers here surveyed allow that Jesus and Paul are linked by a Petrine continuity in principle, in practice none of them carries this through to any significant analytical engagement beyond the answers given by previous generations of scholars. For Sanders this is because Paul and Peter were opposed to each other; Crossan thinks (at least in his earlier work) that in addition each is opposed to Jesus. For Wright and Dunn it seems to be mainly a lack of sustained reflection on the problem: although they have written more on both subjects than most people have time to read, it is almost as if in their mind's eye the Third Quest and the New Perspective are largely separate compartments of NT scholarship, passing as ships in the night. The same, I suspect, would be seen to be true if we broadened our remit to those authors who have made major contributions

134. James D. G. Dunn, "Social Memory and the Oral Jesus Tradition," Durham-Tübingen Conference Papers (Durham, 2004), 180-81; cf. 242.

135. Birger Gerhardsson, Rainer Riesner, and Samuel Byrskog are criticized along these lines in Dunn, *Jesus Remembered,* 198-99, and then largely dismissed; contrast the more positive appraisal in Dunn, "Social Memory and the Oral Jesus Tradition."

136. E.g. Dunn, "Social Memory," 13, on Dan Ben-Amos and Liliane Weissberg, *Cultural Memory and the Construction of Identity* (Detroit: Wayne State University Press, 1999). It is worth comparing his own conviction (Dunn, "Social Memory," 8) "that the Jesus tradition was not 'memorized' as 'teaching of Jesus'; rather it was absorbed into the consciousness and life-manual of the first churches to become a resource on which they could draw almost instinctively and without having to engage in an act of 'remembering' what Jesus taught."

to just one of these two areas of study.[137] What is more, the relative non-communication between the Pauline and Jesus Quests is further complicated by a lack of agreement about method, topic definition, and criteria that I sketched at the beginning.

Beyond this, however, the work of these scholars is marked by a distinct lack of interest in other early Christian traditions about the relationships between Jesus and Peter or Peter and Paul — relationships that do also need to be understood *historically,* however else one assesses them. As perhaps in Pauline and Jesus scholarship more widely, Peter seems repeatedly reduced to an ideological straw man or literary whipping boy: Paulinists see him through the eyes of Paul as one who accentuates Pauline distinctives; Jesus scholars again see him as a sidekick, a foil to Jesus.

Of the writers surveyed in this chapter, James Dunn in my view comes closest to having cleared the ground for a genuine breakthrough here; but to date this potential remains unfulfilled — partly because it is not a high priority for any of his major projects, and partly because of certain weaknesses in method and criteria. In fact, it seems a little ironic that despite thousands of pages on both the New Perspective and the Third Quest, up to now he has never quite implemented the following programmatic statement about Peter that appeared as long ago as 1977 in the conclusion of *Unity and Diversity in the New Testament:*

> Peter was probably in fact and effect the bridge-man who did more than any other to hold together the diversity of first-century Christianity. . . . Peter, as shown particularly by the Antioch episode in Gal. 2, had both a care to hold firm to his Jewish heritage which Paul lacked, and an openness to the demands of developing Christianity which James lacked. . . . Others could link the developing new religion as or more firmly to its founding events and to Jesus himself. But none of them, including none of the rest of the twelve, seem to have played any role of continuing significance for the whole sweep of Christian-

---

137. A quick comparison of the remarkable lack of topical overlap between the respective surveys of Ben Witherington (*The Jesus Quest: The Third Search for the Jew of Nazareth* [Downers Grove: InterVarsity, 1995] and *The Paul Quest: The Renewed Search for the Jew of Tarsus* [Downers Grove: InterVarsity, 1998]) demonstrates this point relatively easily. Paul is not a topic of sufficient prominence to warrant an entry in the extensive subject index of the former book (though the text does discuss Paul repeatedly), nor Jesus in that of the latter; Peter appears in neither.

ity. . . . So it is Peter who becomes the focal point of unity for the whole
Church — Peter who was probably the most prominent among Jesus'
disciples, Peter who according to early traditions was the first witness
of the risen Jesus, Peter who was the leading figure in the earliest days
of the new sect in Jerusalem, but Peter who also was concerned for
mission, and who as Christianity broadened its outreach and character
broadened with it, at the cost to be sure of losing his leading role in Jerusalem, but with the result that he became the most hopeful symbol
of unity for that growing Christianity which more and more came to
think of itself as the Church Catholic.[138]

Perhaps this is somewhat youthful purple prose, which one might choose
to tone down in the cold light of twenty-five years' research on the historical Jesus and the historical Paul. Nevertheless, as far as the correlation of
these two projects goes, Dunn's 1977 conclusion has not yet lived up to its
considerable promise — though there may be more to come in the series
of which *Jesus Remembered* is only the first volume.

If this initial assessment appears gloomy, other signs do nonetheless
suggest the possibility of a genuine sea change in our understanding of
what a post–New Perspective Paul may or may not know about a post–
Third Quest Jesus. The key, ironically, may lie less in the works of scholars
active in both fields than in bringing the most pertinent insights of each
project into conversation with those of the other. Interestingly, recent
scholarship on Peter and Paul, in America and especially in F. C. Baur's native land, has tended to the clear affirmation of Peter as a mediating figure
between Jesus and Paul — seeing their Antioch dispute in terms of a
"managed conflict" rather than as permanent all-out rivalry over the heart
of the gospel.[139]

Nicholas Taylor's thought-provoking recent survey of the "Paul and
Jesus" question argues that the Third Quest has made too little use of re-

---

138. Dunn, *Unity and Diversity in the New Testament*, 385-86.

139. So, e.g., Christfried Böttrich, *Petrus: Fischer, Fels und Funktionär*, Biblische Gestalten 2 (Leipzig: Evangelische Verlagsanstalt, 2001); "Petrus und Paulus in Antiochien (Gal
2.11-21)," *BTZ* 19 (2002): 224-39; and "Petrus — Bischofsamt — Kirche," *ZNT* 7 (2004): 44-51;
cf. similarly Andreas Wechsler, *Geschichtsbild und Apostelstreit: Eine forschungsgeschichtliche
und exegetische Studie über den antiochenischen Zwischenfall (Gal 2,11-14)*, BZNW 62 (Berlin:
de Gruyter, 1991); Joachim Gnilka, *Petrus und Rom: Das Petrusbild in den ersten zwei
Jahrhunderten* (Freiburg: Herder, 2002); and Lutz Doering, "Schwerpunkte und Tendenzen
der neueren Petrus-Forschung," *BTZ* 19 (2002): 203-23.

cent Pauline scholarship, which in turn has become a little more sanguine about what Paul knew of Jesus.[140] On this reading, Paul's Jesus was born as a Jew linked with the Davidic line, whom the apostle regards as having been consciously Israelite and observant of the Torah's covenantal obligations. Paul was aware of conflict with the Jerusalem authorities as a major contributing factor to the crucifixion. He also had some significant knowledge of traditions about Jesus' teaching, delivered to his churches not in letters but in the context of formal catechesis. Paul himself may in Taylor's view have acquired his knowledge of teachings preserved by Mark largely through his extended visit with Peter in Jerusalem (Gal. 1:18).[141]

Among certain other writers on the Third Quest one can find similar indications that Peter could emerge as one catalyst for a link between Jesus and Paul. John P. Meier, for example, devotes much of volume 3 of his *magnum opus* to the disciples, including a section on Simon Peter.[142] The once popular notion that Simon Peter as a witness to the resurrection is discredited by Paul and other major NT authors seems to him so implausible as to be reminiscent of "a snake biting its tail."[143] Meier's portrait of this apostle concludes by observing the extent to which "Peter remains the same in various NT sources, both before and after Easter. . . . He bridges in a singular way the ministry of the historical Jesus and the mission of the early church."[144] That, to be sure, is a tall claim, and not one which even a project of Meier's magnitude will establish to everyone's satisfaction. But it is quite in keeping with the trend in recent scholarship on Peter,[145] which in turn lends some credence to James Dunn's programmatic statement of 1977.

The figure of Peter, in other words, does seem to harbor unrealized potential for relating the two projects we are here examining — the Third Quest for a more coherently Jewish Jesus and the New Perspective on a

---

140. Nicholas H. Taylor, "Paul and the Historical Jesus Quest," *Neot* 37 (2003): 105-26 (see 110, 118, and *passim*).

141. E.g. Taylor, "Paul and the Historical Jesus Quest," 119-20.

142. John P. Meier, *A Marginal Jew: Rethinking the Historical Jesus,* 3 vols. (New York: Doubleday, 1991-2001), 3:41-285, esp. 221-45.

143. Meier, *Marginal Jew,* 3:243. To be fair, Meier's immediate reference in that discussion is the more limited concern with the basic historicity of Peter's denial of Jesus.

144. Meier, *Marginal Jew,* 3:244, 245.

145. In addition to the German language titles cited in n. 139, cf., e.g., Pheme Perkins, *Peter: Apostle for the Whole Church* (Columbia: University of South Carolina Press, 1994).

Paul more articulately engaged with Judaism. Although Peter stands without doubt in a degree of tension with the aims of both Jesus and Paul, he is a unique bridge figure who embodies important connections from Jesus to the Jewish and Gentile missions, both historically and theologically. Part of that Petrine continuity is to represent something of the radical Jewishness of the early Christian search for identity, as it came to such seemingly contradictory expressions in Jerusalem, in Antioch, and in Rome.[146]

As we have seen, the leading players in both recent scholarly efforts have not as yet drawn these links very clearly, perhaps with the partial exception of Dunn. The jury is still out on whether Peter, or for that matter another early Christian figure, could prove a useful catalyst for engagement between the Third Quest and the New Perspective. Meanwhile, I offer this modest contribution in the hope that it may spark some discussion to that end.

146. This point could be fruitfully explored in further dialogue with Boyarin, *Paul*, and *Border Lines*.

Chapter 5

"I Received from the Lord . . .":
Paul, Jesus, and the Last Supper

Francis Watson

Introduction

"For I received from the Lord what I also handed on to you, that the Lord Jesus, on the night on which he was handed over, took bread . . ." (1 Cor. 11:23). By repeating a tradition the Corinthians already know, Paul seeks to reawaken their sense of awe in the presence of holy mysteries: the bread and the cup of the Lord's Supper, through which they participate in the Lord's own body and blood, imbued with the supernatural power of his risen life.[1] To eat this bread and to drink this wine as if they were ordinary bread and wine, heedlessly and without preparation, is to risk converting their life-giving power into a poison that causes weakness, illness, or death.[2] The abused bread and wine can become the agents of the Lord's judgment — a judgment that intends final salvation rather than condemnation but which one would still wish to avoid.[3] Some at Corinth are already guilty of an abuse of this kind, ungraciously going ahead with the

---

1. The Eucharistic bread and wine are "spiritual food" and "spiritual drink" (1 Cor. 10:3-4), in the sense that they enable participation in "the blood of Christ" and "the body of Christ" (10:16; cf. 11:27) — that is, in the heavenly existence of the crucified and risen Lord who is "lifegiving spirit" (15:45).

2. Cf. 1 Cor. 11:28-30.

3. Cf. 1 Cor. 11:31-32.

I am grateful to my student Jeff Spivak for the initial suggestion about 1 Cor. 11:23 that is developed in this paper.

meal without waiting for the whole congregation to be assembled.[4] By the time the latecomers arrive, the food and drink have all been consumed so that they are left hungry and humiliated.[5] Perhaps those responsible will plead that the hour was late and that they too were hungry? In that case, they should have taken something to sustain them before they left home.[6] Only when the whole congregation is gathered together can the Lord's Supper truly be celebrated.[7]

This apparently trivial discourtesy to fellow Christians is symptomatic of a more serious error, the failure to reckon with the invisible presence of the Lord himself in the sharing of bread and cup.[8] The Last Supper tradition is fully integrated into the exhortations and warnings of 1 Cor. 11:17-34, since this tradition underlies Paul's point about the life-

---

4. "So, my brothers and sisters, when you come together to eat, wait for one another" (1 Cor. 11:33). Going ahead with the meal without waiting for latecomers would be a specific instance of the unworthy consumption of the bread and the wine against which the preceding verses warn (vv. 27-32).

5. Paul envisages a situation in which "one is hungry while another is drunk" (11:21), where those who proceed with their meal "shame those who do not have" (11:22). While this is often interpreted as a reference to social stratification, 11:33 suggests that the problem is a failure to wait for the whole congregation to be assembled. The meal is begun prematurely — as *prolambanei* (11:21) also implies, if the temporal force of the prefix is retained here as in Mark 14:8. The alternative view is taken by Gerd Theissen, who argues that at Corinth "the conflict is one between class-specific expectations on the one hand and on the other the norms of a community of love which encompasses people of different social strata" (*The Social Setting of Pauline Christianity*, SNTW [Edinburgh: T&T Clark, 1982], 162). More specifically: "[W]hen the community in Corinth came together for the common *kuriakon deipnon* there was for some, in addition, an *idion deipnon* containing something in addition to bread and wine. Baked goods, fish, and meat would be candidates for such a supplementary dish. . . . [W]ealthier Christians ate other food in addition to the bread and wine" (pp. 159-60). Theissen seems to me to underplay the significance of 11:33-34 and to misread the reference in 11:21 to *to idion deipnon*, the sense of which is determined by the temporal force of *prolambanei*.

6. Paul's repeated suggestion that people should if necessary satisfy their hunger at home (1 Cor. 11:22, 34) confirms that the point at issue is premature participation in the communal meal, not social stratification between haves and have-nots. There is no indication that he is speaking here exclusively to the wealthy (*contra* Theissen, *Social Setting*, 150).

7. Currently the Corinthians do not truly practice "the Lord's Supper" (11:20), since this requires the participation of the whole congregation, so that "*we all* share in the one loaf" (1 Cor. 10:17).

8. For Paul, the Lord is presumably the host at the *kuriakon deipnon* just as he was on the night of his arrest, granting participation in himself by way of the bread and the wine.

giving yet potentially threatening holiness of its reenactment as the Lord's Supper. The question is: where does this tradition come from? When Paul says of this tradition, "*I* received from the Lord what I also handed on to you . . . ," the *egō* is emphatic, as though he wished to emphasize the special link between this tradition and his own person. This *egō* recalls the *egō Paulos* of Gal. 5:2 and the still more assertive *autos de egō Paulos* of 2 Cor. 10:1. But why should Paul claim a unique role in relation to this tradition? When he states that he received this tradition "from the Lord," he surely cannot mean that it was revealed to him personally, directly, and exclusively? If Paul *does* mean this, then this revelation would be the sole origin of the Last Supper tradition; its later Synoptic versions would be variants of a Pauline original. In spite of the consensus that this cannot be the case, it is worth asking whether Paul here could indeed mean what he appears to say: that he, Paul, received the Last Supper tradition from the Lord himself and not from any merely human process of transmission.[9]

The Last Supper Tradition in 1 Cor. 11:23-25: A Revelation to Paul?

The consensus that "from the Lord" cannot imply a claim to direct revelation is impressively unanimous. According to Hans Conzelmann, Paul

---

9. The distinctiveness of the Pauline, "Hellenistic" Eucharist is emphasized by Hans Lietzmann, who contrasts it with a Jerusalem rite in which the congregation reenacted the meals Jesus shared with his disciples, without any reference to his death, his body, or his blood (*Mass and Lord's Supper: A Study in the History of the Liturgy*, ed. Robert D. Richardson, trans. Dorothea H. G. Reeve [Leiden: Brill, 1979], 204-8). Thus, "Paul is the creator of the second type of the Lord's Supper" (p. 208). According to Lietzmann, "The narrative of the last meal of Jesus is familiar to [Paul] from the tradition of the Church, as we have it also in Mark, but the Lord has revealed to him the essential meaning of this story, i.e., that it is the prototype of the Lord's Supper of the Church and must be repeated again and again in remembrance of Jesus" (p. 208). In other words, Jesus did indeed perform symbolic actions relating to his death at his last meal, but it was Paul who ritualized his actions and the accompanying words, authorized by a revelation of the risen Lord. On this view, what Paul "received from the Lord" is (strictly speaking) confined to the command, "Do this in remembrance of me" (1 Cor. 11:24, 25). Lietzmann rightly emphasizes the fundamental role of Paul in the origins of what would become the dominant form of the Eucharist, but still cannot take 1 Cor. 11:23 at face value.

does not mean that he has received this teaching in a vision. He was of course acquainted with it through the mediation of men. Yet it does not merely derive ultimately from the Lord, but also constantly maintains in being passed from hand to hand the immediacy of its origin.[10]

There is, then, a chain of transmission to every link of which the Lord is somehow immediately present. Conzelmann implies that, if "from the Lord" is to be taken seriously, the emphasis must fall on Christ's ongoing involvement in the transmission of tradition; that is why Paul omits to refer to a human mediation, which is nevertheless "of course" presupposed here. In recalling the moment when he received the tradition of the Last Supper from (say) Peter or the Antiochene church, Paul remembers only the presence of his divine Lord and not his human instructor. In that sense, "I received *from the Lord* what I also passed on to you. . . ." If Conzelmann were right, however, Paul's relation to the tradition would be the same as the Corinthians'. If he receives the tradition as "from the Lord," then so too do they: in both cases, human mediation should efface itself in the presence of the exalted Lord who continues to speak in the handing down of the tradition. Yet Paul states that he himself, and not the Lord, mediated the tradition to the Corinthians. Conzelmann is unable to explain why the transmission of tradition seems so different in the two cases. In one case, tradition is received "from the Lord," in the other, from Paul.

A similar view is taken by Wolfgang Schrage, who acknowledges that

[t]he beginning of the verse has caused interpreters certain problems, owing to the use and form of *paralambanein*. On the one hand, Paul explains that he has received the tradition "from the Lord"; on the other hand, it is equally clear that he here draws upon an already formulated tradition. Since, in his use of traditional terminology, Paul himself makes it clear that he is citing a tradition (in almost word-for-word agreement with Luke), it is not possible to interpret *apo tou kyriou* as referring to a direct revelation of the Exalted One, going back directly to the Lord without the mediation of tradition. . . . What is of decisive importance here is only the moment of origin. However great the emphasis on the institution by the Lord and not on the human tradition, the alternative, "human tradition versus revelation of the Ex-

10. Hans Conzelmann, *1 Corinthians*, trans. James W. Leitch, Hermeneia (Philadelphia: Fortress Press, 1975), 196.

alted One," is misconceived, since the tradition itself is understood as the Word of the Kyrios.[11]

It is of course true that Paul here cites an already formulated tradition, but it is wrong to suppose that this tradition could not have originated in a revelation of Christ to Paul himself. Nothing is settled by appealing to the correspondence between 1 Cor. 11:24-25 and the Longer Text of Luke (Luke 22:19b-20), for Luke may here be dependent on a Pauline text written, after all, several decades earlier. Schrage's assumption that Luke and Paul independently attest a pre-Pauline Last Supper tradition merely begs the question.

So far, we have identified two indications that 1 Cor. 11:23 should be taken at face value and that the Last Supper tradition originates in a revelation to Paul. First, the emphatic *egō* ("*I* received . . .") implies a special connection between Paul and this particular tradition. Second, his statement seems to imply a distinction between receiving a tradition from the Lord and from Paul himself; human mediation is explicitly acknowledged in the one case but not in the other. To these we may now add, third, the observation that "I received from the Lord" refers to a *narration* of what Jesus did and said on the night of his arrest. It is not clear that Jesus' action and speech in themselves amount to the transmission of that narration, in spite of the repeated command to "do this in remembrance of me" (1 Cor. 11:24, 25). If transmission takes the form of narration, then the Lord's handing on of this narration does not occur at the Last Supper itself but might have occurred through a visionary appearance to Paul.

Fourth, it is remarkable that Paul's Last Supper tradition contains absolutely no reference to "the Twelve" as participating in this event and as the probable source of the tradition it generated.[12] For Paul, Jesus speaks not to the Twelve, but, through him, to the Corinthians. Jesus' command to "do this, as often as you drink [it], in remembrance of me" (v. 25) is addressed to the Corinthians, as Paul's interpretative gloss makes clear: "For

11. Wolfgang Schrage, *Der erste Brief an die Korinther. II. 1 Kor 6,12–11,16*, EKKNT 7.2 (Zurich: Benziger Verlag, 1995), 29-30; my translation.

12. The phrase "on the night on which he was betrayed" is generally understood as a reference to Judas. But the Greek should probably be understood as alluding to Isa. 53:12 and referring to divine rather than human action — "on the night on which he was handed over" (so J. D. Crossan, *The Birth of Christianity* [San Francisco: HarperSanFrancisco, 1998], 439).

as often as you eat this bread and *drink* the cup, you proclaim the Lord's death until he comes" (v. 26). Paul here reenacts his own mediation of the tradition to the Corinthians, but there seems to be no possibility of a human mediation of the tradition to Paul himself. In the absence of the Twelve, the tradition is *his* tradition.

These four indications suggest that the possibility of a Pauline origin for the Last Supper tradition may be worth considering, but they are not in themselves decisive. For the possibility to be made plausible, it is necessary to demonstrate the following three points:

1. that the use of precisely the same terminology *(paralambanein, paradidonai)* in 1 Cor. 15:3 is compatible with the proposed reading of 11:23;
2. that Paul's statements about his experiences of Christ make it conceivable for him to have claimed a revelation of the risen Lord about what took place at the Last Supper; and
3. that the Markan Eucharistic narratives can be seen as ultimately derived from Paul, rather than being independent of him and at certain points more primitive.

If it proves impossible to make out a plausible case for any one of these three assertions, the hypothesis of a Pauline origin for the Last Supper tradition will have to be abandoned. If, on the other hand, a plausible case can indeed be made, the outcome will simply be to render the hypothesis plausible, not to prove it beyond all reasonable doubt. We can never rule out the possibility that, challenged by one of his Corinthian readers, Paul would have had to concede that the Last Supper tradition came to him through Peter or the church at Antioch. Yet the hypothesis does have the merit of attempting to take Paul's statement in 1 Cor. 11:23 at face value — rather than assuming at the outset that it *cannot* mean what it says. So we may proceed to examine each of our three (still hypothetical) assertions in turn, converting them into questions as we do so.

The Wider Context: Three Questions

➤ Does the reference to the transmission of tradition in 1 Cor. 15:3 rule out the possibility of an unmediated encounter with Christ in 11:23?

In 1 Cor. 15:3, Paul's phraseology is remarkably similar to 11:23:

> For I received [*parelabon*] from the Lord what I also delivered to you [*ho kai paredōka hymin*], that the Lord Jesus . . . (11:23)

> For I delivered to you [*paredōka hymin*] at the first what I also received [*ho kai parelabon*], that Christ . . . (15:3)

In 15:3, Paul does not explicitly claim to have received this tradition "from the Lord." It is arguable that a "revelatory" understanding of 11:23 would entail a similar understanding of 15:3, in which case the risen Christ must at some point have revealed to Paul that he died for our sins according to the Scriptures, that he was buried, that he was raised on the third day according to the Scriptures, and that he appeared to Cephas, the Twelve, and so on (15:3-7). This is not impossible. Paul speaks here of his gospel (vv. 1-2) and of the encounter with the risen Christ that established his apostleship (vv. 8-10), and elsewhere he is insistent that his gospel came to him directly from Christ, without human mediation (Gal. 1:1, 11-17). If that is the case here too, then "what I also received" (1 Cor. 15:3) would mean the same as "I received from the Lord" (11:23).

The problem for this interpretation is simply that in 15:3 Paul makes no explicit claim to have received this tradition from the Lord. He merely says that he received it; he does not say from whom. While, as we have seen, it is possible to harmonize his statement with a "revelatory" interpretation of 11:23, it is not clear that such a harmonization is desirable or necessary. Indeed, harmonization might proceed in the opposite direction; rather than bringing 15:3 into line with 11:23, we might interpret 11:23 in the light of 15:3. In 15:3, it could be argued, Paul shows that he is far less concerned than in Gal. 1 to rule out the human mediation of the tradition he has received and handed on. The lack of explicit reference to the Lord as the source of the tradition indicates that the emphasis lies on Paul's faithful transmission of the tradition, not on its purely divine origin. Since 1 Cor. 15:3 is so similar to 11:23 in its formulation, the conclusion might be that "I received from the Lord" should not be over-interpreted. Such a statement might mean one thing in Galatians but quite another in 1 Corinthians. If 1 Cor. 15:3 does not rule out human mediation, and may imply it, the same could be true of 11:23.[13]

---

13. That *ho kai parelabon* in 1 Cor. 15:3 is compatible with human mediation is apparent from Marcion's excision of these words, which seemed to make Paul dependent on the

Paul's statements in these two texts are so similar that it is tempting to harmonize them — by arguing either that "what I also received" (15:3) implies "from the Lord" (cf. 11:23), or, on the contrary, that human mediation is not seen as a problem in either text. Yet the similarity of the two texts is deceptive: their broader contexts imply quite different views of Paul's own relation to the tradition in question. In 1 Corinthians 15, the tradition about Jesus' death, burial, resurrection, and appearances is common ground between Paul and all the other apostles: "Whether then it was I or they, this is what we preach and this is what you believed" (v. 11). It is to emphasize that the message of the resurrection is common ground that Paul enumerates the various appearances, not just to himself — his was "last of all" (v. 8) — but also and first of all to Cephas, to the Twelve, and so on (vv. 5-7). Paul might have based his argument for the resurrection of the dead solely on his own encounter with the risen Christ, but he does not choose to do so. In stark contrast to Galatians 1–2, references to Cephas, James, and the apostles serve Paul's construction of an "apostolic Christianity" whose impressive unanimity exposes the folly and thoughtlessness of those at Corinth who deny the resurrection of the dead (cf. v. 12). In 1 Corinthians 11, on the other hand, there is no trace of Cephas or the Twelve. The words of institution are addressed not to the Twelve but as if directly to the Corinthians. Through Paul's mediation, the temporal and spatial distances separating the Corinthians from Jesus on the night of his arrest dissolve away, and the Last Supper becomes the enduring substratum of each successive celebration of the Lord's Supper. Paul's relation to the traditions of the Last Supper and of the Easter events is quite different and is fully compatible with a direct revelation from the Lord in the one case and a possible role for human mediation in the other.

> ➤ Do Paul's statements about his experiences of Christ make it conceivable that he should claim to have received the Last Supper tradition from the risen Lord?

Paul bases his claim to apostleship on the fact that he has seen "Jesus our Lord" (1 Cor. 9:1). Others question his apostleship, so the directness of his relationship to the risen Lord is a sensitive issue for him (cf. 9:2). It was not

---

other apostles. On this see Adolf von Harnack, *Marcion: Das Evangelium vom fremden Gott* (1924; repr. Darmstadt: Wissenschaftliche Buchgesellschaft, 1960), 91.

only at his conversion that Paul encountered the risen Lord (cf. 1 Cor. 15:8); on the contrary, he has experienced many "visions and revelations of the Lord," "wonderful revelations" that might have made him proud of his visionary accomplishments had the Lord not taken steps to prevent this (2 Cor. 12:1, 7). These are "revelations of the Lord," that is, of Christ; in them, the Lord is seen, but also speaks. What the Lord says to Paul cannot always be communicated. On one occasion, fourteen years ago as he writes, Paul was taken up into the third heaven (whether physically or spiritually) and "heard unutterable words [*arrēta rhēmata*] which it is not lawful for a man to speak" (2 Cor. 12:4).[14] But Paul does here tell of another encounter in which Christ spoke with him, and on this occasion he is permitted to pass on Christ's words, which were: "My grace is sufficient for you, for my power is perfected in weakness" (2 Cor. 12:9).

Here, the Lord's words to Paul are concerned with the re-enactment in Paul's own life of the dialectic of weakness and power that is disclosed in the Lord's own crucifixion and resurrection. The Christological basis of the Lord's utterance is made clear in 2 Cor. 13:4, where Paul offers the following gloss on the word spoken to him:

> For he was crucified in weakness, but he lives by the power of God. For we too are weak in him, but to you we shall live with him by the power of God. (2 Cor. 13:4)

Thus, in the verbal assurance that "my power is perfected in weakness," the risen Christ discloses that his ongoing action in the world is determined by the pattern of human weakness and divine power manifested in his own death and resurrection. In speaking of the sufficiency of his

---

14. The framing of the description of this event in 2 Cor. 12:1, 6 appears to make it certain that the "man in Christ" of v. 2 is Paul himself — although, for reasons explained in v. 5, Paul's rhetoric deliberately leads his readers to question this identification. Another factor may be that he here "adopts a pseudepigraphical stance" in accordance with a convention prohibiting discussion of one's own mystical experiences (cf. *m. Hag.* 2:1); that would explain "why Jewish mystics consistently picked pseudepigraphical literary conventions to discuss their religious experience, unlocking the entire phenomenon of pseudepigraphical writing" (Alan Segal, *Paul the Convert: The Apostolate and Apostasy of Saul the Pharisee* [New Haven: Yale University Press, 1990], 58-59). Segal also notes that the subsequent experience in which Paul speaks to Christ three times about his infirmity "implies a communication greater than petitionary prayer" — even if the earlier "heavenly ascent to the enthroned presence of Christ" is not repeated on this occasion (p. 36).

grace for Paul, Christ speaks of the divine power released into the world by his own crucifixion. The power that is perfected in Paul's weakness is in the first instance a salvific power. God's power operates through "earthen vessels," who are constantly

> carrying in the body the killing [*nekrōsin*] of Jesus, so that the life of Jesus might be manifested in our body. For we who live are always given up to death for Jesus' sake, so that the life of Jesus might be manifested in our mortal flesh. So death is at work in us, but life in you. (2 Cor. 4:10-12)

Here, the power of Jesus' resurrection is salvific; but it may also be punitive. Paul anticipates with foreboding the prospect of a third visit to Corinth, during which he will not spare those who undermine his authority — "since you desire proof that Christ speaks in me, who is not weak towards you but powerful among you" (13:3). The divine power of which the exalted Christ speaks arises from his death, manifests itself in and through Paul's own weaknesses and sufferings, and, intending salvation, can nevertheless issue in dire punishment for the disobedient. Paul has learned all this from the words of Christ: "My grace is sufficient for you, for my power is perfected in weakness" (12:9).

The analogies with Paul's Eucharistic tradition are inexact but intriguing:

1. In both cases, the exalted Christ speaks directly to Paul. While Jesus also spoke to Cephas and other disciples during his earthly ministry, as the living one he continues to speak, and Paul is a privileged addressee of this ongoing revelatory discourse. He has been taken up into paradise to meet with Christ; he has heard there mysteries intended for his ears only — and that was just one of the many "visions and revelations of the Lord" that he has experienced (2 Cor. 12:1, 7). Each of the visions and revelations presumably has its own specific rationale and content. In the first of the series, for example, Paul was called to preach the Christ he had formerly persecuted (Gal. 1:15-16; 1 Cor. 15:8-10). In another case, he was told to go up to Jerusalem to lay his gospel before the authorities there (Gal. 2:2). At least in the earlier stages of his career as a Christian, being directly addressed by Christ was for Paul an entirely normal occurrence.[15]

---

15. The first vision or revelation can be seen as distinct from all the others, belonging to a canonical sequence which it brings to a close (cf. 1 Cor. 15:8-10). Elsewhere, however, it is

2. In both cases, what the exalted Christ says relates to his death. The "weakness" in which the divine power is to be manifested is indeed Paul's weakness, but in the first instance it is Christ's: "For he was crucified in weakness" (2 Cor. 13:4). Paul's usage of the term *astheneia* is informed by the image of utter passivity and degradation represented by the crucified Jesus.[16] In the utterance to Paul recorded in 2 Cor. 12:9, the Lord himself alludes to his own suffering in speaking of the "weakness" of Paul, afflicted with his "thorn in the flesh" (vv. 7-8). In the Eucharistic tradition, the Lord speaks concretely of the night of his handing over, and of how his own imminent death was signified in the breaking of bread and the outpouring of wine.

3. In both cases, the exalted Christ speaks of the meaning of his death for the present. It is Paul's ongoing ministry that will display the pattern of divine power perfected in human weakness. It is the Corinthian congregation that is addressed in the words of institution and invited and commanded to reenact the Last Supper in its own congregational meals. In his revelatory utterances to Paul, the risen Lord imposes the pattern of his dying on the apostle and his congregations alike. His death was an utterly concrete past event (cf. 1 Cor. 11:23; 2 Cor. 13:4). Yet, through the risen Jesus' subsequent revelatory words, this event possesses a capacity to shape the present.

4. In both cases, this capacity to shape the present is the power of Jesus' resurrection. Jesus "lives by the power of God" (2 Cor. 13:4): thus he can claim that it is "my power" — the power of his risen life — that is perfected in Paul's weakness. In the Eucharist, the bread and the wine are "spiritual food" and "spiritual drink" (1 Cor. 10:3-4), imbued with the power of "the last Adam" who "became lifegiving Spirit" (1 Cor. 15:45). The congregation participates in the blood of Christ and the body of Christ (10:16) and does so as an act of remembrance of the occasion on which he died (11:24, 26). Yet the Eucharist is not simply a memorial to a dead Christ; it is also an encounter with the living Christ. The body and blood of Christ proceed not

---

not distinguished terminologically from later experiences: if it is a "revelation of Jesus Christ" (Gal. 1:12), so too are they (cf. Gal. 2:2; 2 Cor. 12:1). N. T. Wright's attempt to distinguish an initial "real 'seeing' with [Paul's] ordinary eyes" from later "extraordinary moments of spiritual elevation" does not seem to me to be successful (*The Resurrection of the Son of God* [Minneapolis: Fortress, 2003], 383, 387). For an alternative view, see Alan Segal's compelling discussion of "Paul's Ecstasy" in *Paul the Convert*, 34-71.

16. The term occurs five times in the concluding chapters of 2 Corinthians (11:30; 12:5, 9 [twice]; 13:4) and five times elsewhere in Paul (1 Cor. 2:3; 15:43; Rom. 6:19; 8:26; Gal. 4:13).

only from his death but also from his present life; they descend from heaven like the manna in the wilderness. The Eucharist remains the "Lord's Supper" (*kuriakon deipnon* [11:20]), the cup and the table remain "the Lord's table" and "the Lord's cup" (10:21), for it is the Lord who continues to preside, as he did on the night on which he was handed over.

5. In both cases, the Lord's words to Paul have an imperative force. Since "my grace is sufficient for you" and since "my power is made perfect in weakness," Paul must live by that all-sufficient grace and accept his own weakness as a necessary condition of his apostolic ministry. In particular, there are to be no further repetitions of his request that the thorn in his flesh be removed: although it is "an angel of Satan" (2 Cor. 12:7), he must learn to live with it. In this context, the Lord's words to Paul have the force of a command and a prohibition. The Eucharistic narrative is also essentially a command of the risen Lord, who instructs Paul's congregations to "do this [. . .] in remembrance of me" — that is, to eat the bread and drink from the cup as a proclamation of the Lord's saving death (1 Cor. 11:24, 26).

6. In both cases, Paul's renderings of what the Lord said to him have shaped his own linguistic usage in the immediate context. The Lord told him, "My grace is sufficient for you, for my power is perfected in weakness" (2 Cor. 12:9a), and this saying immediately generates the following interpretative comments:

> I will all the more gladly boast in my weaknesses, so that the power of Christ may rest upon me. So I delight in weaknesses, insults, hardships, persecutions, and disasters, for Christ's sake; for when I am weak, then I am powerful. (2 Cor. 12:9b-10)

Here, Paul's language is modeled on Christ's. In 1 Corinthians 11, there is a similarly seamless transition between the words of Christ and Paul's interpretative comments. On the night of his handing over, the Lord Jesus

> took bread and giving thanks he broke [it] and said, "This is my body which is for you. Do this in remembrance of me. . . . This cup is the new covenant in my blood, Do this, as often as you drink it, in remembrance of me." For *as often as you* eat the bread and *drink the cup,* you proclaim the Lord's death until he comes. So whoever eats the bread or *drinks the cup of the Lord* unworthily will be guilty of *the body and the blood of the Lord.* (11:25-27)

In addition to the (italicized) verbal allusions to the words of the Lord, it should also be noted that "you proclaim the Lord's death until he comes" is Paul's gloss on "Do this [. . .] in remembrance of me." Paul also alludes to the Eucharist tradition in 1 Corinthians 10, in the context of warnings against idolatry:

> *The cup* of blessing which *we bless,* is it not a sharing of *the blood of Christ? The bread which we break,* is it not a sharing of *the body of Christ?* Because there is one bread, we the many are one body, because we all share the one bread. (10:16-17)

> Can you *drink the cup of the Lord* and the cup of demons? Can you share in the table of the Lord and the table of demons? (10:21)

Here, the reference to blessing alludes to the blessing or "thanksgiving" preceding the bread and (by implication) the cup sayings in the Eucharistic narrative. "My body" and "my blood" in the words of institution become, "the body of Christ" and "the blood of Christ," and the parallelism between the bread and the cup sayings is imitated in Paul's identically constructed rhetorical questions.[17] In addition, Paul offers an allegorizing interpretation of the Eucharistic bread, in which the one loaf symbolizes the oneness of the congregation, to whom the term "body" is here transferred.[18] As in 2 Corinthians 12, Paul presents himself as the faithful interpreter of revelations he received from the Lord.

The reference in 2 Cor. 12:1 to "visions and revelations of the Lord" provides a general context for the revelatory event of which Paul appears to speak in 1 Cor. 11:23. The Lord's response to Paul's requests concerning his "thorn in the flesh" offers a partial analogy to the revelation concerning the Lord's Supper.

---

17. Christian Wolff distinguishes between the identification of the cup with "the blood of Christ" (10:16) and with "the new covenant in my blood" (11:25) and finds in the former the influence of the tradition taken up by Mark and Matthew (*Der erste Brief des Paulus an die Korinther* [THKNT 7.2; Berlin: Evangelische Verlagsanstalt, 1982], 51). Yet the symmetry of 10:16 can be adequately explained on the basis of "my body" and "my blood" in 11:24-25.

18. Compare *Did.* 9.4, where the oneness signified by the loaf is the eschatological oneness of the worldwide church. Further points of contact with Paul occur in the prayer over the cup in *Did.* 9.2 (cf. 1 Cor. 10:16, "the cup of blessing which we bless") and in the reference to "spiritual food and drink" (*pneumatikēn trophēn kai poton*) in *Did.* 10:3 (cf. 1 Cor. 10:3-4).

➤ Can the Markan Eucharistic narratives be seen as ultimately dependent on Paul?

It is widely assumed that the Eucharistic narratives of Paul and Mark are independent of each other and that both derive from earlier oral tradition whose wording can still be tentatively reconstructed by subtracting evidently secondary elements from both texts. Where Paul speaks of Jesus "giving thanks" *(eucharistēsas)* over the bread, Mark has him "blessing" *(eulogēsas);* Mark's term may conform more closely to Aramaic usage. On the other hand, Mark shows a tendency to assimilate the words over the bread and over the cup: "This is my body," "this is my blood of the covenant," in contrast to Paul's "This is my body which is for you," but "this cup is the new covenant in my blood." The non-assimilated form is perhaps the more original, although the motif of the "new" covenant could be a Pauline addition inspired by Jeremiah 31. An analysis along these lines shows that these texts *can be* read as independent developments of an earlier tradition.[19] The question is whether they *have to be* read as such. If we suppose that Mark had at his disposal something like the tradition as handed down by Paul, as Luke did, can we make sense of the evidence of the texts on that basis? Or is it highly improbable that all the Markan variants should have arisen from a tradition originating with Paul?

In the analysis that follows, Pauline priority will be regarded as a working hypothesis. While it will not be possible to demonstrate beyond reasonable doubt that this hypothesis is true, it may be possible to show that it is not implausible. The relevant passages appear on p. 117, with the hypothetical Markan deviations from Paul indicated by italics (or by a blank space in the case of omissions).

If Mark is directly or indirectly dependent on Paul, he has modified the Pauline tradition at the following points:

1. Mark locates the institution of the Eucharist at the Passover meal: it takes place "as they ate" (14:22) and follows an account of the preparations for the Passover (14:12-16) and the identification of the traitor, which occurs during the meal (14:17-21). While Paul can associate the death of Je-

---

19. The classic version of this analysis is in Joachim Jeremias, *The Eucharistic Words of Jesus* (London: SCM Press, 1966), 160-203. The Pauline and Markan accounts "go back . . . to a common Eucharistic tradition lying behind both forms of the text" (p. 186).

1 Cor. 11:23-25	Mark 14:22-25
The Lord Jesus . . . took bread and giving thanks he broke and said	*And as they ate,* taking bread [and] *blessing* he broke *and gave to them* and said
"This is my body which is for you, do this in remembrance of me."	*"Take,* this is my body."
Likewise also the cup after supper,	And taking a cup and giving thanks *he gave to them, and they all drank of it.* And he said *to them,*
saying, "This cup is the new covenant in my blood. "Do this whenever you drink in remembrance of me."	*"This is my blood of the covenant poured out for many."*
	Amen I say to you, I shall no longer drink from this fruit of the vine until that day when I drink it new in the kingdom of God.

sus with the Passover (cf. 1 Cor. 5:6-8), he does not suggest a continuity between Passover and Eucharist.[20]

2. In introducing the saying relating to the bread, Mark replaces "thanksgiving" with "blessing" (14:22), although he does speak of Jesus as "giving thanks" in connection with the cup. The two introductory statements are close parallels: "Taking bread [and] blessing he broke and gave to them" (v. 22); "Taking a cup [and] giving thanks he gave to them . . ." (v. 23). Blessing and giving thanks are clearly synonymous and interchangeable. Similarly, in the first of Mark's feeding stories, it is said that Je-

20. The secondariness of Mark's link between Passover and Eucharistic institution is noted by Rudolf Bultmann, who finds in Mark 14:22-25 "the cult legend of the Hellenistic circles about Paul made to serve as an organic continuation of vv. 12-16 . . ." (*The History of the Synoptic Tradition,* trans. John Marsh, 3d ed. (Oxford: Blackwell, 1972], 265). In attempting to connect the Eucharist with the Passover, Jeremias implausibly interprets the words of institution as referring not only to the bread and the wine but also to the Passover lamb: bread and wine = Passover lamb = Jesus, who is "the eschatological Passover lamb" (Jeremias, *Eucharistic Words,* 223).

sus, "taking the five loaves and the two fish [and] looking up into heaven, *blessed* and broke the loaves and gave to his disciples" (Mark 6:41). In the second story it is said that, "taking the seven loaves and *giving thanks,* he broke and gave to his disciples . . ." (8:5), but also that he "blessed" the fish (8:7). The alternation between "blessing" and "giving thanks" in the Eucharistic narrative is simply a Markan idiom; it is fully compatible with the hypothesis of Pauline priority.[21]

3. In the case of both the bread and the cup, the statement that Jesus "gave to them" (his disciples) is a Markan addition, again conforming closely to the language of the feeding stories (14:22; cf. 6:41; 8:5). Here and elsewhere, Mark introduces Jesus' disciples into the narrative: it is they who are the recipients of the bread and the cup and the addressees of the words of institution. As we have seen, the disciples are absent in Paul.

4. Mark adds references to the consumption of the bread and wine, in the form of a command ("Take . . ." [14:22]), or of reported action ("And they all drank of it" [14:23]). This again serves to emphasize the participation of Jesus' disciples in this event.

5. Paul's "This is my body which is for you [*to hyper hymōn*]" may be compared with Mark's "This is my blood of the covenant poured out for many [*hyper pollōn*]" (14:24). The shift in the position of the *hyper* phrase may be occasioned by Mark's attempt to achieve a better balance between the two sayings. In substituting "for many" for the Pauline "for you," Mark draws on the earlier saying in which it was said that "the Son of man" would "give his life as a ransom for many [*anti pollōn*]" (Mark 10:45). The use of *hyper* rather than *anti* in Mark 14:24 may betray the influence of the Pauline formulation.

6. Like their introductions, the sayings relating to the bread and the cup are parallel in Mark: "this is my body" and "this is my blood . . ." (14:22, 24), as opposed to the asymmetrical Pauline "this is my body which is for you" and "this cup is the new covenant in my blood" (1 Cor. 11:24a, 25a). Arguably, the Pauline version represents the "harder reading" and is more likely to be original.[22]

---

21. *Contra* Jeremias, for whom the Pauline *eucharistēsas* is a "graecizing" substitute for an original *eulogēsas* (Jeremias, *Eucharistic Words,* 175).

22. According to Jeremias, "[t]he words, 'This is my blood' were susceptible to the misunderstanding that they spoke of the drinking of blood, which, particularly for born Jews, was a dark animistic abomination"; Paul's cup-saying is therefore a secondary attempt to avoid this misunderstanding (Jeremias, *Eucharistic Words,* 170). Jeremias does not explain

7. Mark omits the twofold command to repeat, "Do this [. . .] in remembrance of me" (1 Cor. 11:24b, 25b). This is of a piece with his tendency to "historicize" this event, also evident in his emphasis on the participation of Jesus' disciples. There is in Mark no mandate to repeat Jesus' actions.

8. Mark also omits Paul's assertion that the cup was passed round only "after supper" (1 Cor. 11:25). Paul's tradition may correspond to a practice of the Eucharist in which a communal evening meal opens with the breaking of bread and concludes with the sharing of the cup. Mark again shows himself to be uninterested in the liturgical dimensions of the tradition. What matters to him is to integrate this tradition into his broader account of the events that led to Jesus' death.

9. Mark's "This is my blood of the covenant . . ." replaces the Pauline reference to Jeremiah's "new covenant" with an allusion to Exod. 24:8, where it is recounted how Moses, "taking the blood, sprinkled the people and said, 'Behold, the blood of the covenant which the Lord has made with you. . . .'" Mark 14:23 echoes not only the phrase "the blood of the covenant" (*to haima tēs diathēkēs*, into which *mou* is inserted) but also the introduction to Moses' announcement: "Taking . . . and said [*labōn . . . kai eipen*]." (Mark's "This is . . ." may also be compared to Moses' "Behold. . . .") This use of the Exodus text produces a stronger scriptural basis for the cup saying than in Paul's version. The substitution of Exodus 24 for Jeremiah 31 finds a partial parallel in Hebrews 8–9. Here, although Jer. 31:31-34 is quoted at length (Heb. 8:8-12; 10:15-17), the lack of reference to sacrifice limits its usefulness to the author, who offers only brief interpretative comments (cf. 8:13; 10:18). On the other hand, Exod. 24:8 is cited to underline the law's typologically significant emphasis on blood sacrifice (Heb. 9:15-22).[23] A sacrificial understanding of Jesus' covenant-making death can be derived from Exodus but not from Jeremiah.[24]

---

why Paul did not also rewrite the equally objectionable "this is my body . . ." or how he can refer elsewhere to a participation in the blood of Christ (10:16).

23. As cited in Heb. 9:20, Exod. 24:8 reads, *touto to haima tēs diathēkēs . . .* (LXX: *idou . . .*), in close parallel to the Markan cup saying. Jeremias's attempt to reconstruct Jesus' Hebrew or Aramaic *ipsissima verba* (*dam beriti* or *adam keyami:* "my covenant blood") overlooks the clear Markan allusion to Exodus (Jeremias, *Eucharistic Words*, 193-95).

24. N. T. Wright interprets the bread-and-cup-sayings in connection with the end of Israel's exile and finds in the cup-saying an allusion to Zech. 9:9-11 as well as to Exod. 24:8 (*Jesus and the Victory of God* [London: SPCK, 1996], 561). Here, after speaking of the world-dominion of the messianic king, God promises Zion that, "because of the blood of my cove-

10. Mark adds the saying in which Jesus renounces "the fruit of the vine" (14:25), which is obviously secondary in this context. "I will no longer drink . . ." may refer back to "they all drank of it" (v. 23) — all, that is, apart from Jesus himself. Yet the connection is artificial, as is the juxtaposition of sacrificial and eschatological symbolism. The saying does make it clear, however, that this is indeed the *last* meal that Jesus will share with his disciples until their reunion in the kingdom of God. It can be compared with other Markan sayings in which Jesus speaks of what lies ahead — notably his announcement of the future worldwide fame of the woman who anointed him at Bethany (14:9), his betrayal by one of the twelve (14:18), and his denial by Peter (14:30). Like 14:25, these prophetic sayings all open with the formula "Amen I say to you. . . ."

On the hypothesis of Pauline originality, the main tendency evident in Mark's redaction is to integrate this tradition into his overall account of Jesus' last days in Jerusalem. This would explain Mark's decision to set this tradition in the context of the Passover meal (point 1, above), his harmonizing it with earlier stories in which Jesus presides at a meal (point 2), his un-Pauline emphasis on the disciples' participation (points 3, 4), his omission of liturgical elements (points 7, 8), and his insertion of another in the series of Jesus' prophetic utterances about his own fate (point 10). Mark historicizes a tradition that, in its Pauline form, speaks of the institution of a liturgical practice. Given the nature of the text Mark is writing, this redactional tendency is entirely understandable. But that means that the hypothesis of Pauline originality and Markan secondariness can indeed be shown to be plausible. Competing hypotheses — Markan originality or independent use of prior oral tradition — are not finally excluded by these considerations. At the very least, however, we have seen that the Markan Last Supper narrative poses no problems for the hypothesis of Pauline originality.

Further support for this hypothesis may be found in Luke's redaction of the Markan narrative — assuming that the better attested longer text is the original one (Luke 22:15-20).[25] The longer text makes excellent sense

nant with you, I will set your prisoners free from the waterless pit . . ." (Zech. 9:11 NRSV, as cited by Wright). The Hebrew here reads *bdm brytk,* "because of the blood of your covenant," which is less close to Mark 14:24 than the NRSV paraphrase would suggest.

25. On this see Joseph A. Fitzmyer, *The Gospel according to Luke,* 2 vols., AB 28-28A (New York: Doubleday, 1981, 1985), 1387-89; Bruce M. Metzger, *A Textual Commentary on the Greek New Testament* (New York: United Bible Societies, 1975), 173-77; Heinz Schürmann, *Traditionsgeschichtliche Untersuchungen zu den synoptischen Evangelien* (Düsseldorf:

on the assumption that Luke wishes to reestablish the Pauline form of the tradition and has serious reservations about Mark. For Luke, the Pauline account is definitive, the Markan one is problematic: in addition to his excessively free rewriting of Paul, Mark does not adequately integrate the Eucharistic narrative into its Passover setting, and the relation between the Eucharist and the Passover meal is left obscure. In addition, the symbolism of the fruit of the vine saying is out of keeping with the Eucharistic cup. Luke therefore takes Mark's fruit of the vine saying (Mark 14:25) and constructs from it the following scene:

> And he said to them: "With desire have I desired to eat this Passover with you before my suffering. For I say to you that I will no more eat it until it is fulfilled in the kingdom of God." And taking a cup and giving thanks he said: "Take this and share it among yourselves. For I say to you, from now on I will not drink from the fruit of the vine until the kingdom of God comes." (Luke 22:15-18)

Luke models the statement about Jesus' last Passover on the fruit of the vine saying and provides it with an introduction (v. 14) that serves to connect the previous scene (the preparation for the Passover, 22:7-13) with the Eucharistic narrative.[26] The fruit of the vine saying is now attached to a distribution of the cup belonging in the context of the Passover meal, not the Eucharist. The Passover is thereby provided with an eschatological interpretation, which may also serve to explain why, for Luke, Christians need no longer observe it. For Luke, it seems that the Passover is a festival that belongs essentially to the past and to the eschatological future; for the present, it is supplanted by the Eucharist, whose institution Luke now proceeds to narrate:

Patmos-Verlag, 1968), 159-97. The Shorter Text seems to have originated in an attempt to replace the sequence cup-bread-cup with the sequence cup-bread (D it[a,d,ff2,i,l]), subsequently reversed by inserting v. 19 before vv. 17-18, in a shorter (it[b,e]) or longer (syr[c,s,p]) form. The cup-bread-cup sequence is only problematic if one overlooks the fact that the first cup saying (vv. 17-18) is attached to the Passover (vv. 15-16), the second to the Eucharist (v. 20). The full sequence is therefore: Passover lamb — cup; Eucharistic bread — cup.

26. For Luke 22:15-18 as a reworking of Mark 14:25, see Gerhard Schneider, *Das Evangelium nach Lukas* (Gütersloh: G. Mohn; Würzburg: Echter, 1977), 444. The prediction of the betrayal, which in Mark is inserted between the preparation for the Passover (Mark 14:12-16) and the institution narrative (14:22-25), is in Luke abbreviated and postponed until after the institution (Luke 22:21-23).

> And taking bread and giving thanks, he broke and gave to them, saying, "This is my body which is given for you. Do this in remembrance of me." And the cup likewise after supper, saying: "This cup is the new covenant in my blood, poured out for you." (Luke 22:19-20)

This account of the institution of the Eucharist is drawn almost exclusively from Paul. Surviving Markan elements are confined to the breaking and distribution of the bread and the addition of "poured out for you" to the cup saying.[27] In fact, this addition is only partially Markan, since it has also been influenced by "which is given for you" in the Pauline bread saying. The only point at which Luke wishes to improve on Paul is in this assimilation of the two sayings.

With only minor exceptions, Luke thus replaces the Markan narrative with the Pauline one. Presumably it is his view that the Pauline narrative is original and definitive and that the Markan rewriting was unjustified. Luke himself appears to hold the hypothesis of Pauline originality and Markan secondariness.

Conclusion

"I received from the Lord what I also handed on to you": we have found in Paul, Mark, and Luke no reason not to take this statement at face value. While I have generally tried to show only that the hypothesis of Pauline originality is plausible, without claiming to be able to demonstrate it, the cumulative force of the analysis offered here is considerable. Also considerable are its wider implications. We conclude with some brief comments on the significance of this hypothesis for Paul's Christology.

How does Paul understand the relationship between the earthly Jesus and the exalted Lord? In his later discussion of the resurrection of the dead, Paul appears to emphasize the non-identity of the earthly with the risen Jesus. To bury a corpse is, he argues, to plant a seed:

> It is sown in corruption, it is raised in incorruption. It is sown in dishonor, it is raised in glory. It is sown in weakness, it is raised in power.

---

27. Although Mark here has "poured out for many" (Mark 14:24). The widespread view that "there is . . . no evidence that Luke had ever read any of Paul's letters" (Fitzmyer, *Luke*, 28) deserves reconsideration.

It is sown an ensouled body [*sōma psuchikon*], it is raised a spiritual body. If there is an ensouled body, there is also a spiritual one. For thus it is written: "The first man Adam became a living soul" — the last Adam a lifegiving spirit. (1 Cor. 15:42-45)

At the resurrection, God will bestow a new body, out of the unlimited resources of God's creativity; and the glory of the new body will be like the glory of the heavenly bodies, the sun, the moon, and the stars, rather than the fleshly bodies of this lower world (cf. 15:38-41, 50). In his resurrection, Jesus, the first fruits of the eschatological harvest, experiences a transformation. In him, the earthly has already given way to the heavenly, the ensouled body to the spiritual body. But this raises a question: are we still speaking about Jesus? Or is the transformation so profound that "the last Adam" who is "lifegiving spirit" is in fact someone other than Jesus? In his resurrection, does Jesus lose his identity?

In the Eucharistic narrative, Paul claims that he "received from the Lord . . . that the Lord Jesus on the night on which he was handed over took bread . . ." (1 Cor. 11:23). The exalted Lord here reveals the Eucharist to Paul, based as it is on an event at the close of Jesus' earthly life. There is here a straightforward continuity between the one who speaks to Paul and the one who spoke at the Last Supper: for the one who speaks to Paul speaks of what he himself did at the Last Supper and commands that what took place then should be reenacted now and into the future, until the day of his own return. The one who is Lord now was Lord then: it was "the Lord Jesus" who took bread, and the death that followed shortly afterwards was "the Lord's death" (11:23, 26). There is here a single identity, not a dual one, and this identity is constituted in part by continuity of consciousness and memory. In commanding the remembrance of his own death, the risen Lord must himself remember. Speaking to Paul, the Lord recounts the story of his own Last Supper and repeats the words he uttered over the bread and the cup. Is it the earthly Jesus who speaks in the words of institution or the heavenly Lord? For Paul it is both, and the two are one: for there is one "Lord Jesus," not an earthly Jesus transformed into someone other, into an anonymous exalted Lord. If it is a purely historical Jesus who speaks in the words of institution, it is impossible to understand how the bread and wine he offers can be identified with his body and his blood. If it is an anonymous exalted Lord who speaks in these words, it is hard to see a connection between the heavenly food and drink that comes to us in the

Eucharist and the death of Jesus. The agent in the Last Supper must be the same as the agent in the Lord's Supper, in which that last meal is reenacted: the earthly Jesus *as* the exalted Lord, the exalted Lord *as* the earthly Jesus.

In the Eucharist, the death and resurrection of Jesus represent not two successive events but the single reality of the Lord who is simultaneously crucified and risen, lowly and exalted, weak and powerful. The bread and the wine are the body and blood of the crucified Jesus as the risen one, whose spiritual body comes to us as lifegiving food and drink in the form of bread and wine.

Chapter 6

Interpreting the Death of Jesus Apocalyptically: Reconsidering Romans 8:32

BEVERLY ROBERTS GAVENTA

Introduction

During the winter of 2003, with the advance publicity for and the advance controversy around Mel Gibson's *The Passion of the Christ,* discussion of the death of Jesus briefly migrated into the public arena from its customary home in the ecclesiastical and scholarly worlds. By the time Lent and Holy Week arrived, some pastors of my acquaintance were actually heard lamenting the fact that they were receiving the answers to their prayers. Although they had always wanted people to take the passion and death of Jesus more seriously, they had not wanted to engage in endless discussions about a particular filmmaker's interpretation of that event. Central to these discussions was and is the question of responsibility for Jesus' death. Heated debates about the movie's depiction of the Temple leadership, of Herod and Pilate, and of the Roman soldiers almost inevitably circled back to the question of who instigated Jesus' crucifixion. The question of historical fact became paramount: Who killed Jesus?

I am indebted to Charles B. Cousar, Martinus C. de Boer, J. Louis Martyn, J. Ross Wagner, and Patrick J. Willson for reading and commenting on an earlier draft of this article, as well as to Craig B. Carpenter and Carla Works for careful assistance with research. This paper was written during a sabbatical leave at the Center of Theological Inquiry, to which I am grateful for hospitality and scholarly conversation. I especially appreciate the gracious and constructive response of participants in the Drumwright Colloquium at George W. Truett Theological Seminary.

Debate flourished again around the various Gospel accounts of Jesus' arrest, trial, and crucifixion, with conflicting interpretations of relative accuracy, biases, and their theological agenda. To be sure, the Gospels are the natural battleground for this question. And yet few would dispute the claim that the *earliest sources of written evidence* concerning the death of Jesus are the letters of the Apostle Paul. For that reason, it seems appropriate to ask what Paul has to say about responsibility for the death of Jesus. To put the matter directly: Who, in Paul's view, killed Jesus of Nazareth?

The evidence can be canvassed in just a few sentences. However rightly we characterize Paul as a theologian of the cross,[1] we must also acknowledge that his assertions about *responsibility* for the death of Jesus Christ are few and far between. In what many regard as the earliest of his letters, Paul writes in 1 Thessalonians 2 that "Jews killed the Lord Jesus and the prophets," an assertion so extraordinary within the Pauline corpus that it has produced numerous suggestions of interpolation.[2] 1 Cor. 2:8 claims that it is the "rulers of this age" who crucified "the Lord of glory." Gal.2:20 attributes Jesus' death to his own act of "handing himself over" (see also

---

1. On Paul's theology of the cross, an excellent starting place is the work of Charles B. Cousar, *The Theology of the Cross: The Death of Jesus in the Pauline Letters,* OBT (Minneapolis: Fortress, 1990).

2. Translations are those of the author unless otherwise noted. On the question of interpolation in 1 Thessalonians 2, see Birger A. Pearson, "1 Thessalonians 2:14-16: A Deutero-Pauline Interpolation," *HTR* 64 (1971): 79-94; Hendrikus Boers, "The Form-Critical Study of Paul's Letters: 1 Thessalonians as a Case Study," *NTS* 22 (1976): 140-58; Daryl Schmidt, "1 Thess. 2.13-16: Linguistic Evidence for an Interpolation," *JBL* 102 (1983): 269-79; and Helmut Koester, "I Thessalonians — Experiment in Christian Writing," in *Continuity and Discontinuity in Church History: Essays Presented to George Huntston Williams on the Occasion of His 65th Birthday,* ed. F. Forrester Church and Timothy George, Studies in the History of Christian Thought 19 (Leiden: Brill, 1979), 33-44, esp. 38. Those who argue for the authenticity of the passage include the following: John C. Hurd, "Paul Ahead of His Time: 1 Thess. 2:13-16," in *Anti-Judaism in Early Christianity: Paul and the Gospels,* ed. Peter Richardson and David M. Granskou, Studies in Christianity and Judaism 1 (Waterloo: Wilfrid Laurier University Press, 1986), 21-36; Jon A. Weatherly, "The Authenticity of 1 Thessalonians 2.13-16: Additional Evidence," *JSNT* 42 (1991): 79-98; Karl P. Donfried, "Paul and Judaism: 1 Thessalonians 2:13-16 as a Test Case," *Int* 38 (1984): 242-53; Christopher M. Tuckett, "Synoptic Traditions in 1 Thessalonians?" in *The Thessalonian Correspondence,* ed. Raymond F. Collins, BETL 87 (Leuven: Leuven University Press, 1990), 160-82; R. Schippers, "The Pre-Synoptic Tradition in I Thess II 13-16," *NovT* 8 (1966): 223-34; Carol J. Schlueter, *Filling Up the Measure: Polemical Hyperbole in 1 Thessalonians 2:14-16,* JSNTSup 98 (Sheffield: Sheffield Academic Press, 1994); and Abraham J. Malherbe, *The Letters to the Thessalonians,* AB 32B (New York: Doubleday, 2000), 164-79.

Gal. 1:4), and Rom. 8:32 says that God "handed him over" (see also Rom. 3:25). Elsewhere the death of Jesus is referred to in the passive voice, with no agent specified (as in Rom. 4:25: "he was handed over on account of our trespasses"; see also 1 Cor. 11:23; and perhaps also 1 Cor. 5:7; 2 Cor. 13:4); and sometimes the death of Jesus is expressed in the active voice, but with no comment about responsibility ("Christ died," 1 Cor. 15:3; see also Rom. 5:6, 8 [although note the earlier part of the verse]; 1 Cor. 8:11; 2 Cor. 5:14-15; 1 Thess. 5:10).

It is customary to review these passages, to note how little Paul actually says about responsibility for the death of Jesus, and then move on to elaborate Paul's understanding of the atonement, that is, to the question of what is accomplished in Jesus' death. In this study, however, I want to linger with *the role Paul ascribes to God*. For in Paul's letters, in contrast to the debate generated by *The Passion of the Christ*, it is neither the Jewish leaders (despite 1 Thessalonians 2) nor the Roman officials who crucify Jesus. It is God — the God of Israel, the Father of Jesus Christ, the very one who brings life from the dead — who hands Jesus over to the powers of Sin and Death to bring about his crucifixion, thereby setting in motion their own final defeat.

We begin with Rom. 8:32, paying special attention to the use of παραδίδωμι ("deliver" or "hand over") elsewhere in Romans and its implications for understanding this verse. Then we consider the impact of Rom. 8:32 for understanding the death of Jesus in Paul. What I hope to show is that, when Paul says that God handed over his own Son, he means that God handed him over to *anti-god powers*. This is not simply a giving up to human forces or a giving away in love, but a unique and determinative event in the struggle between God and the powers, an event that has cosmic consequences even as its consequences lovingly rescue humankind from captivity to Sin and Death. It is in this sense, then, that I identify Paul's interpretation of Jesus' death as apocalyptic. In the conclusion I consider briefly ways in which Luke may share some aspects of Paul's understanding of Jesus' death and why that understanding has urgent importance in the present.

Conventional Readings of Rom. 8:32

Beginning with Rom. 8:18, Paul acknowledges the subjection and struggle of all creation at the present time and anticipates its glorious redemption.

He then introduces in v. 31 a question that sums up at least the entirety of this passage, if not the whole of chs. 1–8:

> Therefore, what shall we say about these things?
> If God is for us, who is against us?

In v. 32 he begins to answer the question with yet another question:

> The one who did not withhold even his own Son but handed him over on behalf of us all, how will he not also graciously give us all things together with him?

Historically, discussions of this verse largely focus on its relationship to the story of Abraham and Isaac in Genesis 22. At least as early as Origen, the statement that God "did not withhold his own Son" was connected with the angel's statements to Abraham in Genesis 22.[3] In the LXX, the same verb (φείδομαι) is used in both instances (although below I will question the significance of that parallel). Some scholars also contend that the discussion of Abraham in Romans 4 reinforces the strength of this allusion.[4]

Controversy arises over exactly what relationship obtains between the story of Abraham and Isaac on the one hand and that of God and Jesus Christ on the other. Scholars often posit only a rather loose analogy between the two: Abraham's obedient willingness to give up his son finds its completion in God's actual gift of Jesus Christ.[5] Nils Dahl argued for a much more specific connection, namely, that the handing over of Jesus is God's *reward* to Abraham and his offspring for Abraham's handing over of Isaac.[6] Some scholars have shared with Dahl the notion that Rom. 8:32 re-

---

3. *Homilies on Genesis* 8. Irenaeus makes a connection between the two events, if not between the two texts explicitly, see n. 6 below.

4. Although, as Daniel R. Schwartz notes, Romans 4 does not specifically mention Isaac; see "Two Pauline Allusions to the Redemptive Mechanism of the Crucifixion," *JBL* 102 (1983): 259-68 (esp. 264-65).

5. See, for example, William Sanday and Arthur C. Headlam, *A Critical and Exegetical Commentary on the Epistle to the Romans*, 5th ed., ICC (Edinburgh: T&T Clark, 1902), 220; C. E. B. Cranfield, *The Epistle to the Romans*, 2 vols., ICC (Edinburgh: T&T Clark, 1975, 1979), 1:436; Brendan Byrne, *Romans*, SP 6 (Collegeville: Liturgical Press, 1996), 275.

6. Nils A. Dahl, "The Atonement: An Adequate Reward for the Aqedah?" in *Jesus the Christ: The Historical Origins of Christological Doctrine*, ed. Donald H. Juel (Minneapolis: Fortress, 1991), 137-51. In this connection, notice the comment of Irenaeus that Abraham

flects the early development of Jewish and Christian traditions having to do with the "binding" (the *Akedah*) of Isaac, but others have claimed that the influence moves in the other direction, namely, it was Christian soteriology that influenced the development of Jewish tradition.[7]

Not everyone is confident that 8:32 alludes to the sacrifice of Isaac or that the allusion has particular force for understanding the passage.[8] A few problems merit our attention, although I want to be clear that I am less concerned to dismantle the connection between Romans 8 and Genesis 22 than to suggest that *the allusion does not exhaust the content of this passage.* In Gen. 22:12 and 16 (LXX), the angel says to Abraham, "you did not withhold *your beloved* son from me," while Rom. 8:32 speaks of "*his own* son." The shift from the second person "your" to the third person "his" is easy to understand, because the angel addresses Abraham directly (second person) but Paul speaks about God (third person). It is less clear why the LXX's "beloved" is not retained. More important, much of the argument for an allusion has been based on the use of the same verb φείδομαι (usually translated as "spare" or "withhold") in both texts, but φείδομαι is not a particularly rare word. Indeed, its usage elsewhere in the LXX and beyond suggests another nuance may be at work here (see below).

If the exegetical tradition includes multiple proposals for connecting this verse to its scriptural antecedents, there is nevertheless agreement that *what Paul writes here concerns God's love.* For example, Brendan Byrne characterizes v. 32 as "an assertion of the love and favor of God shown in the Christ-event."[9] To be sure, God's love is an active concern in v. 32, yet the verse ascribes to God three *distinct* actions:

"followed the command of the Word of God, and with a ready mind delivered up, as a sacrifice to God, his only-begotten and beloved son, in order that God also might be pleased to offer up for all his seed His own beloved and only-begotten Son, as a sacrifice for our redemption" (*Against Heresies* 4.5.4 [*ANF*]).

7. Contrast Robert J. Daly, "The Soteriological Significance of the Sacrifice of Isaac," *CBQ* 39 (1977): 45-75, with Philip R. Davies and Bruce D. Chilton, "The Aqedah: A Revised Tradition History," *CBQ* 40 (1978): 514-46.

8. See, e.g., Heinrich Schlier, *Der Romerbrief*, HTKNT 6 (Frieburg: Herder, 1977), 277; C. K. Barrett, *A Commentary on the Epistle to the Romans*, HNTC (New York: Harper & Brothers, 1957), 99; Ernst Käsemann, *Commentary on Romans*, trans. and ed. Geoffrey W. Bromiley (Grand Rapids: Eerdmans, 1980), 247.

9. Byrne, *Romans*, 275.

God did "not spare" his own son (φείδομαι).
God "handed him over" (παραδίδωμι).
God will "graciously give" (χαρίζομαι) all things.

Many contemporary translations collapse these last two verbs, translating both with forms of the English verb "give." To take two widely adopted translations, the NRSV reads:

He who did not withhold his own Son, but *gave* him up for all of us, will he not with him also *give* us everything else?

The NIV is almost identical,

He who did not spare his own Son, but *gave* him up for us all — how will he not also, along with him, graciously *give* us all things?[10]

The difficulty with translating παραδίδωμι as "gave up" is not simply that it blurs the presence of two different Greek verbs. It also creates the impression that God's giving up has to do only with "giving" for the sake of human beings. Yet Paul does not otherwise employ παραδίδωμι to refer to gracious giving; he uses it of concession, of handing over in a situation of conflict, and there are good reasons to take that nuance into account in this passage. Gal. 2:20 is the single occasion in Paul's letters where "love" and "hand over" appear conjunctively, and even there it is not obvious that they constitute a single action. In what follows, I hope to show that love is not the only action involved here. When the two actions are collapsed into one, the full range of Paul's understanding of Jesus' death recedes from view.

"God Handed Him Over": παραδίδωμι in Romans

In order to see those implications, it is important to begin by examining other passages in Romans that use the verb παραδίδωμι ("hand over"). The verb has already appeared in connection with the death of Jesus in 4:25, a passage many think reflects a pre-Pauline tradition which associated

---

10. The NLT and NIB likewise translate both verbs with "give," as did the RSV. The NASB and NKJV make a distinction, reading "delivered up" instead of "give."

Jesus' death with Isaiah 53.[11] Verse 25 reads that he "was *handed over* [παραδίδωμι] on account of our trespasses and raised on account of our rectification." Yet the initial appearance of the verb "hand over" in Romans occurs in the first chapter of the letter with the repeated clauses that refer to God's action in response to human rebellion:

> 1:24 Wherefore *God handed them over*
> because of the desires of their hearts
> to uncleanness. . . .
> 1:26 For this reason *God handed them over*
> to dishonorable passions. . . .
> 1:28 *God handed them over*
> to an unfit mind. . . .

Seldom do discussions of 8:32 notice the usage of παραδίδωμι in Romans 1, and those that do tend to comment on the differences between the two passages rather than on a possible relationship.[12] Dunn notes that this final "handing over" rounds off the argument, but it does more than that.[13] It refers back to that ominous repetition in ch. 1, connecting the handing over of the Son with that of rebellious humankind.

παραδίδωμι is used here, as it is elsewhere, to refer to the turning over of someone or something to a third party, often in a situation of conflict.[14] The use of παραδίδωμι to refer to the act of handing someone or something over into the custody of another or to surrender in a military

---

11. E.g., Douglas Moo, *The Epistle to the Romans*, NICNT (Grand Rapids: Eerdmans, 1996), 288.

12. Among the most important discussions is that of Karl Barth, who connects the "handing over" in Rom. 1 and Rom. 8 with the betrayal of Judas (*Church Dogmatics II.2: The Doctrine of God*, eds. Geoffrey W. Bromiley and Thomas T. Torrance [Edinburgh: T&T Clark, 1957], 480-506). Some commentators note in passing that the same verb appears in both passages: Matthew Black, *Romans*, NCB (London: Oliphants, 1973), 120; Cranfield, *Romans*, 1:436; Fitzmyer, *Romans*, 532; Byrne, *Romans*, 279; Adolf Pohl, *Der Brief des Paulus an die Römer* (Wuppertal: R. Brockhaus, 1998), 180. Otto Michel does observe that the fact of the use of the same verb in both passages and in 4:25 indicates the gravity of the situation; see *Der Brief an die Römer*, 4th ed., KEKNT (Göttingen: Vandenhoeck & Ruprecht, 1966), 214.

13. James D. G. Dunn, *Romans 1–8*, WBC 38A (Dallas: Word Books, 1988), 500.

14. This section draws heavily on my chapter, "God Handed Them Over," in *Our Mother Saint Paul* (Louisville: Westminster John Knox, 2007), 113-23, 194-98.

context appears in a variety of sources, both biblical and non-biblical.[15] In the LXX, παραδίδωμι consistently refers to the surrendering of an individual or a people to the power of another agent. παραδίδωμι appears over twenty times in Deuteronomy, almost always of God "handing over" a territory or a people to the possession of Israel (e.g., 2:24, 30, 31, 33; 3:2, 3; 7:2, 23, 24; 20:13, 20; 28:7). The pattern in Joshua is similar, as the story of the conquest credits God with handing over to Israel the city of Jericho (2:14, 24; 6:2, 16) or Ai (7:7; 8:18) or Gibeon (10:8, 12).[16] The prophetic literature, not surprisingly, frequently uses παραδίδωμι to refer to handing Israel itself over to captivity, as when Jeremiah pronounces God's decree that Jerusalem will be handed over to Babylon (Jer. 21:10; see also 22:25; 24:8; 39:28), or when Ezekiel declares that Israel's possessions will be given over to "the wicked of the earth" (Ezek. 7:21; see also 11:9; 16:27; 21:31; 23:28; 25:4). In these instances, as in Romans 1, an explicit connection is made between faithlessness or disobedience and the "handing over."

Nothing in this brief sketch is particularly startling, although it is noteworthy that "handing over" virtually always involves *handing over to another agent*.[17] In the LXX, conflict with another agent or power regularly appears in the textual vicinity of παραδίδωμι (e.g., King Sihon, the King of Babylon, the hands of foreigners, Satan).[18] Paul's letters reflect this usage as well. To be sure, he employs the verb to refer to the handing over of tradition or instruction (1 Cor. 11:2, 23; 15:3), but in several instances παραδίδωμι is associated with handing over to another power. The most notable example is that of 1 Cor. 5:5 — Paul's instruction that the man who is living with his father's wife should be handed over to Satan for (or perhaps "until") the destruction of the flesh. The passage is a notorious inter-

---

15. For examples outside biblical literature, see PHib 92.11, 17; PLille 3.50; PTebt 38.6; Herodotus 1.45.1; 3.13.3; Xenophon, *Cyropaedia* 5.1.28; 5.4.51; Pausanias, *Graeciae descriptio* 1.2.1. See also the discussions in M-M 482-83, DBAG 761-63, and LSJ 1308.

16. See also 10:32, 35; 11:6, 8; 21:44, 4, 10, 11, 33.

17. I had already completed my own investigation of παραδίδωμι when I learned of the work of Gabriella Berényi, who comes to the same conclusion regarding this verb: "Παραδίδωμι, therefore, is used to describe the action of delivering a person or a group into the power of another who disposes of that person or group according to his own will," "Gal 2,20: a Pre-Pauline or a Pauline Text?" *Bib* 65 (1984): 490-537.

18. Job 2:6 offers a fascinating and important exception to this generalization, since most commentators agree that, although God delivers Job to the Satan (in the LXX, ὁ διάβολος), the Satan is not an enemy but an aspect of the divine itself. Yet the *Testament of Job* shows that the tradition early on identifies the action of the Satan as hostile.

pretive crux,[19] yet it seems clear that "turning over" in this context involves a surrender of power, since Satan consistently appears in Paul's letters as an enemy both of God and of the community (e.g., Rom. 16:20; 1 Cor. 7:5; 2 Cor. 2:11; 11:14; 12:7; 1 Thess. 2:18; and cf. 1 Tim. 1:20); the community is to hand the offender over to the powerful enemy, Satan. First Corinthians 15:24 also reflects the regular use of the LXX, as Paul looks forward to the time when the risen and triumphant Christ will "hand over" the kingdom to God, when Christ has himself destroyed "every authority and power," that is, at the culmination of conflict with the anti-god powers.

Of course, if the παραδίδωμι clauses in Romans 1 imply that God turns humanity over to the control of another agent or power, then we must return to the text to learn the identity of that power. The three phrases that complete each of these clauses provide us with clues to that identity:

He handed them over to ἀκαθαρσία/uncleanness or impurity,
he handed them over to πάθος ἀτιμίας/dishonorable passions,
and he handed them over to ἀδόκιμος νοῦς/unfit mind.

Upon initial inspection, these do not appear to be the names or descriptions of agents. They seem instead to be what we would identify as aspects of the human being and human behavior, thought, attitude. In other words, they seem to be characteristics that inhere entirely within the human.

Later passages in Romans open up the possibility that Paul can construe them as powers, however. The first term, ἀκαθαρσία/uncleanness, appears only one other time in Romans. In 6:19, Paul recalls that the addressees previously "presented your members as slaves to uncleanness," back when they "were slaves of sin." Here "uncleanness" offers an alternate way of speaking of the power of Sin itself. The second term, πάθος or "passion," occurs nowhere else in Romans, but the closely related expression, τὰ παθήματα τῶν ἁμαρτιῶν ("sinful passions"), in 7:5 stands as the subject of the verb "to be at work" (ἐνεργέω), referring to the sinful passions that work through the law to bring about death. The third phrase, ἀδόκιμος νοῦς/unfit mind, also does not appear elsewhere in Romans, but a functionally equivalent phrase occurs in Rom. 8:6-7 referring to the "mind" of the flesh that is death and that is set over against God. All of these expres-

19. For an overview of the exegetical issues involved, see Raymond F. Collins, *First Corinthians*, SP 7 (Collegeville: Liturgical Press, 1999), 205-16.

sions, then, have in view *the enslavement of humanity to powers that oppose the power of God.* Uncleanness, dishonorable passions, and unfit mind are instances of synecdoche; they are ways of referring to anti-god powers, most especially the power of Sin. Because of human refusal to recognize God, God turns humanity over — concedes humanity for a time — to another power, the power of Sin.

To be sure, Paul nowhere uses the phrase "anti-god powers"; this shorthand expression serves to draw together the various ways in which Paul reflects an understanding that God has enemies, and these include other-than-human enemies.[20] As mentioned above, Satan is named among these enemies. In 1 Corinthians 2, Paul observes that the "rulers of this age" were responsible for the crucifixion (1 Cor. 2:6, 8; see also "the god of this world" in 2 Cor. 4:4). Elsewhere he writes of the sacrifices that are made to "demons, not to gods" (1 Cor. 10:20) and of slavery to things that are not God (Gal. 4:8; and see also 1 Cor. 8:5). The argument of 1 Corinthians 15 makes little sense apart from some concrete notion that God has enemies that must finally be defeated, chief among which is Death itself (1 Cor. 15:26, 54-57).

Reconsidering Rom. 8:32

Romans 1 reveals that anti-god powers achieved their grasp of humanity because God responded to humanity's rebellion by turning humanity over to anti-god powers, including Sin and Death. Because of this handing over, Sin and Death and other anti-god powers achieve the captivity of humankind, captivity of Gentiles, and even of those who follow God's own Law. In fact, among the most frightening symptoms of Sin's power is its ability to take even God's "holy and just and good" law and twist it toward evil.[21] In Rom. 8, Paul refers to the final stage in this hand-over as God's handing over his own Son to these same powers.

20. On this point, see the important work of Martinus C. de Boer, *The Defeat of Death: Apocalyptic Eschatology in 1 Corinthians 15 and Romans 5*, JSNTSup 22 (Sheffield: JSOT Press, 1988); and his "Paul and Apocalyptic Eschatology," in *The Encyclopedia of Apocalypticism, Vol. 1: The Origins of Apocalypticism in Judaism and Christianity*, ed. John J. Collins (New York: Continuum, 1998), 345-83.

21. Paul W. Meyer, "The Worm at the Core of the Apple: Exegetical Reflections on Romans 7," in *The Word in This World: Essays in New Testament Exegesis and Theology*, ed. John T. Carroll, NTL (Louisville: Westminster John Knox, 2004), 57-77.

My case rests not only on the verb παραδίδωμι, but also on the word "spare" or "withhold" as the NRSV renders it (Gk.: φείδομαι). In Rom. 8:32, recall, Paul not only says that God turned over his own Son, but that God *did not spare him, did not withhold him*. Not surprisingly, given that interpreters have been preoccupied with the relationship between 8:32 and Genesis 22, little or no attention has been given to the frequent appearance of φείδομαι (like παραδίδωμι) in contexts having to do with conflict. This usage occurs as early as Homer, where withholding or not, as the case may be, takes place in the aftermath of military confrontation.[22] Particularly noteworthy is the frequent use of this verb in Paul's near-contemporary Josephus, where more often than not it refers to the sparing of human life in a context of military conflict.[23]

In the LXX also, and with some frequency, "withholding" or "sparing" refers to the taking or saving of human lives as a consequence of battle.[24] For instance, Deut. 7:16 (LXX) explicitly commands that Israel will not spare (οὐ φείσεται) any of the people given them (δίδωσιν) by God. And in the LXX of 1 Sam. 15:3, Samuel delivers to Saul the Lord's instructions to attack Amalek:

> Now go and strike Amalek . . . and do not spare (φείδομαι) him and kill male and female, child and infant, sheep and camel and donkey.

In other instances, it is Israel that is not to be spared. The LXX of 2 Chr. 36:17 summarizes the result of God's judgment against Jerusalem:

> [The king of the Chaldeans] killed their young men . . . and he did not spare (φείδομαι) any . . . and he had no pity on their young women and he led away their elders captive. He handed over (παραδίδωμι) everything into their hands.

The author of Lamentations describes Zion's defeat (2:17 [LXX]):

> The Lord accomplished what he planned, he accomplished his decrees that were established long ago, he destroyed and he did not withhold (φείδομαι). . . .

22. *Iliad* 15.215; 21.101; 24.158; *Odyssey* 9.277; 22.54; see LSJ 1920.
23. E.g., *J. W.* 1.352; 4.82; 4.197; 4.310; 6.345; *Ant.* 14.480; 18.359; 19.141; *Ag. Ap.* 2.213.
24. In addition to these examples, see also 2 Sam. 21:7; Ps. 77:50 (LXX); *Pss. Sol.* 13:1; 17:12; 1 Sam. 24:10; 2 Sam. 18:5; Jer. 28:3; Ezek. 20:17; Zech. 11:6; Isa. 13:18.

This pattern at least reinforces the possibility that the activity to which Paul refers here is similarly located: God did not spare or withhold his own Son in a situation of conflict with anti-god powers.

To be sure, Rom. 8:32 does not explicitly claim that God handed Jesus over to another power. In that sense, the statement differs from many of those adduced above. Yet chs. 5 and 6 speak plainly about the dominion of Sin (5:21; 6:6, 16-17, 20). Paul has already observed in ch. 8 that creation itself was subjected to futility (8:20). Soon he will offer a veritable litany of the powers: death, life, angels, rulers, things present, things to come, powers, height, depth; so, this conclusion is not hard to draw. His intense affirmation that none of these powers can bring about separation from the love of God in Christ Jesus implies that they actually undertake to do just that; they *intend* to separate humanity from its proper Lord, and they array themselves against God.[25]

To bring a few strands together: in Rom. 8:32 Paul places the death of Jesus in the context of God's own conflict with Death and Sin and all other anti-god powers. Having introduced the question, "Who can be against 'us'?", Paul begins his answers by recalling that God did not withhold from these enemies even God's own Son but handed him over on behalf of all humankind. On this construal of the text, *it is not sufficient to describe God's handing over only as a loving, sacrificial act, a gracious giving up; it is also an event in the ongoing struggle between God and anti-god powers.* God brings to an end the "handing over" of humanity to Sin and Death by means of another handing over, this time of God's Son. The consequences of this act are, of course, the reversal of the captivity so terrifyingly outlined in ch. 1; this handing over results in the release of captive humanity and defeat of these powerful foes of God.

---

25. It is hard to understand James D. G. Dunn's conclusion that Paul has little to say about the "heavenly powers" and that the references in Rom. 8:38-30 and 1 Cor. 15:24 "look as though they were added almost for effect," that Paul did not have "a very strong, or at least very clear, belief regarding these heavenly powers," *The Theology of Paul the Apostle* (Grand Rapids: Eerdmans, 1998), 109. A similar position was argued by Wesley Carr in *Angels and Principalities: The Background, Meaning, and Development of the Pauline Phrase* hai archai kai hai exousiai, SNTSMS 42 (Cambridge: Cambridge University Press, 1981). For compelling arguments to the contrary, see G. H. C. MacGregor, "Principalities and Powers: The Cosmic Background of Paul's Thought," *NTS* 1 (1954-55): 17-28; and G. B. Caird, *Principalities and Powers: A Study in Pauline Theology* (Oxford: Clarendon, 1956).

Coherence with Other Pauline Texts

To be sure, this is not the usual reading of Paul's language in 8:32 or his statements in 1:24, 26, and 28. It is, in fact, a radical claim about the cosmic, apocalyptic character of Jesus' death, asserting that Paul's answer to the question "Who put Jesus to death?" is not only "God did," but that God did it by conceding his own Son to cosmic powers. Because I have detected it in two slender passages, it is important to take notice of corroborating evidence elsewhere in Romans and in other Pauline letters.

To begin with, in Paul's first statement in this letter about Jesus' death he writes that all people

> are now justified by his grace as a gift, through the redemption that is in Christ Jesus, whom God put forward as a sacrifice of atonement by his blood, effective through faith. (3:24-25 NRSV)

In this pivotal statement, Paul introduces the death of Christ with the word "redemption" (following the NRSV's rendering of ἀπολύτρωσις). Douglas Campbell has argued convincingly that this is one of the key words in this passage — that God's righteousness is revealed in this act. Campbell also argues that the nuance at work here is not that of ransom (i.e., the payment of a price), but of liberation, as in liberation from slavery. This view is reinforced when we observe that v. 25 refers to the passing over or "release" (almost certainly not "forgiveness") from former sins.[26] Whatever else Rom. 3:21-26 does, then, it depicts the death of Jesus Christ as bringing about release from captivity, the very captivity to which God hands humanity in Romans 1. Or, as Paul puts it succinctly in 11:32: "God confined all in disobedience that he might have mercy on all."

Romans 6 can be read as an explication of this same point. As Paul reflects on the analogy between Jesus' death and that of the believer in baptism, he claims that the believer has died to slavery to Sin. Here he affirms that Christ

> being raised from the dead, will never die again; *death no longer has dominion over him.* The death he died, *he died to sin,* once for all; but the life he lives, he lives to God. (6:10 NRSV)

26. Douglas A. Campbell, *The Rhetoric of Righteousness in Romans 3.21-26*, JSNTSup 65 (Sheffield: JSOT Press, 1992), 116-30.

137

That death no longer has power over the resurrected Christ may be taken straightforwardly; however one construes the power of death, resurrection clearly involves its defeat. But what does it mean to say that Christ "died to sin"? It seems highly unlikely that Paul wants to suggest that *Christ himself was a sinner in the sense that he transgressed and now does so no longer.*[27] Paul may well mean that Christ died to Sin's power — but, again, what does that mean, if not that Sin manifested itself in behaviors such as those adumbrated in Rom. 1? It might mean, consistent with the interpretation offered here, *that Christ died to the realm of Sin, to which even he had been handed over.* In common with all of humanity, Jesus also is handed over to the sphere of Sin and Death.

At this point, we turn to the several places where Paul simply says that Christ was handed over, without specifying an agent. I refer, of course, to:

> Rom. 4:25: [Jesus our Lord] was handed over for our trespasses and was raised for our justification.

And also to

> 1 Cor. 11:23: The Lord Jesus, on the night when he was handed over, took bread. . . .

Even if we affirm, along with much exegetical precedent, that these are expressions Paul received from earlier Christian tradition, they may nevertheless, at least in their Pauline context, reflect the divine passive: it was God who handed over Jesus Christ.

Finally, notice should be taken here of 1 Cor. 2:8, where Paul specifies that the wisdom he declares has not been revealed to the "rulers of this age":

> None of the rulers of this age knew [about God's mystery]. For if they had known, they would not have crucified the Lord of glory.

The category of "rulers of this age" may *include* those human beings in Jerusalem who made certain decisions and carried out certain actions against Jesus of Nazareth, although it is more likely that those residents of

---

27. See the discussion in Moo, *Romans,* 379.

Jerusalem are but pawns in the control of the real "rulers." The context demands that Paul is talking about rulers whose power extends only over the present evil age. If they had known about God's mystery, they would not have crucified Jesus.

Perhaps we should prescind from reading this text alongside Romans 8, but the suggestion presents itself that here Paul shows us the death of Jesus from another angle. Having received Jesus Christ because God handed him over to their realms, the powers crucified Jesus Christ through their human agents, but they would have known better if they had understood the "mystery." Paul's comment here is scarcely a complimentary concession to the rulers of this age, in which he imagines that, had they really known who Jesus was, they would not have crucified him. Instead, the "mystery" somehow refers to the victory of the resurrection and its anticipated consequences in Jesus Christ's triumphant return. If the powers had known that their momentary grasp of God's Son meant, not their victory but their defeat by virtue of his resurrection, they would not have carried out the crucifixion.

To return to the opening question: Who is responsible for the death of Jesus? According to Paul, Christ Jesus dies because God has turned him over to anti-god powers. This act enables those powers to have him put to death, but it also ultimately proves to be the undoing of those same powers. God's resurrection of Jesus from the dead not only frees Jesus Christ from the powers, but it sets in motion the defeat of Sin and Death that will culminate when all of God's enemies are placed in subjection.

Other Apocalyptic Readings of Jesus' Death: A Glimpse at Luke-Acts

Because we do not customarily speak of God handing Jesus over to the powers of Sin and Death, to anti-god powers, this will seem a strange notion, one concocted from tiny shreds of evidence. Yet it is worth noticing that Paul's understanding of Jesus' death is not without counterpart elsewhere in early Christian tradition. Colossians 2 juxtaposes the cross with the disarming of the rulers and authorities, resulting in their downfall (vv. 14-15). And this argument would sound entirely plausible to Irenaeus, who dramatically depicts the death of Jesus as binding the strong man, spoiling his goods, abolishing death, and rescuing humankind from its captivity to Satan.[28]

This evidence is scarcely surprising, given that the author of Colossians is at least associated with the circle around Paul, and Irenaeus draws heavily on Paul's letters. A more challenging question is how this argument would sound to Luke, to take the evangelist who writes about Paul and who has frequently been regarded as having a theology that is distinctly at odds with Paul's own. Space permits only some preliminary observations, the first of which must be an admission of the sheer difficulty of the question. Scholars approach the study of Lukan theology from strikingly different vantage points, with some identifying as evidence of "Lukan" theology only the evangelist's editing of the sources he received and others identifying all of the Third Gospel and Acts as "Lukan," regardless of its origin. More important, any observation that compares Luke with Paul crosses genres in a way that is problematic, since Luke's comments about Jesus' death take the form of narrative, which makes for difficult comparison with Paul's letters. Setting aside these problems for the moment, and returning to our opening question of responsibility for Jesus' death, we may find some points at which Luke also appears to understand Jesus' death as having to do with God's own action, an action that takes place in the face of God's enemies.

The most prominent Lukan rubric for understanding the death of Jesus is that of the divine plan. With various linguistic signals, including especially the word δεῖ ("it is necessary") and the phrase βουλὴ τοῦ θεοῦ ("plan of God"), Luke presents all the "things that have been fulfilled among us" (Luke 1:1) as the result of God's own will.[29] Understandably, the death of Jesus features prominently in God's plan, a plan that Luke

---

28. E.g., *Against Heresies* 3.8.3; 3.18.7; 3.23.1; 3.24.1; 3.40.1; 5.24.3; the discussion of Irenaeus in Gustaf Aulén's classic study of the atonement remains important: *Christus Victor: An Historical Study of the Three Main Types of the Idea of the Atonement* (New York: Macmillan, 1969). See also Brian Daley's informative discussion of the dramatic presentation of Jesus' death not only in Irenaeus but elsewhere ("'He Himself Is Our Peace' [Ephesians 2:14]: Early Christian Views of Redemption in Christ," in *The Redemption: An Interdisciplinary Symposium on Christ as Redeemer,* ed. Stephen T. Davis, Daniel Kendall, and Gerald O'Collins [Oxford: Oxford University Press, 2004], 149-76, esp. 161-64).

29. On this motif in Luke-Acts, see Charles H. Cosgrove, "The Divine ΔΕΙ in Luke-Acts," *NovT* 26 (1984): 168-90, and John T. Squires, *The Plan of God in Luke-Acts,* SNTSMS 76 (Cambridge: Cambridge University Press, 1993).

early on interprets as intended for the salvation of Israel and the Gentiles (Luke 2:32). To be sure, there are human characters who figure in the death of Jesus, and Luke is careful to identify those. The Lukan Passion narrative distinguishes the actions of the religious leaders from the chorus of "the people" (ὁ λαός), who support Jesus until the trial before Pilate, when "the people" join their leaders in demanding Jesus' death.[30] The early speeches of Acts appear to hold both leaders and followers accountable. On Pentecost, Peter addresses all those gathered in Jerusalem with the accusation that "you crucified and killed" Jesus (Acts 2:23). Similarly, in 3:13-15 Peter pointedly asserts that "you killed the author of life," and Paul in 13:27-28 blames the "residents of Jerusalem and their leaders." In one sense, then, Luke appears to understand the death of Jesus as the result of human error, yet Luke also consistently places that claim within the larger view that these human actions are part of God's plan (e.g., Luke 24:46, 44-48; Acts 2:23; 3:14-18; 4:27-28). As with much else in Luke, there are multiple threads to this story, however, and there is more to the death of Jesus in Luke-Acts than false human judgment that is interpreted as part of God's larger plan. Luke also understands that God has enemies who feature in this plan, even as they attempt to subvert that plan for their own ends.

For Luke, the most prominent and powerful opponent of God's plan is Satan or the Devil. First entering the story in the temptation narrative of Luke 4, Satan declares that everything has been handed over to him (παραδίδωμι). In common with the rest of Satan's claims in this scene, this assertion of authority is surely false, but it does set the stage for understanding Satan as a character obsessed with his own power and prepared to enter into conflict for that power. At the close of the temptation narrative, Luke comments that Satan "departed from him [Jesus] for a time" (4:13).[31] From that point on throughout the ministry of Jesus, Satan appears in Luke only indirectly within Jesus' own comments about him (8:12; 10:18; 11:18; 13:16). When he does reappear, it is at the outset of the passion narrative, when Luke ominously reports that "Satan entered Judas, the one

---

30. On the Lukan passion narrative and secondary literature pertaining to it, see the helpful work of John T. Carroll and Joel B. Green, *The Death of Jesus in Early Christianity* (Peabody, Mass.: Hendrickson, 1995), 60-81.

31. Neither Mark nor Matthew has parallels to either of these statements, making them particularly important for those who are interested in Lukan redaction.

named Iscariot, who was one of the Twelve" (22:3), prompting Judas's betrayal.[32] At the Last Supper, Jesus turns to address Peter with the words,

> Simon, Simon, look! Satan demanded you so that he might sift you as
> if you were wheat. But I asked on your behalf, so that your faith won't
> run out. And you, when you have turned back again, strengthen your
> brothers. (22:31-32)

That Satan and Jesus are both making requests for Peter's allegiance recalls
the role of Satan in the book of Job, where Satan is the accuser in the heavenly court (1:6-12). Yet Satan in Luke is a far more malignant character, as
is demonstrated in his attempt to bring Jesus under his own power in Luke
4 as well as in his successful take-over of Judas. It is Satan who stands behind the betrayal of Jesus, who places his own power over against that of
God, trying to undermine God's plan for human salvation. Jesus himself
gives voice to this accusation at his arrest, "This is your hour and the
power of darkness" (Luke 22:53).

This conflict cannot be projected into the heavenly sphere, as if it had
vague or no implications for human beings. Judas and Peter are held in Satan's grasp, as already noted above. In the story of the healing of the bent-
over woman, Jesus declares that she had been bound by Satan (Luke 13:16).
When Peter confronts Ananias, he asks, "Why did Satan fill your heart?"
(Acts 5:5). Later, Paul gives Bar-Jesus yet another name (in addition to Bar-
Jesus, he is Elymas the magician), that of "son of the Devil" (Acts 13:10). In
his final defense speech in Acts 26, Paul recapitulates the risen Jesus' commission to him, this time including the charge to "turn the people from
darkness to light and from the power of Satan to that of God." To be sure,
Luke does not quite use Paul's language of the rule of Sin and Death (Rom.
5:12-21) or the defeat of death (1 Cor. 15:54-57), but he nevertheless at
points seems to understand Satan as holding humanity in his grasp.

In Luke-Acts the death and resurrection of Jesus constitute a defeat
for Satan, although that conclusion must be inferred from the story. Similarly, the numerous points at which Satan's power is defeated constitute indications that Satan will not finally triumph (e.g., Acts 5:1-11; 13:4-12).[33]

---

32. None of the Synoptics attributes Judas's action to Satan, but notice John 6:70-71;
13:2, 27.

33. Susan R. Garrett, *The Demise of the Devil: Magic and the Demonic in Luke's Writing*
(Minneapolis: Fortress, 1989).

The most elusive and yet perhaps the most important indication of Satan's defeat comes in Luke 10, when Jesus himself announces proleptically that he has watched Satan fall from heaven (10:17).

Without exaggerating the similarities between Luke's presentation of Jesus' death and that found in Paul's letters, it does seem that their understandings are comparable. Jesus' death results from God's own decision in both cases. And in both cases, that death figures prominently in a cosmic battle between God and God's enemies, identified in Luke's narrative as Satan or the Devil, identified in Romans as Sin and Death.

Reading the Death of Jesus Apocalyptically Today: Some Closing Observations

Why does it matter that we attend to this aspect of Paul's interpretation of Jesus' death? Especially if I am correct in thinking that there is a cosmic conflict lurking in the background, that Paul understands Jesus' death as resulting from God's handing over of Jesus to anti-god powers — why would anyone want to draw attention to that line of thinking? Some would say that there is enough embarrassing literalism at work in American Protestantism as it is. Others — among them good friends of mine — simply say that they cannot believe such things and would prefer not to have them discussed.

My first response to these objections is that, if what I am arguing is in the text, then we must take it seriously. And, as I think the history of interpretation (or even five minutes on the World Wide Web) will confirm, these challenging cosmic and apocalyptic texts will be taken up by someone, often by people who are ill-equipped to interpret them. Let us not persist in our practice of simply conceding the cosmic character of NT texts to those who will make that cosmic character into a weapon for attacking others.

Second, and far more important, Paul's understanding that there are powers in the cosmos that actively resist the power of God — including powers named Sin and Death — *coheres with our experience of the world.* I do not know how Christians can talk about the recurrent nightmare of genocide, to take a single example, without some vocabulary that includes anti-god powers. Nor do I know how to think about the persistent crises of the Middle East apart from some acknowledgment that the intransigent

143

nature of the conflict cannot be explained by history or psychology or even economics alone. That is not at all to eschew the contributions that are made by other disciplines, but it is to say that when we consider our world, we need to confess that we are in the grips of powers that are larger than ourselves. We see this not only on the world stage but much closer to home. Those who have watched a loved one ravaged by cancer or who have wrestled with addiction or mental illness know that the language of cells and body chemistry does not entirely suffice. Nor does it suffice to say that human beings who lived in Jerusalem in the first century put Jesus to death. God handed Jesus over to death, handed him over to these same powers in order to bring about their defeat and the eventual deliverance of all creation.

Third, we may find that the cosmic framework of Paul and other early Christian writers offers an important countering voice to the rampant narcissism in American religious life, which I take to be characterized on all sides by concern about the individual self. That is to say, quickly and baldly, that Paul (in common with the rest of the biblical canon) forcefully reminds us that the story is not *about* us. Even though Paul's letters are profoundly *for* the communities to whom he writes, they are not *about* those communities, but about a gospel that has its beginning and will have its culmination in the action of God in Jesus Christ.

In addition, the cosmic, even apocalyptic, character of Paul's interpretation of the gospel is profoundly pastoral in its implications because it relocates our concerns in their rightful context. For example, many of us expended massive energy in 2004 with the presidential election — reading about it, talking about it, composing e-mails, monitoring television and radio coverage. These are responsible actions of citizens in a democracy, and I do not wish to disparage them. And yet there has been a strand in the discourse — often an overt strand — that misunderstands whose world it is and what powers are actually involved. God is not on *our side*, neither are the anti-god powers *on our side* — whether the conflict is that of the election or the crisis in the Middle East or the struggle against HIV-AIDS. All of those are instances of God's own battle for us and all creation.

Does that mean we simply throw up our hands, retreating into our private selves while God finishes off the battle? Emphatically not. If we take this language of cosmic battle seriously, it means that we understand that the outcome is secure in God's hands. As P. T. Forsyth put it nearly a century ago, "The devils we meet were all fore-damned in the Satan Christ ruined. The wickedness of the world is, after all, 'a bull in a net', a chained beast kicking himself to death."[34] Confidence in that final triumph of God is what enables us to live courageously, declaring with Paul that nothing separates us from the love of God in Christ Jesus our Lord.

34. P. T. Forsyth, *The Glorious Gospel* (London: Livingstone Press, 1945), 7. Quoted in MacGregor, "Principalities and Powers," 24.

Works Cited

Allison, Dale C. *Jesus of Nazareth: Millenarian Prophet.* Minneapolis: Fortress, 1998.

————. "Jesus and the Covenant: A Response to E. P. Sanders." *JSNT* 29 (1987): 57-78.

————. "The Contemporary Quest for the Historical Jesus." *IBS* 18 (1996): 174-94.

Aulén, Gustaf. *Christus Victor: An Historical Study of the Three Main Types of the Idea of the Atonement.* New York: Macmillan, 1969.

Auvinen, Ville. *Jesus' Teaching on Prayer.* Åbo: Åbo Akademisk Förlag, 2003.

Avemarie, Friedrich. *Tora und Leben: Untersuchungen zur Heilsbedeutung der Tora in der frühen rabbinischen Literatur.* TSAJ 55. Tübingen: Mohr Siebeck, 1996.

Bailey, Kenneth. *Jacob and the Prodigal.* Downers Grove: InterVarsity, 2003.

————. *Poet and Peasant.* Grand Rapids: Eerdmans, 1976.

Barclay, John M. G. "Jesus and Paul." Pages 492-503 in *Dictionary of Paul and His Letters.* Edited by Gerald F. Hawthorne, Ralph P. Martin, and Daniel G. Reid. Downers Grove: InterVarsity, 1993.

————. "Paul's Story: Theology as Testimony." Pages 133-56 in *Narrative Dynamics in Paul: A Critical Assessment.* Edited by Bruce W. Longenecker. Louisville: Westminster/John Knox, 2002.

Barrett, C. K. "Jesus and the Word." Pages 213-23 in *Jesus and the Word, and Other Essays.* Edinburgh: T&T Clark, 1995.

Barth, Karl. *Church Dogmatics II.2: The Doctrine of God.* Edited by Geoffrey W. Bromiley and Thomas T. Torrance. Edinburgh: T&T Clark, 1957.

Ben-Amos, Dan, and Liliane Weissberg. *Cultural Memory and the Construction of Identity.* Detroit: Wayne State University Press, 1999.

Berényi, Gabriella. "Gal 2,20: A Pre-Pauline or a Pauline Text?" *Bib* 65 (1984): 490-537.

Bernheim, Pierre-Antoine. *James, Brother of Jesus.* Translated by John Bowden. London: SCM, 1997.

Betz, H. D. *Galatians.* Hermeneia. Philadelphia: Fortress, 1979.

Black, Matthew. *Romans.* NCB. London: Oliphants, 1973.

Blank, Josef. *Paulus und Jesus: eine theologische Grundlegung.* SANT 18. München: Kösel-Verlag, 1968.

Bockmuehl, Markus. "1 Thessalonians 2:14-16 and the Church in Jerusalem." *TynBul* 52 (2001): 1-31.

———. "Simon Peter and Bethsaida." Pages 55-91 in *The Missions of James, Peter, and Paul: Tensions in Early Christianity.* Edited by Bruce D. Chilton and Craig A. Evans. NovTSup 115. Leiden: Brill, 2005.

———. *Jewish Law in Gentile Churches: Halakhah and the Beginning of Christian Public Ethics.* Edinburgh: T&T Clark, 2000.

———. Review of James D. G. Dunn, *Jesus Remembered.* *JTS* 56 (2005): 140-49.

Boers, Hendrikus. "The Form-Critical Study of Paul's Letters: 1 Thessalonians as a Case Study." *NTS* 22 (1976): 140-58.

Borg, Marcus J. "An Appreciative Disagreement." Pages 227-43 in *Jesus & the Restoration of Israel: A Critical Assessment of N. T. Wright's Jesus and the Victory of God.* Edited by Carey C. Newman. Downers Grove: InterVarsity, 1999.

Böttrich, Christfried. "Petrus — Bischofsamt — Kirche." *ZNT* 7 (2004): 44-51.

———. "Petrus und Paulus in Antiochien (Gal 2,11-21)." *BTZ* 19 (2002): 224-39.

———. *Petrus: Fischer, Fels und Funktionär.* Biblische Gestalten 2. Leipzig: Evangelische Verlagsanstalt, 2001.

Boyarin, Daniel. *A Radical Jew: Paul and the Politics of Identity.* Berkeley: University of California Press, 1994.

———. *Border Lines: The Partition of Judaeo-Christianity.* Divinations. Philadelphia: University of Pennsylvania Press, 2004.

Brown, Dan. *The Da Vinci Code: A Novel.* 1st ed. New York: Doubleday, 2003.

Bultmann, Rudolf. "Jesus and Paul." Pages 183-201 in *Existence and Faith.* London: Hodder & Stoughton, 1961.

———. *Jesus and the Word.* London: Nicholson & Watson, 1935.

———. *The Theology of the New Testament.* London: SCM, 1952.

———. "The Significance of the Historical Jesus for the Theology of Paul." Pages 220-46 in *Faith and Understanding.* New York: Harper & Row, 1966.

———. *The History of the Synoptic Tradition.* Translated by John Marsh. 3d ed. Oxford: Blackwell, 1972.

Byrne, Brendan. *Romans.* SP 6. Collegeville, Minn.: Liturgical Press, 1996.

Byrskog, Samuel. "A New Perspective on the Jesus Tradition: Reflections on James D. G. Dunn's *Jesus Remembered.*" *JSNT* 26 (2004): 459-71.

Caird, George B. *Principalities and Powers: A Study in Pauline Theology.* Oxford: Clarendon, 1956.

Campbell, Douglas A. *The Rhetoric of Righteousness in Romans 3.21-26.* JSNTSup 65. Sheffield: JSOT Press, 1992.

Carleton Paget, James. "Quests for the Historical Jesus." Pages 138-55 in *The Cambridge Companion to Jesus.* Edited by Markus Bockmuehl. Cambridge: Cambridge University Press, 2001.

Carr, Wesley. *Angels and Principalities: The Background, Meaning, and Development of the Pauline Phrase* hai archai kai hai exousiai. SNTSMS 42. Cambridge: Cambridge University Press, 1981.

Carroll, John T., and Joel B. Green. *The Death of Jesus in Early Christianity.* Peabody, Mass.: Hendrickson, 1995.

Carson, D. A., Peter T. O'Brien, and Mark A. Seifrid, eds. *Justification and Variegated Nomism: A Fresh Appraisal of Paul and Second Temple Judaism.* 2 vols. WUNT 2/140, 181. Tübingen: Mohr Siebeck, 2001, 2004.

Carter, Warren. *Matthew and the Margins: A Sociopolitical and Religious Reading.* Sheffield: Sheffield Academic Press, 2000.

Castelli, Elizabeth A. *Imitating Paul: A Discourse of Power.* Louisville: Westminster/ John Knox, 1991.

Catchpole, David. "Q's Thesis and Paul's Antithesis." Pages 347-66 in *Forschungen zum Neuen Testament und seiner Umwelt: Festschrift für Albert Fuchs.* Edited by C. Niemand. Linzer Philosophisch-Theologische Beiträge 7. Frankfurt: Peter Lang, 2002.

Chilton, Bruce. "Jesus and the Repentance of E. P. Sanders." *TynBul* 39 (1988): 1-18.

Collins, Raymond F. *First Corinthians.* SP 7. Collegeville, Minn.: Liturgical Press, 1999.

Conzelmann, Hans. *1 Corinthians.* Translated by James W. Leitch. Hermeneia. Philadelphia: Fortress, 1975.

Cosgrove, Charles H. "The Divine ΔEI in Luke-Acts." *NovT* 26 (1984): 168-90.

Cousar, Charles B. *The Theology of the Cross: The Death of Jesus in the Pauline Letters.* OBT. Minneapolis: Fortress, 1990.

Cranfield, C. E. B. *The Epistle to the Romans.* ICC. 2 vols. Edinburgh: T&T Clark, 1975, 1979.

Crossan, John Dominic. *The Birth of Christianity: Discovering What Happened in the Years Immediately after the Execution of Jesus.* San Francisco: HarperSanFrancisco; Edinburgh: T&T Clark, 1998.

————. *The Historical Jesus: The Life of a Mediterranean Jewish Peasant.* San Francisco: HarperSanFrancisco; Edinburgh: T&T Clark, 1991.

————. *Jesus: A Revolutionary Biography.* San Francisco: HarperSanFrancisco, 1994.

Crossan, John Dominic, and Jonathan L. Reed. *In Search of Paul: How Jesus's Apostle Opposed Rome's Empire with God's Kingdom. A New Vision of Paul's Words and World.* San Francisco: HarperSanFrancisco, 2004.

Dahl, Nils A. "The Atonement: An Adequate Reward for the Aqedah?" Pages 137-51 in *Jesus the Christ: The Historical Origins of Christological Doctrine.* Edited by Donald H. Juel. Minneapolis: Fortress, 1991.

Daley, Brian. "'He Himself Is Our Peace' [Ephesians 2:14]: Early Christian Views of Redemption in Christ." Pages 149-76 in *The Redemption: An Interdisciplinary Symposium on Christ as Redeemer.* Edited by Stephen T. Davis, Daniel Kendall, and Gerald O'Collins. Oxford: Oxford University Press, 2004.

Dalman, Gustaf. *The Words of Jesus.* Edinburgh: T&T Clark, 1902.

Daly, Robert J. "The Soteriological Significance of the Sacrifice of Isaac." *CBQ* 39 (1977): 45-75.

Davies, Philip R., and Bruce D. Chilton. "The Aqedah: A Revised Tradition History." *CBQ* 40 (1978): 514-46.

Davies, W. D., and Dale C. Allison. *A Critical and Exegetical Commentary on the Gospel according to Saint Matthew.* 3 vols. Edinburgh: T&T Clark, 1988, 1991, 1997.

de Boer, Martinus C. "Paul and Apocalyptic Eschatology." Pages 345-83 in *The Encyclopedia of Apocalypticism.* Vol. 1 of *The Origins of Apocalypticism in Judaism and Christianity.* Edited by John J. Collins. New York: Continuum, 1998.

———. *The Defeat of Death: Apocalyptic Eschatology in 1 Corinthians 15 and Romans 5.* JSNTSup 22. Sheffield: JSOT Press, 1988.

Doering, Lutz. "Schwerpunkte und Tendenzen der neueren Petrus-Forschung." *BTZ* 19 (2002): 203-23.

Donfried, Karl P. "Paul and Judaism: 1 Thessalonians 2:13-16 as a Test Case." *Int* 38 (1984): 242-53.

Dunn, James D. G. "4QMMT and Galatians." *NTS* 43 (1997): 147-53.

———. *A New Perspective on Jesus: What the Quest for the Historical Jesus Missed.* Grand Rapids: Baker Academic, 2005.

———. *Christology in the Making: A New Testament Inquiry into the Origins of the Doctrine of the Incarnation.* 2d ed. London: SCM, 1989.

———. "Introduction." Pages 1-15 in *The Cambridge Companion to St Paul.* Edited by James D. G. Dunn. Cambridge: Cambridge University Press, 2003.

———. *Jews and Christians: The Parting of the Ways, A.D. 70 to 135.* WUNT 66. Tübingen: Mohr Siebeck, 1992.

———. *Jesus and the Spirit.* London: SCM, 1975.

———. *Jesus, Paul, and the Law: Studies in Mark and Galatians.* Louisville: Westminster/John Knox, 1990.

———. *Jesus Remembered.* Vol. 1 of *Christianity in the Making.* Grand Rapids: Eerdmans, 2003.

———. "Jesus Tradition in Paul." Pages 155-78 in *Studying the Historical Jesus: Evaluations of the State of Current Research.* Edited by Bruce Chilton and Craig A. Evans. NTTS 19. Leiden: Brill, 1994.

————. "Noch einmal 'Works of the Law': The Dialogue Continues." Pages 273-90 in *Fair Play: Diversity and Conflicts in Early Christianity. Essays in Honour of Heikki Räisänen*. Edited by I. Dunderberg et al. NovTSup 103. Leiden: Brill, 2002.

————. "Paul's Knowledge of the Jesus Tradition: The Evidence of Romans." Pages 193-207 in *Christus bezeugen: Festschrift für Wolfgang Trilling zum 65. Geburtstag*. Edited by K. Kertelge et al. ETS 59. Freiburg: Herder, 1990.

————. "Prolegomena to a Theology of Paul." *NTS* 40 (1994): 407-32.

————. *Romans*. 2 vols. WBC 38A-B. Dallas: Word Books, 1988.

————. "Social Memory and the Oral Jesus Tradition." Durham-Tübingen Conference Papers. Durham, 2004.

————. *The Epistle to the Galatians*. BNTC. London: A&C Black, 1993.

————. "The New Perspective on Paul." *BJRL* 65 (1983): 95-122.

————. *The Partings of the Ways between Christianity and Judaism and Their Significance for the Character of Christianity*. London: SCM; Philadelphia: TPI, 1991.

————. *The Theology of Paul the Apostle*. Grand Rapids: Eerdmans, 1998.

————. *Unity and Diversity in the New Testament: An Inquiry into the Character of Earliest Christianity*. London: SCM, 1977.

Dunn, James D. G., ed. *Paul and the Mosaic Law*. WUNT 89. Tübingen: Mohr Siebeck, 1996.

Eddy, Paul R. "The (W)Right Jesus: Eschatological Prophet, Israel's Messiah, Yahweh Embodied." Pages 40-60 in *Jesus & the Restoration of Israel: A Critical Assessment of N. T. Wright's Jesus and the Victory of God*. Edited by Carey C. Newman. Downers Grove: InterVarsity, 1999.

Ellis, E. Earle, and Erich Grässer, eds. *Jesus und Paulus: Festschrift für Werner Georg Kümmel zum 70. Geburstag*. Göttingen: Vandenhoeck & Ruprecht, 1975.

Esler, Philip F. *Community and Gospel in Luke-Acts*. SNTSMS 57. Cambridge: Cambridge University Press, 1987.

Fitzmyer, Joseph A. *The Gospel according to Luke*. AB 28-28A. 2 vols. New York: Doubleday, 1981, 1985.

Forsyth, P. T. *The Glorious Gospel*. London: Livingstone Press, 1945.

Fung, R. Y. K. *The Epistle to the Galatians*. NICNT. Grand Rapids: Eerdmans, 1988.

Furnish, Victor Paul. *Jesus according to Paul*. Understanding Jesus Today. Cambridge: Cambridge University Press, 1993.

————. "The Jesus-Paul Debate: From Baur to Bultmann." Pages 17-50 in *Paul and Jesus: Collected Essays*. Edited by A. J. M. Wedderburn. JSNTSup 37. Sheffield: Sheffield Academic Press, 1989.

Garland, David E. *Reading Matthew: A Literary and Theological Commentary on the First Gospel*. London: SPCK, 1993.

Garrett, Susan R. *The Demise of the Devil: Magic and the Demonic in Luke's Writing.* Minneapolis: Fortress, 1989.

Garrow, Alan J. P. *The Gospel of Matthew's Dependence on the Didache.* JSNTSup 254. London/New York: T&T Clark, 2004.

Gaventa, Beverly Roberts. "God Handed Them Over." In *Our Mother Saint Paul.* Louisville: Westminster John Knox, 2007.

Gerhardsson, Birger. *The Ethos of the Bible.* Philadelphia: Fortress, 1981.

———. "The Secret of the Transmission of the Unwritten Jesus Tradition." *NTS* 51 (2005): 1-18.

Gnilka, Joachim. *Petrus und Rom: Das Petrusbild in den ersten zwei Jahrhunderten.* Freiburg: Herder, 2002.

Goodman, Martin. *Mission and Conversion.* Oxford: Clarendon, 1994.

Green, Joel B. "Good News to Whom? Jesus and the 'Poor' in the Gospel of Luke." Pages 59-74 in *Jesus of Nazareth: Lord and Christ.* Edited by Joel B. Green and Max Turner. Carlisle: Paternoster, 1994.

Hands, A. R. *Charity and Social Aid in Greece and Rome.* London: Thames & Hudson, 1968.

Henderson, Suzanne Watts. "'If Anyone Hungers . . .': An Integrated Reading of 1 Cor 11.17-34." *NTS* 48 (2002): 195-208.

Hengel, Martin, and Anna Maria Schwemer. *Paul between Damascus and Antioch: The Unknown Years.* Translated by John Bowden. London: SCM, 1997.

Hengel, Martin, and Roland Deines. *The Pre-Christian Paul.* Translated by John Bowden. London: SCM, 1991.

Holgate, David A. *Prodigality, Liberality and Meanness: The Prodigal Son in Greco-Roman Perspective.* JSNTSup 187. Sheffield: Sheffield Academic Press, 1999.

Hoppe, Leslie J. *There Shall Be No Poor among You: Poverty in the Bible.* Nashville: Abingdon, 2004.

Hurd, John C. "Paul Ahead of His Time: 1 Thess. 2:13-16." Pages 21-36 in *Anti-Judaism in Early Christianity: Paul and the Gospels.* Edited by Peter Richardson and David Granskou. Vol. 1 of *Studies in Christianity and Judaism.* Waterloo: Wilfrid Laurier University Press, 1986.

Jeremias, Joachim. *The Eucharistic Words of Jesus.* London: SCM, 1966.

Jülicher, Adolf. *Paulus und Jesus.* Religionsgeschichtliche Volksbücher für die deutsche christliche Gegenwart 1.14.1.-10. Tübingen: Mohr, 1907.

Jüngel, Eberhard. *Paulus und Jesus: Eine Untersuchung zur Präzisierung der Frage nach dem Ursprung der Christologie.* HUT 2. 2d ed. Tübingen: Mohr (Siebeck), 1964.

Käsemann, Ernst. *Commentary on Romans.* Translated and edited by Geoffrey W. Bromiley. Grand Rapids: Eerdmans, 1980.

Keesmaat, Sylvia C. *Paul and His Story: (Re)interpreting the Exodus Tradition.* JSNTSup 181. Sheffield: Sheffield Academic Press, 1999.

Kim, Seyoon. *Paul and the New Perspective: Second Thoughts on the Origin of Paul's Gospel.* Grand Rapids: Eerdmans, 2002.

Klausner, Joseph. *From Jesus to Paul.* Translated by W. F. Stinespring. New York: Macmillan, 1943.

Knox, John. *Chapters in a Life of Paul.* London: SCM, 1950. (Rev. ed. 1989).

Koester, Helmut. "1 Thessalonians — Experiment in Christian Writing." Pages 33-44 in *Continuity and Discontinuity in Church History: Essays Presented to George Huntston Williams on the Occasion of His 65th Birthday.* Edited by F. Forrester Church and Timothy George. Studies in the History of Christian Thought 19. Leiden: Brill, 1979.

Lampe, Peter. "The Roman Christians of Romans 16." Pages 216-30 in *The Romans Debate.* Edited by Karl P. Donfried. Rev. ed. Peabody, Mass.: Hendrickson, 1991.

———. *From Paul to Valentinus: Christians at Rome in the First Two Centuries.* Edited by Marshall D. Johnson. Translated by Michael Steinhauser. Minneapolis: Fortress, 2003.

Lietzmann, Hans. *Mass and Lord's Supper: A Study in the History of the Liturgy.* Translated by Dorothea H. G. Reeve. Leiden: Brill, 1979.

Longenecker, Bruce W. *Rhetoric at the Boundaries: The Art and Theology of New Testament Chain-Link Transitions.* Waco: Baylor University Press, 2005.

———. *The Triumph of Abraham's God: Transformation and Identity in Galatians.* Edinburgh: T&T Clark, 1998.

Luz, Ulrich. *Matthew 1–7.* Minneapolis: Augsburg, 1989.

———. *Matthew 8–20.* Minneapolis: Fortress, 2001.

MacGregor, G. H. C. "Principalities and Powers: The Cosmic Background of Paul's Thought." *NTS* 1 (1954-55): 17-28.

Malherbe, Abraham J. *The Letters to the Thessalonians.* AB 32B. New York: Doubleday, 2000.

Marsh, Clive. "Quests of the Historical Jesus in New Historicist Perspective." *BibInt* 5 (1997): 403-37.

Martin, Ralph P. *James.* WBC 48. Waco: Word, 1988.

Martyn, J. Louis. "Epistemology at the Turn of the Ages." Pages 89-110 in *Theological Issues in the Letters of Paul.* Edinburgh: T&T Clark, 1997.

Meggitt, Justin J. *Paul, Poverty and Survival.* SNTW. Edinburgh: T&T Clark, 1998.

Meier, John P. *A Marginal Jew.* 3 vols. New York: Doubleday, 1991, 1994, 2001.

———. "The Present State of the 'Third Quest' for the Historical Jesus: Loss and Gain." *Bib* 80 (1999): 459-87.

Metzger, Bruce M. *A Textual Commentary on the Greek New Testament.* London/New York: United Bible Societies, 1975.

Meyer, Ben F. *The Aims of Jesus.* London: SCM, 1979.

Meyer, Paul W. "The Worm at the Core of the Apple: Exegetical Reflections on

Romans 7." Pages 57-77 in *The Word in This World: Essays in New Testament Exegesis and Theology.* Edited by John T. Carroll. NTL. Louisville: Westminster John Knox, 2004.

Michel, Otto. *Der Brief an die Römer.* 4th ed. KEKNT. Göttingen: Vandenhoeck & Ruprecht, 1966.

Moo, Douglas. *The Epistle to the Romans.* NICNT. Grand Rapids: Eerdmans, 1996.

Moore, Stephen D. *God's Beauty Parlour: And Other Queer Spaces in and around the Bible.* Stanford: Stanford University Press, 2001.

Neill, Stephen, and N. T. Wright. *The Interpretation of the New Testament: 1861-1986.* Oxford/New York: Oxford University Press, 1988.

Neusner, Jacob. "Review Article: Comparing Religions." *HR* 18 (1979): 177-91.

Oakman, Douglas E. Review of Ville Auvinen, *Jesus' Teaching on Prayer. CBQ* 66 (2004): 470-71.

Pearson, Birger A. "1 Thessalonians 2:14-16: A Deutero-Pauline Interpolation." *HTR* 64 (1971): 79-94.

Perkins, Pheme. *Peter: Apostle for the Whole Church.* Columbia: University of South Carolina Press, 1994.

Pohl, Adolf. *Der Brief des Paulus an die Römer.* Wuppertal: R. Brockhaus, 1998.

Porter, Stanley E. *The Criteria for Authenticity in Historical-Jesus Research: Previous Discussion and New Proposals.* JSNTSup 191. Sheffield: Sheffield Academic Press, 2000.

Powell, Mark Allen. *The Jesus Debate: Modern Historians Investigate the Life of Christ.* Oxford: Lion, 1998.

Sanday, William, and Arthur C. Headlam. *A Critical and Exegetical Commentary on the Epistle to the Romans.* ICC. 5th ed. Edinburgh: T&T Clark, 1902.

Sanders, E. P. *Jesus and Judaism.* London: SCM, 1985.

———. *Jewish Law from Jesus to the Mishnah: Five Studies.* London: SCM; Philadelphia: TPI, 1990.

———. *Judaism: Practice and Belief, 63 BCE–66 CE.* London: SCM; Philadelphia: TPI, 1992.

———. *Paul: A Very Short Introduction.* Oxford/New York: Oxford University Press, 2001.

———. *Paul and Palestinian Judaism.* London: SCM, 1977.

———. *Paul, the Law, and the Jewish People.* Philadelphia: Fortress, 1983.

———. "Puzzling Out Rabbinic Judaism." Pages 65-79 in *Approaches to Ancient Judaism* 2. Edited by William S. Green. Chico: Scholars Press, 1980.

———. *The Historical Figure of Jesus.* London: Penguin, 1993.

Schippers, R. "The Pre-Synoptic Tradition in I Thess II 13-16." *NovT* 8 (1966): 223-34.

Schlier, Heinrich. *Der Romerbrief.* HTKNT 6. Freiburg: Herder, 1977.

Schlueter, Carol J. *Filling Up the Measure: Polemical Hyperbole in 1 Thessalonians 2:14-16.* JSNTSup 98. Sheffield: Sheffield Academic Press, 1994.

Schmidt, Daryl. "1 Thess. 2.13-16: Linguistic Evidence for an Interpolation." *JBL* 102 (1983): 269-79.

Schneider, Gehard. *Das Evangelium nach Lukas.* Gütersloh: G. Mohn; Würzburg: Echter, 1977.

Schrage, Wolfgang. *Der erste Brief an die Korinther. II. 1 Kor 6,12–11,16.* EKKNT 7.2. Zurich: Benziger, 1995.

Schürmann, Heinz. *Traditionsgeschichtliche Untersuchungen zu den synoptischen Evangelien.* Düsseldorf: Patmos-Verlag, 1968.

Schwartz, Daniel R. "Two Pauline Allusions to the Redemptive Mechanism of the Crucifixion." *JBL* 102 (1983): 264-65.

Seccombe, D. "Was There Organised Charity in Jerusalem before the Christians?" *JTS* 29 (1978): 140-43.

Segal, Alan F. *Paul the Convert: The Apostolate and Apostasy of Saul the Pharisee.* New Haven: Yale University Press, 1990.

Seifrid, Mark A. *Christ, Our Righteousness: Paul's Theology of Justification.* Leicester: Apollos; Downers Grove: InterVarsity, 2000.

Squires, John T. *The Plan of God in Luke-Acts.* SNTSMS 76. Cambridge: Cambridge University Press, 1993.

Stanton, Graham N. *Jesus and Gospel.* Cambridge: Cambridge University Press, 2004.

Stark, Rodney. *The Rise of Christianity: A Sociologist Reconsiders History.* Princeton: Princeton University Press, 1996.

Stendahl, Krister. *Paul among Jews and Gentiles.* London: SCM, 1976.

Stowers, Stanley K. *A Rereading of Romans.* New Haven: Yale University Press, 1994.

Stuhlmacher, Peter, and Donald A. Hagner. *Revisiting Paul's Doctrine of Justification: A Challenge to the New Perspective.* Downers Grove: InterVarsity, 2001.

Taylor, Nicholas H. "Paul and the Historical Jesus Quest." *Neot* 37 (2003): 105-26.

Theissen, Gerd. *The Social Setting of Pauline Christianity.* Edited and translated by John H. Schütz. SNTW. Edinburgh: T&T Clark, 1982.

Thompson, Michael B. *The New Perspective on Paul.* Grove Biblical Series 26. Cambridge: Grove Books, 2002.

Tuckett, Christopher M. "Synoptic Traditions in 1 Thessalonians?" Pages 160-82 in *The Thessalonian Correspondence.* Edited by Raymond F. Collins. BETL 87. Leuven: Leuven University Press, 1990.

Vermes, Geza. *Jesus the Jew.* London: SCM, 1973.

―――. *The Religion of Jesus the Jew.* London: SCM, 1993.

von Harnack, Adolf. *Marcion: Das Evangelium vom fremden Gott.* 1924. Repr. Darmstadt: Wissenschaftliche Buchgesellschaft, 1960.

Watson, Francis. *Paul and the Hermeneutics of Faith.* London: T&T Clark, 2004.

Weatherly, Jon A. "The Authenticity of 1 Thessalonians 2.13-16: Additional Evidence." *JSNT* 42 (1991): 79-98.

Wechsler, Andreas. *Geschichtsbild und Apostelstreit: Eine forschungsgeschichtliche und exegetische Studie über den antiochenischen Zwischenfall (Gal 2,11-14).* BZNW 62. Berlin/New York: de Gruyter, 1991.

Wedderburn, A. J. M. "Paul and Jesus: Similarity and Continuity." Pages 117-43 in *Paul and Jesus: Collected Essays.* Edited by A. J. M. Wedderburn. JSNTSup 37. Sheffield: Sheffield Academic Press, 1989.

Weiss, Johannes. *Paul and Jesus.* Translated by H. J. Chaytor. London/New York: Harper, 1909.

Wenham, David. *Paul and Jesus: The True Story.* London: SPCK, 2002.

———. *Paul and the Historical Jesus.* Cambridge: Grove Books, 1998.

———. *Paul: Follower of Jesus or Founder of Christianity?* Grand Rapids: Eerdmans, 1995.

Westerholm, Stephen. *Jesus and Scribal Authority.* Lund: C. W. K. Gleerup, 1978.

———. *Perspectives Old and New on Paul: The "Lutheran" Paul and His Critics.* Grand Rapids: Eerdmans, 2004.

———. "The Righteousness of the Law and the Righteousness of Faith in Romans." *Int* 58 (2004): 257-59.

Wilson, Todd A. "Wilderness Apostasy and Paul's Portrayal of the Crisis in Galatians." *NTS* 40 (2004): 550-71.

Winter, Bruce W. *Seek the Welfare of the City: Christians as Benefactors and Citizens.* Grand Rapids: Eerdmans, 1994.

Witherington, Ben. *The Jesus Quest: The Third Search for the Jew of Nazareth.* Downers Grove: InterVarsity, 1995.

———. *The Paul Quest: The Renewed Search for the Jew of Tarsus.* Downers Grove: InterVarsity, 1998.

Wolff, Christian. *Der erste Brief des Paulus an die Korinther.* THKNT 7.2. Berlin: Evangelische Verlagsanstalt, 1982.

Wrede, William. *Paul.* London: P. Green, 1907.

Wright, N. T. *Jesus and the Victory of God.* London: SPCK, 1996.

———. *Paul for Everyone: Galatians and Thessalonians.* 2d ed. London: SPCK; Louisville: Westminster John Knox, 2004.

———. *Paul for Everyone: Romans.* 2 vols. 2d ed. London: SPCK; Louisville: Westminster John Knox, 2004.

———. *The Epistles of Paul to the Colossians and to Philemon.* TNTC 12. Leicester: InterVarsity; Grand Rapids: Eerdmans, 1986.

———. "The Letter to the Romans: Introduction, Commentary, and Reflections." Pages 373-795 in *NIB.* Vol. 10. Nashville: Abingdon, 2002.

———. *The Resurrection of the Son of God.* Christian Origins and the Question of God 3. London: SPCK, 2003.

———. *What Saint Paul Really Said: Was Paul of Tarsus the Real Founder of Christianity?* Oxford: Lion, 1997.

Index of Authors and Subjects

Index of Scripture and Other Ancient Literature